STORIES ABOUT JESUS IN THE SYNOPTIC GOSPELS

The Storyteller's Companion to the Bible™

Dennis E. Smith and
Michael E. Williams, editors

VOLUME NINE

STORIES ABOUT JESUS IN THE SYNOPTIC GOSPELS

Abingdon Press
Nashville

STORIES ABOUT JESUS IN THE SYNOPTIC GOSPELS

Copyright © 2005 by Abingdon Press

This book is printed on acid-free paper.

Library of Congress Cataloging-in-Publication Data

The Storyteller's companion to the Bible.
  Includes indexes.
  Contents: v. 1. Genesis—v. 2. Exodus-Joshua—[etc.]—v. 9. Stories about Jesus in the Synoptic Gospels—[etc.]—v. 13. New Testament Women.

  1. Bible—Paraphrases, English. 2. Bible—Criticism, interpretation, etc. I. Williams, Michael E. (Michael Edward), 1950-
BS550.2.S764   1991   220.9'505   90-26289
ISBN 0-687-39670-0 (v. 1 : alk. paper)
ISBN 0-687-39671-9 (v. 2 : alk. paper)
ISBN 0-687-39672-7 (v. 3 : alk. paper)
ISBN 0-687-39674-3 (v. 4 : alk. paper)
ISBN 0-687-39675-1 (v. 5 : alk. paper)
ISBN 0-687-00838-7 (v. 6 : alk. paper)
ISBN 0-687-00120-X (v. 7: alk. paper)
ISBN 0-687-00101-3 (v. 9: alk. paper)
ISBN 0-687-05585-7 (v. 10: alk. paper)
ISBN 0-687-08249-8 (v. 12: alk. paper)
ISBN 0-687-08272-2 (v. 13: alk. paper)

08 09 10 11 12 13 14   10 9 8 7 6 5 4 3
MANUFACTURED IN THE UNITED STATES OF AMERICA

Contributors

Jo-Ann Elizabeth (Little) Jennings, who holds a B.A. degree from Culver-Stockton College and an M.Div. degree from Phillips Theological Seminary, is a mother, pastor, teacher, writer, and newspaper reporter. *(Storyteller)*

Pam McGrath is pastor of Brookhaven Christian Church in Tulsa, Oklahoma, and an M.Div. student at Phillips Theological Seminary. She is an affiliate of Group Process Consulting, Greensboro, North Carolina, a storyteller, workshop leader, and member of the National Storytelling Network. *(Storyteller)*

Mikeal C. Parsons, Professor and Macon Chair in Religion at Baylor University in Waco, Texas, specializes in the study of the Gospels. His latest book is *Illuminating Luke: The Infancy Narrative in Italian Renaissance Painting* (2003, with Heidi Hornik). *(Commentator)*

Dennis E. Smith is professor of New Testament at Phillips Theological Seminary and primary editor of the New Testament volumes of *The Storyteller's Companion to the Bible*. His latest book is *From Symposium to Eucharist: The Banquet in the Early Christian World* (2003). *(Editor of this volume)*

Michael E. Williams, a storyteller, writer, and pastor of Blakemore United Methodist Church in Nashville, Tennessee, is the founding editor of *The Storyteller's Companion to the Bible. (Founding editor; storyteller for this volume)*

Contents

A Storyteller's Companion

Dennis E. Smith

In the church where I grew up, we used to sing the hymn "Tell Me the Story of Jesus." Telling the story of Jesus has been a part of Christian practice for nearly 2,000 years. In fact, one of the earliest forms of Christian preaching was storytelling, or telling Jesus stories. These early stories/sermons provided the raw material for the Gospel narratives. Because the Gospel writers wrote down these early stories and preserved them, today we can *read* the story of Jesus in the Bible. Yet when we sing "Tell Me the Story of Jesus," we are really talking about something else; we are expressing an age-old longing to *hear* the story told, in the same manner as it has been told by generations of storytellers from ages past.

This volume is designed to help you do just that. Here we have taken a representative collection of stories about Jesus from the Synoptic Gospels (Matthew, Mark, and Luke) and provided for each story a new analysis that illuminates how it works as a story. Paired with each analysis is a creative retelling of the story by a professional storyteller-preacher. The goal is to provide you, the reader, with insights into the biblical story and suggestions on how it might be retold for audiences today.

The editor for this volume is Dennis E. Smith. He is Professor of New Testament at Phillips Theological Seminary in Tulsa, Oklahoma, and primary editor for all five of the New Testament volumes in the *Storyteller's Companion to the Bible* series. He combines scholarship in New Testament studies with a strong commitment to the world of storytelling.

The Stories

Each chapter begins with the story itself just as the Bible tells it. We have used *The Revised English Bible* as our translation because it presents us with a fresh telling of the stories in modern English. Rereading the text in a modern translation can help bring the stories to life once more and provide the interpreter with new insights into their meanings.

Comments on the Stories

The commentator for this volume is Mikeal C. Parsons, who is Professor and Macon Chair in Religion at Baylor University in Waco, Texas. Mikeal is a specialist in the narrative analysis of the Gospels, a relatively new branch of New Testament studies that concentrates on understanding how the Gospel narratives work as stories. This approach gives us new insights into the Gospel stories so that our modern retellings can better capture the sense and power of the original. Mikeal has published many books and articles on the Gospels, including *Illuminating Luke: The Infancy Narrative in Italian Renaissance Painting* (2003, with Heidi Hornik), *Acts: A Handbook on the Greek Text* (2003, with Martin Culy), and *Rethinking the Unity of Luke and Acts* (1993, with Richard I. Pervo). He is both a scholar and a churchman, one who is able to apply the best of current scholarship to the interpretation of the text and, at the same time, bring out its meaning for church and society today.

Retelling the Stories

To help you develop your own stories, we have provided a sample story with each biblical text. These are intended to serve as models for how a retelling can be done, but they are not expected to exhaust the possibilities in each story.

Various approaches have been used in the retellings. Sometimes the retelling will take the point of view of a character in the original story and develop it further. The retelling may follow the original plotline of the biblical story, it may expand on one detail of the plot, or it may explore the aftereffects of the original story. Retellings may utilize the first-century setting as their starting point, or they may be placed in modern settings. In some cases, a folktale or family story or even a historical narrative may be found to offer a parallel to the biblical story. The possibilities are many, and you are encouraged to develop your own retellings according to a format and style that works for you.

Three storytellers have contributed the stories included here. Their stories are all new, original works created specifically for this publication.

Jo-Ann Jennings contributed the first ten stories. Jo-Ann is a recent graduate of Phillips Theological Seminary with an M.Div. degree. She has wide experience as a writer and teacher, including serving as a reporter and editor for a local newspaper. Combining her skills as a creative writer with her training as a pastor and biblical interpreter, Jo-Ann has provided here an outstanding collection of insightful and poignant retellings of biblical stories.

Pam McGrath, who also contributed ten stories, recently began her studies at Phillips Theological Seminary after a long and eventful career as a professional storyteller and storytelling coach in Atlanta, Georgia. She brings the insights of a "natural born" storyteller to bear on the text and constantly surprises us with new wrinkles on old and often all-too-familiar stories. There is never a stale story in Pam's repertoire.

Michael E. Williams can justly be called the "dean" of biblical storytelling,

10

since he is the founding editor of the *Storyteller's Companion to the Bible* series and a long-time storyteller/pastor. He has practiced the art of storytelling in a variety of settings across the nation, ranging from storytelling festivals to local churches. In presenting the final five stories in this volume, he has utilized insights from his long career in a ministry of storytelling.

Parallel Stories

None of the biblical stories developed in a vacuum. They came out of a rich storytelling culture. The parallel stories are provided to bring to our attention the storytelling milieu out of which these stories came. Their purpose is to acquaint us with the ancient world of storytelling so that we can better understand the storyteller's craft and the context in which the stories were originally told and heard. This information will aid the modern storyteller in adapting these stories to fit the sensibilities and experiences of a modern audience.

How to Use this Book

Bible stories share many characteristics with traditional stories. As every storyteller knows, there is no one way to retell a story, yet a storyteller cannot retell a story just any old way.

On the one hand, it is often difficult for people of faith to think that Bible stories can be retold imaginatively. We tend to think of the Bible in rigid terms—as having one, clear, unimpeachable meaning. Yet the plurality of the Gospels themselves leads us to a different conclusion. They tell the same stories in different ways, and thus illustrate that it is not only possible but also appropriate to retell the same basic story in different ways.

On the other hand, the possibilities for retelling are not endless; it is possible to tell a story in a form that is not appropriate to the original story. Successful biblical storytelling involves a delicate balance between the meanings inherent in the ancient story, the boundaries of understanding in the modern community within which the story is told, and the imagination of the storyteller who puts it all together. The storyteller must first start with sound methods of interpretation of the biblical text and its meaning in its original context. Then the storyteller's task will be to recast the story into a form that allows it to have meaning in today's context that is consistent with its ancient meaning.

This book is intended to be a resource to promote the telling of Bible stories. But there is an important component that is not present within these pages. That is what you, the reader, bring to the text. Your experiences and understandings are vital to your own creation of viable retellings of the biblical stories. Only in this way can these ancient stories become real and pertinent to the lives of people today.

Synoptic Stories about Jesus:
A Narrative Introduction

Mikeal C. Parsons

Since the second-century effort of Tatian's *Diatessaron*, Christians have been drawn to "harmonies" of the four Gospels. One thinks especially of the harmonies produced by Augustine and Calvin. A harmony is an edited version of the Gospels that puts them together to tell one story rather than the four stories they tell when read separately. The structure of this volume resembles a Gospel harmony in several respects. For example, if one were to read the comments from beginning to end one would have covered the canonical "life" of Jesus from annunciation to ascension. But, as is the case with any harmony, one would have read an account of Jesus' career that does not exist in any extant Christian Gospel.

This volume, however, tries to avoid the pitfalls of the harmony approach to the Gospels. A real attempt has been made to deal with each Gospel on its own terms, even with those stories that are found in common in all three Synoptic Gospels—Matthew, Mark, and Luke. Here our choice of texts was based on 1) texts that seemed to have interesting rhetorical and storytelling features; 2) texts that (at least in one of the synoptic versions) were featured as a reading in the Revised Common Lectionary; 3) texts that had not been treated in another volume in this series; and 4) balance among the Gospels. Of the twenty-five stories included here, thirteen are found in all three Synoptics, three are in two Gospels, six are unique to Luke, two are unique to Matthew, and one is unique to Mark. With regard to those stories that appear in two or three Gospels, the reader will note that, in some cases, I specifically focus on one of the accounts, making only passing reference to the other(s). Thus, while only one story is unique to Mark per se (#5 "The Beginning of the Gospel"), Mark's version is often the sole focus of my analysis of other stories (see, e.g., #10 "Jairus's Daughter and a Woman's Faith"; #14 "The Confession at Caesarea Philippi"; #16 "The Healing of Bartimaeus"; and #23 "The Empty Tomb"). In other instances, I treat aspects of the various accounts in order to highlight the differing emphases that the synoptic writers place on the same story (see, e.g., #6 "The Temptation"; #9 "The Stilling of the Storm"; #15 "The Transfiguration"; and #20 "Jesus Taken Captive").

With most scholars, I assume that Mark was written first and that, where stories appear in all three accounts, Luke and Matthew can be understood as responses to Mark, in many cases providing different interpretations of the same event, sometimes subtly so. Furthermore, I am interested in the interrelationships of the Gospels, not from the point of view of their *composition*, but rather of their *reception*; in other words, the focus is on the *first reception* of the *final form* of the text, not on how that text came to be in that final form. Shifting from the point of view of the Gospel writer and how he compiled various stories to the way the audience hears the story means we are not interested in the minute changes of single words or slight changes of word order (unless they would prove to be significant to a listening audience), but rather focus on those changes that the authorial audience (the audience the writer had in mind when he wrote) would not have missed. Then we ask: what would be the rhetorical impact of such modifications on this authorial audience?

In order to understand this question, we need to be reminded that the reading of the Gospels in the early church was presumably an aural and communal experience. The texts were read aloud in some kind of community gathering. Though we cannot know the specifics, a reading or "performance" of a Gospel after a shared meal or the Eucharist (or both), in a context that parallels the public reading of literature after banquets or symposia, is certainly an attractive option.

Understanding the "performance" of the text means exploring the rhetorical devices and strategies of the text (repetition of terms, echoes of Old Testament stories, links to other parts of the story). Understanding *how* the story is told is key to understanding *what* the story is about. Furthermore, understanding the original context of the Gospel storyteller and his audience allows us to make explicit connections to the modern storyteller of the Synoptic Gospels and her audience. This approach may provide clues to how the modern storyteller might "perform" the story again in ways that are faithful and free—faithful to the original context, yet free to express it in fresh new ways. Focusing on the Gospels as stories allows one to explore the narratives in terms of their plot, sequence, characterization, motifs, and themes. What emerges from such readings are four distinct portraits of Jesus that Gospel harmonies tend to elide into one.

Given the close similarities between and among Matthew, Mark, and Luke, their differences are sometimes overlooked. The Synoptic Gospels take their name, "Synoptic," from the Greek word *synoptaō*, meaning "to see together." Indeed, these three Gospels do seem to tell the story of Jesus from the same basic perspective, especially when compared to John's Gospel. In the Synoptics, Jesus tells parables; in John he does not, speaking rather in long discourses or speeches. In the Synoptics, Jesus exorcises demons; in John, he does not. In the Synoptics, the cleansing of the Temple occurs near the end of the story and is the precipitating event for Jesus' arrest; in John, the Temple cleansing is near the beginning of his public ministry. Characters significant to John's story are completely missing from the Synoptics: Nicodemus (John 3), the Samaritan woman (John 4), the blind man (John 9), Lazarus (John 11), and the "disciple whom Jesus loved" (by that name) are entirely absent from the Synoptic Gospels. The list of contrasts could continue, but the point is made. In contrast to John's story of Jesus, Matthew, Mark, and Luke share verbatim and near-verbatim agreements across large stretches of narrative. Someone has calculated that as much as 90 percent of Mark's Gospel appears in one or the other or both of the remaining Synoptics.

Nonetheless, we must not allow these similarities to mask the fact that upon closer analysis, the Synoptics themselves present distinct pictures of Jesus, and it is a mistake to speak, as some often do, of *the* Synoptic story of Jesus or of *the* theology of the Synoptics. Blending the stories together in this way produces an unrecognizable picture of Jesus and distorts the portrait of each writer. Ultimately, the church rejected Tatian's published harmony of the Gospels as an inadequate and impoverished substitute for the full and rich, and often divergent, witness of the four-fold Gospel of Matthew, Mark, Luke, and John. We would do well to follow the wisdom of church tradition at this point and seek to understand each Gospel writer's story on its own terms. At the risk of oversimplification, let me provide a thumbnail sketch of those portraits with the understanding that these synoptic portraits certainly have richer and deeper colors and hues in their fullest expression than I can articulate here.

Mark's Gospel attempts to unfold the "messianic secret" regarding Jesus' identity as the "Christ" and "son of God" (see chapter on "The Beginning of the Gospel"). To achieve this end, the plot of Mark is moved along by a series of conflicts, first between Jesus and the religious authorities (Mark 1–8) over the issue of his authority (as in Mark 2:7), and later between Jesus and his own disciples over the nature and purpose of his vocation (see the disciples' reaction to the passion predictions in Mark 8, 9, and 10). To accept Jesus as a miracle worker without coming to terms with the suffering dimension of his mission is to misunderstand him completely, according to Mark. The so-called "messianic secret" in Mark, whereby Jesus commands that his identity be kept secret (1:34, 44; 3:12; 5:43; 8:30), boils down to this: Better to say nothing about Jesus than to say something that is incomplete and therefore distorted! The various responses by Markan characters to Jesus are conveniently catalogued in the parable of the sower and its interpretation (Mark 4:1-20). Some, like the hardened path, refuse to receive Jesus' word, and Satan comes and takes it away; think of the religious authorities who refuse to acknowledge Jesus' teaching and authority (2:6; 3:5-6). Some, like the rocky soil, receive the word but it takes no root, so that when persecution comes they fall away; think of the disciples who respond positively at first, but when persecution comes,

15

they all fall away (see Mark 14:27, 50). Some are like the thorns who allow the cares of the world, the delight in riches, and the desire of other things to choke out the word; think of the Markan characters with religious, economic, and civil power—Herod (6:14-29), the rich young ruler (10:17-22), Judas (14:10-11)—who allow their cares, delights, and desires to extinguish their initial attraction to Jesus. Finally, the response of the "good soil" is found in the reaction of the minor characters in Mark's Gospel to the character of Jesus: the friends of the paralytic (Mark 2), the woman with the flow of blood (Mark 5), the Syrophoenician woman (Mark 7), blind Bartimaeus (Mark 10), and the woman who anoints Jesus (Mark 14), among others.

Matthew takes a different tack from Mark. His Gospel is more didactic, revolving around the five major speeches of Jesus. If Mark reveals the character of Jesus in what he does, Matthew reveals the character of Jesus by what he says! This will come as no surprise to those who understand that, in Matthew, Jesus is depicted as a new Moses who has come not to destroy the law but to fulfill it (Matt. 5:17). The overall structure of Matthew is intended to reflect the books of Moses. Just as there are five books in the Pentateuch attributed to Moses, so Matthew contains five major discourses by Jesus (each of which is brought to closure with the same formulaic expression "and when Jesus had finished"; see 7:28; 11:1; 13:53; 19:1; 26:1). The "five books of Jesus" correspond to the "five books of Moses," and Jesus is depicted as the new Moses who comes to complete Israel's story of redemption. Matthew ties Jesus' story to Israel's story through various means, including explicit Old Testament quotation formulae (see "The Visit of the Magi") and allusions. In so doing, Matthew is like the "scribe trained for the kingdom of heaven," a householder "who brings out of his treasure what is new and what is old" (Matt. 13:52 NRSV). Many of the stories about Jesus, couched between these discourses, serve to underscore this view of Jesus as the fulfillment of Old Testament expectations. Despite this characterization, however, it would be a mistake to think of Matthew, as many have, as the "Jewish Gospel," as though Matthew has no interest in the inclusion of Gentiles into the people of God. Rather, an interest in the place of non-Jews in the history of salvation is evident both in the beginning of Matthew's Gospel, with its inclusion of non-Israelite women in Jesus' genealogy (see "The Genealogy and Birth of Jesus") and Gentile Magi in the story of Jesus' birth (see "The Visit of the Magi"), and the end of the Gospel, with its emphasis in the Great Commission of going to all the "nations," or rather "Gentiles" (Matt. 28:19-20; see "The Death on the Cross").

Finally, Luke presents yet another portrait of Jesus. Here, Jesus is a prophet on the move. In a Gospel dominated by a travel narrative (Luke 9–19) and where, in its sequel, the followers of Jesus are known as "the Way" (Acts 9:2), the journey motif is quite pronounced. This journey is part of fulfilling the "plan of God" (Acts 2:23). But this journey is filled with twists and turns; often things are not what they seem. In Luke's theme that we call "the great reversal," the high and mighty are brought down, the hungry are filled, and the lowly are exalted (Luke 1:51-53; 6:20-26). This interest in the social outcasts and marginalized is seen throughout Jesus' teachings and actions (see, e.g., "Zacchaeus"). Still, it would be a mistake to label Luke the "Gentile" Gospel, as though Luke had no interest in Israel's story. For example, the announcements of the births of John the Baptist and Jesus echo the Old Testament commissioning stories of Moses and Gideon, among others (see "Prophecies of Jesus' Birth").

Furthermore, each Gospel writer intends for the audience to accept his portrait of Jesus as "true." So, while the evangelists understand that they are conveying information (historical, cultural, and theological) about Jesus, they are no less intent on transforming the audience's point of view of Jesus to conform to their own. Thus, the Gospels are both informational and transformational. But then *all* good stories potentially have this power to transform. We rarely tell or listen to stories purely for the information they contain. We certainly do not repeat stories that are "merely" factual; it is, rather, the affective dimension of stories that causes us to return to them time and time again, seeking to find our story in that story. Good storytellers know this desire on the part of their audience and shape their stories accordingly. The synoptic writers were good storytellers, and the purpose of the biblical commentary in this volume is to make transparent the power of the transformational rhetoric that each Gospel presents.

What Are New Testament Parallel Stories?

Dennis E. Smith

If a story is told about a modern-day president in which he eventually says, "I cannot tell a lie," we might think immediately of the first such story, the one about George Washington and the cherry tree. Stories are like that. They often draw on traditional formats or motifs or plots. It is the stock-in-trade of a good storyteller to utilize shared cultural data to make her stories come alive.

The stories in the New Testament work the same way. They are often adapted to standard plots and motifs from the culture. Stories about Jesus as a miracle worker, for example, tend to follow patterns of miracle stories from the culture. Similarly, other stories about Jesus, such as the stories of his birth and death, tend to be modeled on similar stories about heroes in Greek, Roman, and Jewish tradition.

"Parallel stories" are provided here to help us trace some of the background and foreground of the stories about Jesus. They are intended to give us a sense of the cultural cues within a story that would have been noticed by the ancient audience. They also help to illuminate the "building blocks" out of which a story was built. Armed with this information, we are better able to appreciate the art of storytelling as it was practiced by the biblical storytellers.

Storytelling Motifs

There was a standard way in which certain types of stories were told in the world of the New Testament. In particular, stories about heroes contained common patterns and motifs that were influential in the development of stories about Jesus. As mentioned above, these patterns can be seen especially in the miracle stories and in the stories about the birth and death of Jesus. To use such traditions would give more credibility to the story being told, because the story would then fit the expectations of the audience. The parallel stories provide examples of such traditional story motifs.

Social and Cultural Motifs

The Gospel stories also reflected their world in other ways. The ancient storyteller could take it for granted that the ancient audience would be familiar with the social customs of the day, such as meal customs or burial customs, that might be referenced in the story. Modern hearers, however, need help in understanding these relevant pieces of the story. The parallel stories will often explain or illustrate these features of the ancient story.

Jewish Traditions

The Gospels are full of references to Jesus as the fulfillment of an Old Testament prophecy or pattern or messianic theme. They often tell their stories in such a way that they echo Old Testament stories. Some of these echoes are mentioned in the commentary and some are illustrated with references in the parallel stories. Jewish storytelling tradition did not end with the Old Testament, however; it continued in other Jewish literature as well, as illustrated by excerpts from apocryphal and pseudepigraphic literature, Philo, Josephus, and rabbinic literature. This tradition formed the backdrop for many of the stories about Jesus as seen in examples collected in the parallel stories.

Today, an opening phrase such as "once upon a time" will immediately set the stage for the kind of story to follow. So also ancient storytellers had standard ways in which they structured stories that were understood by their audiences. The parallel stories will help us recognize these aspects of the biblical stories and aid us in constructing new versions of these stories for today's culture.

Learning to Tell Bible Stories

A Self-Directed Workshop

1. Read the story aloud at least twice. You may choose to read the translation
   included here or the one you are accustomed to reading. We recommend
   that you examine at least two translations as you prepare, so you can hear
   the differences in the way they sound when read aloud.

   Do read them *aloud*. Yes, if you are not by yourself, people may give
   you funny looks, but this really is important. Your ear will hear things
   about the passage that your eye will miss. Besides, you can't skim when
   you read aloud. You are forced to take your time, and you might notice
   aspects of the story that you never saw (or heard) before.

   As you read, pay special attention to *where* the story takes place,
   when the story takes place, *who* the characters are, *what* objects are
   important to the story, and the general *order of events* in the story.
2. Now close your eyes and imagine the story taking place. This is your
   chance to become a playwright/director or screenwriter/filmmaker
   because you will experience the story on the stage or screen in your imagination. Enjoy this part of the process. It takes only a few minutes, and the
   budget is within everybody's reach.
3. Look back at the story briefly to make sure you haven't left out any
   important people, places, things, or events.
4. Try telling the story. This works better if you have someone to listen
   (even the family pet will do). You can try speaking aloud to yourself or to
   an imaginary listener. Afterward ask your listener or yourself what questions arise as a result of this telling. Is the information you need about the
   people, places, things, or language in the story? Is it appropriate to the
   age, experiences, and interests of those who will be hearing it? Does the
   story capture your imagination? One more thing: You don't have to be
   able to explain the meaning of a story to tell it. In fact, those of the most
   enduring interest have an element of mystery about them.
5. Read the "Comments on the Story" provided for each passage. Are some
   of your questions answered there? You may wish also to look at a good
   Bible dictionary for place names, characters, professions, objects, or words
   that you need to learn more about. *The Interpreter's Dictionary of the
   Bible* (Nashville: Abingdon Press, 1962) and *The Anchor Bible Dictionary*

(New York: Doubleday, 1992) are the most complete sources for Bible study. A good one-volume source is the *HarperCollins Bible Dictionary* (San Francisco: HarperSanFrancisco, 1996).

6. Read the "Retelling the Story" section for the passage you are learning to tell. Does it give you any ideas about how you will tell the story? How would you tell it differently? Would you tell it from another character's point of view? How would that make it a different story? Would you transfer it to a modern setting? What places and characters will you choose to correspond to those in the biblical story? Remember, the retellings that are provided are not meant to be told exactly as they are written here. They are to serve as springboards for your imagination as you develop your own telling.

7. Read the "parallel stories" that accompany each passage. These give you insights into the raw materials used by the original storyteller in putting together the biblical story. An appreciation for the "craft" of the ancient storyteller will help you develop your own craft as a storyteller.

8. Once you have the elements of the story in mind and have chosen the approach you are going to take in retelling it, you need to practice, practice, practice. Tell the story aloud ten or twenty or fifty times over a period of several days or weeks. Listen as you tell your story. Revise your telling as you go along. Remember that you are not memorizing a text; you are preparing a living event. Each time you tell the story, it will be a little different, because you will be different (if for no other reason than that you have told the story before).

9. Then "taste and see" that even the stories of God are good—not all sweet, but good and good for us and for those who hunger to hear.

The Genealogy and Birth of Jesus

Matthew's story of Jesus begins with a genealogy that emphasizes the role of women and the dual paternity of Jesus as Son of God/Son of David.

The Story

The genealogy of Jesus Christ, son of David, son of Abraham.

Abraham was the father of Isaac, Isaac of Jacob, Jacob of Judah and his brothers, Judah of Perez and Zarah (their mother was Tamar), Perez of Hezron, Hezron of Ram, Ram of Amminadab, Amminadab of Nahshon, Nahshon of Salmon, Salmon of Boaz (his mother was Rahab), Boaz of Obed (his mother was Ruth), Obed of Jesse; and Jesse was the father of King David.

David was the father of Solomon (his mother had been the wife of Uriah), Solomon of Rehoboam, Rehoboam of Abijah, Abijah of Asa, Asa of Jehoshaphat, Jehoshaphat of Joram, Joram of Uzziah, Uzziah of Jotham, Jotham of Ahaz, Ahaz of Hezekiah, Hezekiah of Manasseh, Manasseh of Amon, Amon of Josiah; and Josiah was the father of Jeconiah and his brothers at the time of the deportation to Babylon.

After the deportation Jeconiah was the father of Shealtiel, Shealtiel of Zerubbabel, Zerubbabel of Abiud, Abiud of Eliakim, Eliakim of Azor, Azor of Zadok, Zadok of Achim, Achim of Eliud, Eliud of Eleazar, Eleazar of Matthan, Matthan of Jacob, Jacob of Joseph, the husband of Mary, who gave birth to Jesus called Messiah.

There were thus fourteen generations in all from Abraham to David, fourteen from David until the deportation to Babylon, and fourteen from the deportation until the Messiah.

This is how the birth of Jesus Christ came about. His mother Mary was betrothed to Joseph; before their marriage she found she was going to have a child through the Holy Spirit. Being a man of principle, and at the same time wanting to save her from exposure, Joseph made up his mind to have the marriage contract quietly set aside. He had resolved on this, when an angel of the Lord appeared to him in a dream and said, 'Joseph, son of David, do not be afraid to take Mary home with you to be your wife. It is through the Holy Spirit that she has conceived. She will bear a son; and you shall give him the name Jesus, for he will save his people from their sins.' All this happened in order to fulfil what the Lord declared through the prophet: 'A virgin will conceive and bear a son, and he shall be called Emmanuel,' a name which means 'God is with us.' When he woke Joseph did as the angel of the Lord had directed him; he took Mary home to be his wife, but had no intercourse with her until her son was born. And he named the child Jesus.

23

Comments on the Story

The opening line of Matthew serves as the title of the work: "The genealogy [in Greek: the book of the beginning (genesis)] of Jesus Christ, son of David, son of Abraham." Like Mark, Matthew includes in this introduction some of the most significant titles assigned to Jesus, "Christ," "son of David," "son of Abraham." Unlike Mark, however, Matthew begins in the past with a genealogy of Jesus' ancestry. Thus Matthew's story explicitly and self-consciously acknowledges its indebtedness to other stories—the stories of God's dealing with the children of Abraham and of David.

This passage, Matthew 1:1-25, divides naturally into two rhetorical units, 1:1-17 and 1:18-25. The three names in 1:1, Christ ... David ... Abraham, are repeated in verse 17, Abraham ... David ... Christ, and form an *inclusio* that any hearer would recognize. Matthew 1:18 repeats the reference to "genesis" (see 1:1) and proceeds to explain how the ancestry from Abraham to Jesus can be traced through Joseph, whom the narrator goes to great lengths to argue is not the biological father of Jesus. We shall take up each unit in turn.

Ancient listeners, and even some modern ones, would have been fascinated by this story that begins with the "book of the genealogy of Jesus," language that recalls that of Genesis 2:4 and 5:1. But still the modern reader may rightly ask, Why does Matthew begin with a genealogy? The summary at the end of this first unit discloses that "there were thus fourteen generations in all from Abraham to David, fourteen from David until the deportation to Babylon, and fourteen from the deportation until the Messiah" (1:17). While scholars have noted the difficulties with wringing a 3 x 14 plan from a list that contains only 41 names, Matthew sees in this 3 x 14 schema the key to "holy history." The numbers are significant Fourteen is, of course, a multiple of seven, the number of perfection (seven days of creation, Sabbath rest, etc.). Thus in these three discrete periods of Hebrew history—ancestral period, monarchy, exile—there are six periods of seven generations according to Matthew's reckoning. Hence the advent of the Messiah is appropriately the beginning of the seventh (and final?) period, the messianic period. Further, the name "David," which in Hebrew was spelled without vowels, has the numeric value of 14 (D-4; V-6; D-4). It is as though DAVID is written across Jewish history. Matthew seems to be arguing that if his audience had only seen what he had seen, they would not be able to escape the conclusion that he himself had reached—all the factors of history were converging on the appearance of Messiah at this very time.

The pattern in Matthew's genealogy is: A is the father of B, B is the father of C, etc., moving from Abraham to Christ. (To this, one might contrast Luke's genealogy, which moves in the opposite direction from Jesus to Adam with the pattern, Z is the son of Y, son of X, etc.) Two breaks in this pattern are noteworthy and surely would have arrested the attention of the hearers of the story.

First, four women are mentioned in the genealogy, breaking the patrilineal rhythm and representing an anomaly in ancestral lineages. Further, these women are not the great matriarchs of Israelite faith, though they do come from different periods: Tamar from the ancestral period, Rahab from the time of the conquest and settlement, Ruth from the period of the judges, and Bathsheba from the Davidic monarchy.

These women never appear together in another list from antiquity. How might the ancient audience have sought some common thread in their appearance here? While many answers have been proposed to this question, two are most compelling. First, these women are all non-Israelites, outsiders to the Israelites. Tamar, whose story is told in Genesis 38, though never identified as a foreigner as such in the biblical text, was clearly recognized as such in post-biblical Jewish texts. Jubilees 41:1 refers to her as an Aramean. Rahab was a Canaanite who lived in Jericho. Ruth was from the despised race of Moab, spawned from Lot's incestuous relationship with his elder daughter (see Gen. 19:30-38). Bathsheba is identified as the wife of Uriah, the Hittite, another non-Israelite.

These women also shared in common a checkered sexual history. Tamar played the prostitute to seduce her father-in-law, Judah, when he refused to send his last son to be her husband. Rahab was a prostitute who ran a brothel in Jericho, though she was heralded in later Christian texts as a mother of the faith (see Heb. 11:31). Ruth was presumed by later rabbis to have engaged in a little seduction of her own when in the middle of the night she uncovered the "feet" of Boaz on the threshing floor, (a)rousing him from sleep. And, of course, the illicit union of David with Bathsheba produced a stillbirth before it produced an heir in Solomon.

While androcentric interpretation of these women has tended to highlight their sinfulness, a more sensitive reading might note that in a patriarchal society where the rights and privileges of women were severely limited, each of these women did what was necessary to survive—ensuring an heir (Tamar), making a living as an unattached woman (Rahab), securing a husband and an heir (Ruth), and surviving the sexual advances of the most powerful person in the monarchy, the monarch himself (Bathsheba). More important, these women were used mightily by God in the history of salvation that for Matthew culminates in the birth of the Messiah. The stories of these four women then point to the story of a fifth woman, Mary, herself the victim of sexual innuendo in subsequent debates.

The second significant break in the genealogical pattern is precisely here in reference to Mary: "Jacob [was the father] of Joseph, the husband of Mary, who gave birth to Jesus called Messiah" (1:16). Up to this point in the genealogy, the active voice of the verb "to give birth" had been used, as in "Abraham was the father of Isaac," and so on down the list. Here for the first time a passive voice is used, "Mary gave birth to Jesus" (or "Mary to whom Jesus was born"). And while Mary in Matthew is presented neither as a Gentile nor as unchaste, nonetheless the birth of Jesus to an unwed (though betrothed) mother is irregular at the least.

The second unit in this section, 1:18-25, attempts to answer questions that surround the birth of Jesus, especially questions concerning Jesus' dual paternity as "son of God" and "son of David." The virginal conception of Jesus is asserted, not argued, by Matthew. What Matthew does provide is scriptural warrant for Joseph not to divorce Mary by citing Isaiah 7:14 in 1:22-23. This citation, part of the scripture formula employed by Matthew elsewhere in his Gospel (as in Matt. 2:15, 17-18; 2:23b; 4:14-16; 8:17; 12:17-21; 13:35; 21:4-5; 27:9-10), has been the subject of much scholarly debate. Some have accused Matthew of simply reading a messianic prophecy back into a text that in its original historical context has no messianic overtones. While this argument may be true, strictly speaking, one should recognize that (1) Matthew stands in a long Jewish exegetical tradition of treating this passage messianically and (2) what sets Matthew's interpretation apart from other contemporary Jewish interpreters is not his messianic interpretation but his identification of the Messiah as Jesus.

In its original context the "prophetic sign" Isaiah offers Ahaz in Isaiah 7:14 is most likely a reference to one of Isaiah's own children, during whose infancy the kings of Syria and Israel would fall. During the compilation of the book of Isaiah (long noted for its complicated composition history), this "non-messianic" text in Isaiah 7 was placed in close proximity to what is clearly a messianic text in Isaiah 9 ("For a child has been born to us, a son is given to us; he will bear the symbol of dominion on his shoulder ... bestowed on David's throne and on his kingdom"), inviting subsequent interpreters of Isaiah to give the first reference to a child in 7:14 a messianic reading in light of the second reference in 9:6-7. The Greek translators of this passage in the third century B.C.E. did exactly that, making more explicit the messianic overtones by depicting the birth of this child as a supernatural event, translating the rather innocuous Hebrew word *alma* ("young woman") with the more theologically loaded Greek term *parthenos* ("virgin"). Matthew takes the next step in this messianic exegesis by identifying "a virgin" as *the* virgin" and identifying this messianic figure with Jesus. Thus, the divine sonship of Jesus is demonstrated by his virginal conception. And of course the name Emmanuel, "God is with us," given to Jesus here through the prophecy of Isaiah, is fulfilled at the end of Matthew's Gospel through Jesus' words to his disciples, "I will be with you always" (28:20).

The second point Matthew makes is that Jesus is also "son of David." Here, though, is the problem: If Joseph is not the biological father of Jesus, how is it that Jesus can enjoy the benefits of Joseph's Davidic lineage, that is, the other part of his dual paternity? Matthew provides a subtle but persuasive answer. In the message to Joseph, the angel of the Lord informs him that "[Mary] will bear a son; and *you* shall give him the name Jesus" (emphasis added). The naming of Jesus by Joseph is significant, because in Jewish law, when a father names a child, it makes him the child's legal parent (see *Mishna Baba Batra* 8:6). This legal status as son bestows all the paternal benefits that a biological son would enjoy. Jesus is joined to the Davidic lineage through Joseph's legal adoption of him, symbolized by the naming.

The first unit answers who Jesus is: he is the Messiah, "son of David," "son of Abraham." The second unit describes how he received dual paternity: he was born to a virgin, but legally adopted by a descendant of David. Jesus is shown to have all the requisite credentials and pedigrees for Messiah. And so Matthew's story of Jesus, Israel's Messiah, has begun.

Retelling the Story

> Being a man of principle, and at the same time wanting to save her from exposure, Joseph made up his mind to have the marriage contract quietly set aside. (Matthew 1:19)

Joseph waited until dark to go to the tavern, hoping he would see no one that he knew. There are times when a man just wants to crawl into a bottomless bowl of wine and swim around alone without the advice and bantering of friends who think they have all the answers. Such a temporary death could not be all that bad, drowning in intoxication, his questions grape-stained in fermentation. His wasn't a story he could tell just anyone. He wasn't so sure himself he wasn't just as goofy as the old man who lived outside the city who thought of himself as a wolf ... Joseph mulled that thought over. Now that he—Joseph—had heard angels, maybe that old man wasn't so crazy after all.

The donkey of Joseph's friend Shlomo was tied outside the tavern. Joseph sighed, thinking that as much as he didn't want to talk to anyone, if he were forced to tell his story, Shlomo would be the most understanding How could anyone be judgmental who owned a beast like that donkey? He was the most flea-bitten animal in the entire country, having more bare spots than the desert, and one eye never closed.

"Joseph, my friend!" Shlomo called as Joseph walked into the stuffy room, overwhelmed with the onion-y smell of old sweat, made bearable only by the sweet trumpet call of the wine. "My ewes are dropping lambs as if there were no tomorrow," Shlomo continued. "I've given one to the barkeep. He's promised to keep my cup filled until the moon changes. Drink, my friend, drink! The drink is on the lamb!" He tore a shred of bread from a crusty loaf and thrust it at Joseph. "Here," he said, "I'm sure it's not more than a week old!"

27

Joseph let the wine numb his worries before he began to express them. "Mary is showing," he finally said. "It's obvious she's with child."

"And this is reason to be unhappy?" Shlomo shouted, leaning over to nudge Joseph and wink.

"I have never come into her," Joseph replied, motioning for more wine. "I know I'm older than she is, but why would she disgrace me and put herself in such danger? She's humiliating me and her family—my family—and if the town finds out—you know what they'll do! I have earned the love of a pure woman. I don't deserve this kind of blatant insult."

Shlomo was quiet for a moment. "We haven't had a stoning in a long time, Joseph," he finally said. "It could be good for the morale of the people."

Joseph shot Shlomo a glance that caused him to shrug. "It was just a thought," Shlomo said.

Quintilian, a first-century C.E. Roman rhetorician, argued that background information on a celebrated hero, such as a listing of ancestors, was indispensable for narrating the hero's achievements: "In the first place there is a distinction to be made as regards time between the period in which the objects of our praise lived and the time preceding their birth. . . . With regard to things preceding a man's birth, there are his country, his parents and his ancestors, a theme which may be handled in two ways. For either it will be creditable to the objects of our praise not to have fallen short of the fair fame of their country and of their sires or to have ennobled a humble origin by the glory of their achievements." (*Institutio oratoria*, 3.7.10) (from LCL)

"This is *Mary* we're speaking of," Joseph said. "This is the woman I love! Do you think I could live with myself if I allowed her to come to such an end? Who could look into that innocent face and want to kill her? Besides. . ." He covered his face with his hands, hesitating before blurting it out.

"I was visited by an angel," he said.

"Barkeep?" Shlomo said, lifting his hand, pointing to his cup. "Just keep pouring! I think I'm here for the night." He looked again at Joseph—deeply—and chewed on his lip, pondering his words. "And this angel ... did it have wings?"

Joseph nodded. "Beautiful—powerful—magnificent wings," he said.

"And music?" Shlomo asked. "Was there music?"

"I don't think so," Joseph said. "There was—peace—yes, peace in place of music."

"Did you wrestle with him like the prophets?" Shlomo asked.

"No wrestling," Joseph answered thoughtfully. "I was in awe actually, and his voice was so filled with God."

"That would explain why you're not limping," Shlomo said, shaking his head. "I understand it's very difficult to win when wrestling with an angel."

Joseph nodded. "But ... what do you think? Do you believe me?"

Shlomo raised his hand again, motioning to Joseph. "Just pour it directly into his mouth!" he shouted to the barkeep. "He's eaten some bad weeds."

"Do you want to hear what the angel said, or do you want to make jokes?" Joseph asked quietly, not wanting to draw attention to their conversation. It would be easy for a stoning mob to grow from a tavern of drinking men looking for anything that would put excitement into their lives.

"Yes! Yes! Of course I want to know what the angel said," Shlomo said.

"The angel said not to be afraid to take Mary as my wife." Now as the memory enveloped him, Joseph found that his courage was rising. He could feel the grace of the angel as he held him; he pulled strength from the words. "The angel said that the child would save his people from their sins, and that we must name him *Immanuel* because it means *God is with us*. The angel said that Mary

Great men in the Greco-Roman world were often thought to be of divine parentage. Here Alexander the Great is claimed to be a descendant both of the divine Heracles and the god Zeus, who is said to have visited his mother in the form of a thunderbolt: "As for the lineage of Alexander, on his father's side he was a descendant of Heracles through Caranus, and on his mother's side a descendant of Aeacus through Neoptolemus; this is accepted without any question. And we are told that Philip [Alexander's father], after being initiated into the mysteries of Samothrace at the same time with Olympias [Alexander's mother], he himself being still a youth and she an orphan child, fell in love with her and betrothed himself to her at once with the consent of her brother, Arymbas. When, then, the night before that on which the marriage was consummated, the bride dreamed that there was a peal of thunder and that a thunder-bolt fell on her womb, and that thereby much fire was kindled, which broke into flames and traveled all about, and then was extinguished.... Moreover, a serpent was once seen lying stretched out by the side of Olympias as she slept, and we are told that this, more than anything else, dulled the ardor of Philip's attentions to his wife, so that he no longer came often to sleep by her side, either because he feared that some spells and enchantments might be practiced upon him by her, or because he shrank from her embraces in the conviction that she was the partner of a superior being." (Plutarch, *Life of Alexander* 2.1-3.2 [first cent. c.e.]; from Boring-Berger-Colpe, 37, no. 6) is a virgin, that she was not touched by someone else. She has never been known by a mortal."

Shlomo at last was serious. "My friend," he said, putting his hand on Joseph's shoulder, "you believe whatever you must believe to get through this. Yes, I think you are crazier than the old man who thinks he's a wolf, but I think you are crazy with love, and Mary's death would kill my best friend in the world. Your secret is safe with me. I will forever as long as I live swear that the child, even when he grows into a man, looks like the spitting image of you. I will even swear that I witnessed the consummation if you like."

Joseph sighed and shook his head, puzzling over the predicament. Then he turned to Shlomo and said, "My friend, thank you for listening to my story. I know now what I must do."

His steps to the door were slow although he welcomed the thought of fresh air. He turned around just once, giving his friend a look of thanks, but wishing Shlomo had believed him.

There was no doubt in Joseph's mind as he stepped into the moonlight as to whether or not he had really seen the angel. He could not have imagined such a dream. But whether or not it had happened as he remembered it, Shlomo was right. He had to do whatever he could to save Mary and keep her and the child safe. *(Jo-Ann Jennings)*

The Visit of the Magi

Wise men from the east seek the place of the Messiah's birth, and Herod responds with the massacre of the innocents.

The Story

Jesus was born at Bethlehem in Judaea during the reign of Herod. After his birth astrologers from the east arrived in Jerusalem, asking, 'Where is the newborn king of the Jews? We observed the rising of his star, and we have come to pay him homage.' King Herod was greatly perturbed when he heard this, and so was the whole of Jerusalem. He called together the chief priests and scribes of the Jews, and asked them where the Messiah was to be born. 'At Bethlehem in Judaea,' they replied, 'for this is what the prophet wrote: "Bethlehem in the land of Judah, you are by no means least among the rulers of Judah; for out of you shall come a ruler to be the shepherd of my people Israel."'

Then Herod summoned the astrologers to meet him secretly, and ascertained from them the exact time when the star had appeared. He sent them to Bethlehem, and said, 'Go and make a careful search for the child, and when you have found him, bring me word, so that I may go myself and pay him homage.'

After hearing what the king had to say they set out; there before them was the star they had seen rising, and it went ahead of them until it stopped above the place where the child lay. They were overjoyed at the sight of it and, entering the house, they saw the child with Mary his mother and bowed low in homage to him; they opened their treasure chests and presented gifts to him: gold, frankincense, and myrrh. Then they returned to their own country by another route, for they had been warned in a dream not to go back to Herod.

After they had gone, an angel of the Lord appeared to Joseph in a dream, and said, 'Get up, take the child and his mother and escape with them to Egypt, and stay there until I tell you; for Herod is going to search for the child to kill him.' So Joseph got up, took mother and child by night, and sought refuge with them in Egypt, where he stayed till Herod's death. This was to fulfil what the Lord had declared through the prophet: 'Out of Egypt I have called my son.'

When Herod realized that the astrologers had tricked him he flew into a rage, and gave orders for the massacre of all the boys aged two years or under, in Bethlehem and throughout the whole district, in accordance with the time he had ascertained from the astrologers. So the words spoken through Jeremiah the prophet were fulfilled: 'A voice was heard in Rama, sobbing in bitter grief; it was Rachel weeping for her children, and refusing to be comforted, because they were no more.'

After Herod's death an angel of the Lord appeared in a dream to Joseph in Egypt and said to him, 'Get up, take the child and his mother, and go to the land of Israel, for those who threatened the child's life are dead.'

So he got up, took mother and child with him, and came to the land of Israel. But when he heard that Archelaus had succeeded his father Herod as king of Judaea, he was afraid to go there. Directed by a dream, he withdrew to the region of Galilee, where he settled in a town called Nazareth. This was to fulfil the words spoken through the prophets: 'He shall be called a Nazarene.'

Comments on the Story

Matthew 2:1-23 consists of two sections: Matthew 2:1-12 is the story of the magi's search for the Messiah and Herod's response to them; Matthew 2:13-23 details the migration of Joseph to Egypt, Herod's massacre of the Hebrew children, and the return of Joseph and his family to Nazareth. We take up each section in turn.

The unit begins with magi or "astrologers" coming from the east to Jerusalem to inquire about the "newborn king of the Jews" (2:1). Though the term "magi" could be heard as a pejorative reference to magicians or sorcerers (see Acts 13:6), their appearance here in Matthew seems much more positive. Indeed, they are pious seekers after the "king of the Jews." And they are Gentiles; the phrase "king of the Jews" is used of Jesus only by Gentiles in Matthew (as in Matt. 27:11, 29, 37). Why have these Gentiles come to Jerusalem? Because "We observed the rising of his star, and we have come to pay him homage" (2:2). Rather than rejoicing at the news the magi bring, Herod, and indeed "the whole of Jerusalem," was frightened (2:3). He summoned "the chief priests and scribes of the Jews, and asked them where the Messiah was to be born" (2:4). They answer by naming Bethlehem and quoting scripture (Mic. 5:2 with 2 Sam. 5:2).

In addition to the explicit citation of scripture, the first part of this story draws heavily on the Old Testament for its imagery of a Messiah descended from David. In Numbers 22–24, the king of Moab, Balak, called for a famous visionary named Balaam to come from the east (Num. 23:7) to use his magical arts against Moses. Instead of cursing Moses, however, Balaam had this positive prophecy: "a star will come forth out of Jacob, a comet will arise from Israel" (Num. 24:17).

This passage was understood not only to predict the emergence of the Davidic monarchy, but also, in later Judaism (by the time of Matthew), to refer to the coming of the Messiah. In fact, by the time of the second Jewish revolt in 135 C.E., the revolutionary Simon ben Kosibah was hailed by his followers as "Bar Kochba," which means "son of a star" and was meant to refer to his identity as "Messiah." So though the characters in the story, the magi, may not understand the significance of seeing the child's star, the audience, both *in* the text (Herod and "the whole of Jerusalem") and *of* the text (the first and subsequent readers), would no doubt catch the allusion here to the messianic prophecy in Numbers 24.

Matthew knows that during his earthly ministry Jesus came only to minister to the "lost sheep of the house of Israel" (10:5-6), but he finds a compelling way to include Gentiles in his story of salvation from the beginning. These pious Gentiles come to Jerusalem because they have received a revelation through pagan astrology, and they have responded to this "natural revelation." But their revelation is incomplete; they are unable to locate the "king of the Jews" without the aid of the Jews who have the scriptures, which reveal the birthplace of the Messiah. Here is the irony: the Gentiles know of the birth through their pagan sciences and wish to pay homage to the new king; the Jews, through their scriptures, know of the place of the birth, but refuse to worship the new king. Here then is the gospel in miniature: Gentiles come to Jews to learn about God's redeeming work in Jesus Christ. Or as Paul put it: "the Jew first, but the Greek also" (Rom. 1:16).

Herod secretly summons the magi and sends them to Bethlehem (2:7-8). He deceives them with promises of his own desire to see the new child: "Go and make a careful search for the child, and when you have found him, bring me word, so that I may go myself and pay him homage" (2:8*b*). To focus exclusively on the number of magi or the symbolism of their gifts of gold, frankincense, and myrrh, as has been the case for so much of the history of interpretation of this passage, is to miss the overall argument of the text. If the first part of this unit (2:1-8) records the implicit hostility at the news of the Messiah's birth, the second half (2:9-12) records the proper response to the news: the magi pay homage to the newborn king. They may be the first to worship Jesus, but they are not the last: a leper (8:2), a ruler (9:18), the disciples (14:33), a Canaanite woman (15:25), the mother of James and John (20:20), an unnamed woman (26:6-13), the women at the tomb (28:9), and the disciples, in the Gospel's final scene (28:17), all pay homage to Jesus. The appropriate response to Jesus from womb to tomb is to give him the same kind of reverence one would give God.

Herod's first plan is spoiled by two dreams: one in which the magi are warned "not to go back to Herod" (2:12), and another in which Joseph is warned to take his family to Egypt to escape Herod's wrath (2:13). The flight to Egypt (2:13-15) is explained in a fulfillment formula typical of Matthew: "This was to fulfil what the Lord had declared through the prophet: 'Out of

33

Egypt I have called my son'" (2:15). The text cited is Hosea 11:1, in which "son" refers to Israel, but also in the background here is the story of another dreamer named Joseph who traveled to Egypt (see Gen. 37) and the subsequent story of Israel's exodus from Egypt.

Joseph, Mary, and Jesus will likewise make an exodus from Egypt back to the promised land, but not before Herod executes his horrendous "Plan B." In a story reminiscent of the story of Moses' birth, Herod, like the Egyptian pharaoh, "gave orders for the massacre of all the boys aged two years or under, in Bethlehem and throughout the whole district" (2:16; see also Exod. 1:15-22). Like Moses' birth, the birth of Jesus in Matthew is accompanied by deep grief and lament, not by canticles of joy (as in Luke). Several points must be made about this text. First, the parallels between Moses and Jesus do not end with this story. The forty days of Jesus' testing in the wilderness (4:1-11) echo Moses and the Israelites' wandering around in the wilderness for forty years. Jesus' Sermon on the Mount, in which he says he came not "to abolish, but to complete" the law (5:17), echoes Moses' reception of the law on Mount Sinai. In fact, many hold that the overall structure of Matthew is intended to reflect the books of Moses. Just as there are five books in the Pentateuch attributed to Moses, so Matthew contains five major discourses by Jesus, each of which is brought to closure with the same formulaic expression, "when Jesus had finished" (7:28; 11:1; 13:53; 19:1; 26:1). The "five books of Jesus" correspond to the "five books of Moses," and Jesus is depicted as the new Moses who comes to complete Israel's story of redemption.

Second, the action of Herod in Matthew is certainly in keeping with what we know of his paranoia from other texts. Josephus recounts how Herod, fearful of the influence the Hasmonean dynasty still wielded through his wife Mariamme, ordered intermittent executions of members of his own family beginning with his sons and culminating with the execution of Mariamme herself (see Josephus, *Antiquities*, book 15).

Finally, we should note that the fulfillment formula that occurs at the end of this passage is different from all the other fulfillment formulae in Matthew's infancy narrative. The text reads: "So the words spoken through Jeremiah the prophet were fulfilled: 'A voice was heard in Rama, sobbing in bitter grief; it was Rachel weeping for her children, and refusing to be comforted, because they were no more'" (Matt. 2:17-18). The fulfillment formulae usually begin with the Greek word *hina*, "in order that," indicating that the event occurred *so that* scripture would be fulfilled (as in Matt. 1:22; 2:15; 2:23). In our text the causal, "in order that," has been replaced by the word "so." The change is theologically significant. Matthew does not suggest that the murder of the children took place *in order that* scripture might be fulfilled; no, the cause of the children's death was Herod's wickedness, not some divine mandate that prophecy be fulfilled. So rather than trying to explain the brutal event, Matthew found some solace in this passage from Jeremiah. Rather than offering some glib explanation for this tragedy, Matthew encourges his audience to interpret this horrendous event against the backdrop of scripture. The solidarity of suffering with those in the past provides some solace for those grieving in the present.

The unit ends when Herod dies (see the rather extended and gruesome description of his death in Josephus, *Antiquities*, 17.6.5), and Joseph, Mary, and Jesus return. Joseph is told in a dream to "go to the land of Israel, for those who threatened the child's life are dead" (2:19-20). This respite from the threat of death is, as we know, only short-lived. Joseph soon learns that Herod's son, Archelaus, has taken over Judea and leaves again, this time for Nazareth in Galilee. So Jesus leaves Judea to escape death; ironically, the next time Jesus returns to Judea, there are new enemies (from the same old unholy religious/political alignment), and he does die. But Jesus, like Samson, who is also a "Nazorean/nazirite" (Matt. 2:23; see also Judg. 13:5, 7), will deliver his people through the efficacy of his death.

Retelling the Story

> Then they returned to their own country by another route, for they had been warned in a dream not to go back to Herod. (Matthew 2:12)

The ancient man who sat atop his camel in the middle of the desert was pre-posterous. His bushy gray beard was as big as the bejeweled cloth crown that he wore on his head, and his portly body was woven together with clever magic, decorating the rotund results of too many feasts in embroidered silk. It was the cord around his waist that was the most intriguing. The glittering golden rope disappeared somewhere between two rolls of fat. If it were loosened, could he be unwound until there was nothing left but the cord itself, a pile of gold and purple thread, and the elegant crown?

Not far away was a band of men with weapons.

"I am returning from a visit to Bethlehem," he explained dramatically to a merchant who stood below him on the sand, staring up at the gestures of the speaker, who wore a ring on every chubby finger.

The camel's rider let out a booming laugh. "Just call me the wise man," he said. "And you?"

The itinerant salesman shrugged. "Call me the merchant," he replied, mounting his fuzzy camel, which was tied to a string of other heavy-laden beasts of burden. "Those are your bodyguards?" he asked.

The wise man chuckled. "Hand-picked every one of them. Twelve of them are my very own sons ... or more. I stopped counting."

"There's water ahead," the merchant said, nodding.

He motioned to three men behind him who each led six camels, their bodies weighted down with merchandise that scented the scorched afternoon with cinnamon, cloves, and anise, which mixed with the smell of perspiration and animal. "It would be safer if we traveled together."

"You have our protection," said the wise man.

When they reached the oasis, the merchant pulled out dried fruit, dates, a loaf of hard bread, and a leg of lamb from his packs, hoping to impress the bejeweled man he had met. He even found one of his best bags of wine and presented it as an intended gift, but in return the wise man gave him a handful of gold coins. And he had no opportunity to share his salesman stories; it was the wise man who turned out to be the storyteller.

"The baby didn't look like a king!" said the wise man as he wiped grease from his beard with the sleeve of his garment. "If you showed me even two babies, I could not tell you which was the infant king of the Jews. But I would feel it somehow. Yes, I would know if I were again in his presence. I wanted to stay for the circumcision, but there wasn't time."

"What makes you think the baby is the king of the Jews?" the merchant asked, throwing a bone into the campfire. "Even I could make the claim. Anyone can claim."

The wise man was perturbed at the obvious ignorance of the merchant. "Why, it has been prophesied!" he said. "I can't believe you didn't see the star that lit the sky with magnificent light. Fabulous! There has never been anything like it, and I know. I study the stars. I followed it and met up unexpectedly with two other kings who traveled with me to Bethlehem, a perfect place for this birth. We were seeing prophecy come true in our very lifetimes! The three of us who traveled were

> The story of Moses' birth and miraculous escape from the slaughter of Israelite male children was quite popular among the Jews and was often retold. This version, by Josephus, comes from the first century C.E.: "One of the Egyptian priest-scholars—people who can predict the future with great accuracy—announced to the king that there would soon be born among the Israelites someone who, if he reached adulthood, would bring down the dominance of the Egyptians and build up the Israelites, and would surpass everyone in virtue and win everlasting fame. The king was alarmed at this news, and on the advice of the scholar, ordered that every newborn Israelite boy should be done away with by being drowned in the river. He also ordered that pregnant Hebrew women should be watched when they went into labor, and that the Egyptian midwives should watch out for their deliveries." (*Jewish Antiquities*, 2.205-6; from Miller, *Born Divine*, 130)

summoned by King Herod, who also wanted to honor the child. His scribes and priests agreed that the birth was indeed taking place. They, too, were calling the child the Messiah. As we speak, Herod is awaiting word on the location of the birthplace."

"From you?" asked the merchant.

The wise man shrugged sheepishly. "Perhaps."

"So why are you headed in the opposite direction?"

"If you must know—I had a dream that warned me not to return to Herod. So—what other edibles do you have?"

Saving himself several future trips, the merchant pulled a heavy bag from one of the camels and set it close to the wise man. "It's difficult for me to imagine Herod being pleased with the tale of a child who will perhaps compete against him—challenge him," he said, pondering for a moment. "The light you spoke of could have come from the palace where the child was born ... and what was it you said earlier you gave to the child? Frankincense and myrrh?"

Stuffed with dates and lamb, looking like yet another mound of sand in the desert, the wise man lay down flat on his back and sighed, a sound of relief that turned into a loud belch. "There was no palace. The child was in a simple dwelling, born of simple parents."

"I think you've been had," said the merchant, poking at the fire. "The child's father will sell your gifts."

"No, no, it wasn't like that," said the wise man. "When we found the child, we knew immediately that we were in the right place—as poor as it was, as tired and pathetic as the parents looked, as ragged as their belongings. I felt very ... humble. We fell to our knees, all of us. We hadn't planned to, but all

There are several parallels between Matthew's story and the stories that circulated about the divine portents that accompanied the birth of the emperor Augustus as catalogued, for example, by Suetonius: "Having reached this point, it will not be out of place to add an account of the omens which occurred before he was born, on the very day of his birth, and afterward, from which it was possible to anticipate and perceive his future greatness and uninterrupted good fortune. . . . According to Julius Marathus, a few months before Augustus was born a portent was generally observed at Rome, which gave warning that nature was pregnant with a king for the Roman people; thereupon the senate in consternation decreed that no male child born that year should be reared; but those whose wives were with child saw to it that the decree was not filed in the treasury, since each one appropriated the prediction to his own family." (Suetonius, *Lives of the Caesars*, "The Deified Augustus," 2.94 [early second cent. C.E.]; from Boring-Berger-Colpe, 43-44, no. 14.)

strength left our bodies, and we were limp with ... worship, I suppose. After visiting a new king, I should come away with something material, one would think, but I came away with nothing but awe."

"But why?" asked the merchant. "It was a hoax."

"I don't think so," said the wise man, actually looking the part of a king for a moment. "My friend, I would not have started on this long journey if I did not believe what the stars told me and what my heart tells me now. I may not know all the secrets of the universe, but I know something miraculous has happened, and I was able to be there before it was over."

Long after the wise man had fallen asleep and was snoring, the merchant put his things together, summoned his men, and mounted his camel, starting off into the night. Turning around, going in the direction from which he had come, he set off for Bethlehem, hoping it was not too late to see the miracle.

(Jo-Ann Jennings)

LUKE 1:26-55

Prophecies of Jesus' Birth

The birth of Jesus is announced to Mary.

The Story

In the sixth month the angel Gabriel was sent by God to Nazareth, a town in Galilee, with a message for a girl betrothed to a man named Joseph, a descendant of David; the girl's name was Mary. The angel went in and said to her, 'Greetings, most favoured one! The Lord is with you.' But she was deeply troubled by what he said and wondered what this greeting could mean. Then the angel said to her, 'Do not be afraid, Mary, for God has been gracious to you; you will conceive and give birth to a son, and you are to give him the name Jesus. He will be great, and will be called Son of the Most High. The Lord God will give him the throne of his ancestor David, and he will be king over Israel for ever; his reign shall never end.' 'How can this be?' said Mary. 'I am still a virgin.' The angel answered, 'The Holy Spirit will come upon you, and the power of the Most High will overshadow you; for that reason the holy child to be born will be called Son of God. Moreover your kinswoman Elizabeth has herself conceived a son in her old age; and she who is reputed barren is now in her sixth month, for God's promises can never fail.' 'I am the Lord's servant,' said Mary; 'may it be as you have said.' Then the angel left her.

Soon afterwards Mary set out and hurried away to a town in the uplands of Judah. She went into Zechariah's house and greeted Elizabeth. And when Elizabeth heard Mary's greeting, the baby stirred in her womb. Then Elizabeth was filled with the Holy Spirit and exclaimed in a loud voice, 'God's blessing is on you above all women, and his blessing is on the fruit of your womb. Who am I, that the mother of my Lord should visit me? I tell you, when your greeting sounded in my ears, the baby in my womb leapt for joy. Happy is she who has had faith that the Lord's promise to her would be fulfilled!'

And Mary said:
'My soul tells out the greatness of the
    Lord,
my spirit has rejoiced in God my
    Saviour;
for he has looked with favour on his
    servant,
lowly as she is.
From this day forward
all generations will count me blessed,
for the Mighty God has done great
    things for me.
His name is holy,
his mercy sure from generation to
    generation
toward those who fear him.
He has shown the might of his arm,
he has routed the proud and all their
    schemes;
he has brought down monarchs from

39

their thrones,
and raised on high the lowly.
He has filled the hungry with good
   things,
and sent the rich away empty.
He has come to the help of Israel his

servant,
as he promised to our forefathers;
he has not forgotten to show mercy
to Abraham and his children's children for ever.'

Comments on the Story

Luke 1:26-38 is the text used in the Revised Common Lectionary for the Annunciation of the Lord, a special feast day observed on March 25. As such, it is an extremely important text in the liturgical life of the church. The annunciation has also been the subject of innumerable portraits in the visual arts, especially during the medieval and Renaissance periods. For our purposes, it is important to note that this text is a wonderful story that continues the particular story of God's people, Israel, as well as drawing upon more universal human emotions and pathos. A young girl is told she is to become pregnant out of wedlock. Stunned, she resists the angel's message, before finally becoming obedient to the Lord's command. To understand this story more fully, it is helpful to see its connections to Israel's scriptures, as well as its place within the context of the Lukan birth narrative.

Both Luke and Matthew connect their stories of Jesus' birth to the story of Israel. Matthew uses a quotation formula, "All this happened in order to fulfil what the Lord declared through the prophet" (see Matt. 1:22-23; 2:15, 17-18, 23; also comments on Matt. 2:1-23). Luke is subtler in his echoes of the Old Testament. His technique is more like a photograph that has been double-exposed, that allows one to see one set of figures through another. For Luke, most of the stories in the birth narrative have another story from the Old Testament lurking just beneath the surface. So, for example, the barren couple Zechariah and Elizabeth recall the barren couple Abraham and Sarah from Israel's ancestral period. The annunciation of Jesus' birth shares important elements with Old Testament commissioning stories, and Luke's audience was sure to hear these verbal echoes.

Commissioning stories, in which a messenger of God delivers a message to one of God's people, are found throughout the Old Testament and contain a number of elements that remain fairly stable—evidently there was among Israelite storytellers a stereotypical way of telling a commissioning story. The Old Testament commission contained five essential elements: (1) the appearance of an angel; (2) the explicit or implicit expression of fear or resistance on the part of the recipient; (3) the message of commissioning; (4) an objection expressed on the part of the one receiving the commission; and (5) the giving of a sign to confirm the authenticity of the message. We can illustrate these elements by comparing a few Old Testament commissioning stories.

40

In Exodus 3, the story of the commissioning of Moses contains all of the elements of an annunciation story: (1) the appearance of an angel (3:2); (2) the expression of fear on the part of the recipient (3:6); (3) the message of commissioning (3:7-10); (4) an objection by the recipient (3:11); and (5) the giving of a sign (3:12). Likewise the story of the call of Gideon in Judges 6 follows the same form: (1) the appearance of an angel (6:11-12); (2) the expression of resistance on the part of the recipient (6:13); (3) the message of commissioning (6:14); (4) an objection by the recipient (6:15); and (5) the giving of a sign (6:17-21).

The audience familiar with these stories and others like them would recognize all of these elements in the annunciation to Mary:

1. *Appearance of Angel.* "In the sixth month the angel Gabriel was sent by God to Nazareth, a town in Galilee... The angel went in and said to her, 'Greetings, most favoured one! The Lord is with you' " (1:26-28).
2. *Reaction.* "But she was deeply troubled by what he said and wondered what this greeting could mean" (1:29).
3. *Angel's Message.* "Do not be afraid, Mary, for God has been gracious to you; you will conceive and give birth to a son, and you are to give him the name Jesus. He will be great, and will be called Son of the Most High" (1:30-32).
4. *Objection to Message.* "How can this be?" said Mary. "I am still a virgin" (1:34).
5. *Giving of Sign.* "Moreover your kinswoman Elizabeth has herself conceived a son in her old age; and she who is reputed barren is now in her sixth month" (1:36).

The form of this story so closely follows that of the Old Testament commissioning stories that the authorial audience must have heard these echoes. What is the rhetorical effect? First, the connection of the annunciation to its Old Testament pattern helps explain the rather enigmatic note that Mary pondered what kind of greeting this could be. The phrase "the Lord is with you" is found in an angel's message elsewhere only in the Old Testament in the Gideon story (Judg. 6:12). Mary also knows her scripture, and perhaps knows that this same greeting given to Gideon is followed by a commission. Her puzzled pause over these words encourages the audience to do the same. The commissioning pattern also encourages the audience to expect that, like Moses and Gideon, Mary too will be given a task to do. What may surprise them (and us!) is the specific assignment: she will become pregnant with the "Son of the Most High." Her objection, like Gideon and Moses, is expected. Moses says, "Who am I?" Gideon complains he is from the smallest tribe and the least in his own family. Mary objects, "How can this be, since I am a virgin?" In each case, of course, the angel gives a sign to confirm the authenticity of the commission. For Mary, the convincing sign is that her relative Elizabeth, barren all those years, is now in her sixth month of pregnancy.

Not only does this story announcing Jesus' birth share elements in common with Old Testament commissioning stories, the pattern is found repeated in the Lukan birth narrative In the passage just prior to this one is the annunciation of the birth of John the Baptist (1:11-20). This text, too, contains the elements of a commissioning story: (1) the appearance of an angel (1:11); (2) the expression of fear on the part of the recipient (1:12); (3) the message of commissioning (1:13-17); (4) an objection by the recipient (1:18); and (5) the giving of a sign (1:20).

As of old, God has chosen two of his people, an old priest and a young virgin, to carry out his task. For Zechariah, the commission is to father John, who will go before the Lord, making the people ready. For Mary, the assignment is to give birth to Jesus, to whom will be given the throne of his ancestor David. Both initially object, but ultimately Zechariah and Mary join the band of witnesses who have gone before them and who have been faithful to the task given them. This story has little room for sentimental musings about the first Christmas; rather, it demands that its hearers, then and now, discern their own commission, and despite whatever obvious shortcomings, commit themselves to its completion.

Mary's response is expressed in poetic form, in a hymn that has come to be known by its Latin beginning, the Magnificat. This hymn of Mary echoes the song of Hannah at the birth of Samuel (1 Sam. 2:1-10). Like Hannah, Mary marvels at how God has visited a "lowly" servant and sees in that a fulfillment of a longstanding promise that goes back to "our forefathers ... to Abraham and his children's children for ever." The promise of the Messiah is not often remembered in this form at Christmas time, but perhaps it should be. For this is a promise that God will judge the arrogant and powerful and will give attention to the needs of the lowly, the hungry, and the poor. Here the audience is served notice about the nature of the kingship of Jesus and its claim on them as his subjects.

Retelling the Story

"I am the Lord's servant," said Mary; "may it be as you have said." (Luke 1:38)

Joanna's head bowed, tears falling into the watery soup she prepared, knowing she had to pull herself together before her husband and sons came out of the fields. She watched a few bits of gray meat swirl, much like the whirlwind of her life that wouldn't stop churning, the never-ending sickness of fear.

42

She had shared *only two circumstances* with the men in her family, one, that her brother-in-law, Zechariah, had lost his speech. There was not one moment's thought of the cause being a demon, as Zechariah was a priest, but what *had* caused the silence? Joanna's sister Elizabeth, Zechariah's wife, had prepared healing soups and brewed herbs known to cure, treating him for everything from shortness of breath to ingrown toenails. She called on wise women for advice and wrapped his throat; the animals slept close to him; and he was surrounded in prayer, but he still could not speak. It was obvious he had something great to say. Would he ever be able to share the untold message?

The next shocking news was that Elizabeth was expecting a child. Had the news come fifty years earlier, Joanna would have been happy. But when Elizabeth's maid delivered the news, Joanna said only, "My sister is an old woman!"

The young girl smiled and covered her face. "And Zechariah is an old man," she said.

"Elizabeth is ecstatic with chatter," the girl continued. "She says that God has taken away her shame."

As if Elizabeth's condition and Zechariah's loss of speech had not been enough crisis, Joanna's own daughter Mary had come to her with an extravagant tale that would bring the entire family to incredible shame and put Mary's life in danger.

> Augustus Caesar, who reigned as emperor of the Roman Empire from 31 B.C.E. to 14 C.E., was credited with bringing an era of peace to the world. Like other extraordinary men of the time, he was thought to have been sired by a god. Suetonius tells this story of the divine birth of Augustus: "When Atia had come in the middle of the night to the solemn service of Apollo, she . . . fell asleep. . . . On a sudden a serpent glided up to her and shortly went away. When she awoke, she purified herself, as if after the embraces of her husband, and at once there appeared on her body a mark in colors like a serpent, and she could never get rid of it. . . . In the tenth month after that Augustus was born and was therefore regarded as the son of Apollo." (Suetonius, *Lives of the Caesars*, "The Deified Augustus," 2.94 [early second cent. C.E.]; from Boring-Berger-Colpe, 43, no. 14)

In response to her fears Joanna had sent Mary to Elizabeth's for a visit and did not admit to wanting her home, fearing her husband and sons as much as the townspeople. What if they heard that Mary was carrying a child? Would they kill Mary themselves to keep her from being stoned to death or to keep the secret? Women with bastard children lived at the gate and died of starvation if they were not stoned. She would be eaten by the dogs. How long could she hide her condition by staying with Elizabeth?

Mary was engaged. Her wedding dress was almost finished. A feast had been planned. The wine was in storage. Her fiancé Joseph and Mary's father had already decided what price would be paid for the girl.

Joseph.

Oh yes, Joseph. He had come to the door with hurt in his eyes and looked at Joanna with a questioning look.

"You know?" he asked.

She bowed her head, nodding.

"She says an angel spoke to her," Joseph said. "How can I believe such a story? How can I believe that an angel told her this child is the Messiah? But how can I not believe our Mary?"

"I just don't know," Joanna said faintly. "Has she been chosen—or fooled?"

Joanna had not seen Joseph since that conversation.

Mary herself had not confided in her mother at first. She had become hollow-eyed from lack of sleep and had walked around in a dream world. She was nauseated in the morning, and the smell of food caused her to run from the house. When she smelled incense in the market, she hurried past. Joanna became suspicious.

When Mary did speak, she poured out doubts—the fear of telling Joseph; the terror of the people finding out; the anxieties of any young mother who knows she must give birth to a child, not really knowing what to expect, and then care for it.

After Mary confessed the angel story to her mother, however, peace came over her face, and she said, "An angel named Gabriel visited me. It's not as if I should be afraid. This is something God wants, isn't it? I was asked to do this. The child will be safe, won't he?—since this is something God wants?"

> Dio Cassius also told the story of divine omens connected with the birth of Augustus: "Atia [the mother of Augustus] . . . dreamed that her womb was lifted to the heavens and spread out over all the earth. That same night her husband Octavius thought that the sun rose from between her thighs. Shortly after the boy was born, Nigidius Figulus, a senator, immediately prophesied that the child would attain absolute power. . . . On the day the baby was born, Nigidius ran into Octavius, who was late getting to the Senate, which was meeting that day. When Nigidius asked him why he was late and learned the cause, he shouted, "You have fathered a master over us." (*History of Rome*, 45.1.2-5 [early third C.E.]; from Miller, *Born Divine*, 140-41)

Because Mary was engaged, the midwife had come regularly to check on her month-to-month progress, as it was the midwife who would determine the most fertile time for the wedding. She appeared not to be alarmed that Mary had no news for her. She said it was not at all unusual for someone as young as Mary not to bleed on a regular basis, and the stress of the upcoming union itself could take its toll on her schedule. If the midwife did know, and sometimes Joanna thought surely she must since she was the expert in such matters, she was keeping quiet to protect Mary.

A noise at the door interrupted Joanna's thoughts, and she quickly raised her head and wiped her tears, fearful that her husband would find her crying.

"Mother?" Mary's voice said. "I'm home."

In spite of the doubts Joanna held inside, she ran to the doorway to hold Mary in her arms. No words were spoken as they embraced, Joanna's tears falling again, mixing with Mary's as their cheeks touched.

She looked at Mary sadly. "You have the look about you," she said. "Your face is fuller. Your hips are wider. Soon people will know."

Mary nodded. "I'm not afraid," she whispered. "God will see us through this."

As evening came on and the family sat down to eat, Joanna jumped each time there was a noise outside, for fear the townspeople were coming in force to murder her only daughter—to convict her of adultery. She had seen women stoned before, and now she closed her eyes, trying not to remember the anger, hysteria, and mutilation.

Joanna trembled when a knock came at the door. Her legs shivered. She pulled her clothing tightly around her, preparing for the worst. "Oh, God, oh, God," she whispered. "Save my good child from this."

There were no angry shouts as the door opened, and Joseph stood there, humbly looking in at the family.

Joanna sighed with relief, seeing only peace in his eyes.

"I have come to take Mary home," he said. "It is time that our marriage began."

Mary's father continued to eat, nodding, and saying only, "Let it be done." *(Jo-Ann Jennings)*

45

The Birth of Jesus

Jesus is born in a manger and is visited by shepherds.

The Story

In those days a decree was issued by the emperor Augustus for a census to be taken throughout the Roman world. This was the first registration of its kind; it took place when Quirinius was governor of Syria. Everyone made his way to his own town to be registered. Joseph went up to Judaea from the town of Nazareth in Galilee, to register in the city of David called Bethlehem, because he was of the house of David by descent; and with him went Mary, his betrothed, who was expecting her child. While they were there the time came for her to have her baby, and she gave birth to a son, her firstborn. She wrapped him in swaddling clothes, and laid him in a manger, because there was no room for them at the inn.

Now in this same district there were shepherds out in the fields, keeping watch through the night over their flock. Suddenly an angel of the Lord appeared to them, and the glory of the Lord shone round them. They were terrified, but the angel said, 'Do not be afraid; I bring you good news, news of great joy for the whole nation. Today there has been born to you in the city of David a deliverer—the Messiah, the Lord. This will be the sign for you: you will find a baby wrapped in swaddling clothes, and lying in a manger.' All at once there was with the angel a great company of the heavenly host, singing praise to God:

'Glory to God in highest heaven,
and on earth peace to all in whom
he delights.'

After the angels had left them and returned to heaven the shepherds said to one another, 'Come, let us go straight to Bethlehem and see this thing that has happened, which the Lord has made known to us.' They hurried off and found Mary and Joseph, and the baby lying in the manger. When they saw the child, they related what they had been told about him; and all who heard were astonished at what the shepherds said. But Mary treasured up all these things and pondered over them. The shepherds returned glorifying and praising God for what they had heard and seen; it had all happened as they had been told.

Comments on the Story

Luke 2:1-20 describes the birth of Jesus and the visitation of the shepherds. It begins with a reference to a census decreed by the emperor Augustus (2:1). Locating the local events of Judea on the larger world map is typical of Luke

46

in these early chapters (see 1:5; 3:1). The present case raises some historical questions since there is no evidence of a registration of the whole Roman Empire under Augustus. The theological significance, however, is clear. By the time of Luke's Gospel, Augustan propaganda, which praised the peace Augustus had brought to the Roman Empire, was found throughout Roman literature (see Virgil's *Aeneid* and *Fourth Eclogue*) and art (the *Augustus Primaporta* and *Ara Pacis Augustae*) and was no doubt familiar to Luke's audience. An official inscription in Priene boasted: "The birthday of the god [Augustus] marked the beginning of the good news for the world." In Halicarnassus Augustus was called the "savior of the whole world." His birthday was even adopted as the first day of the New Year in parts of Asia Minor.

Luke challenged the conventional wisdom of this propaganda by setting the birth of the Messiah within the context of Augustus's edict. The altar of Christ's peace was a manger; the proclamation of his peace was on the lips of angels: "On earth peace to all in whom he delights" (2:14). Jesus' birthday, not Augustus's, divides the epochs of human history. The savior, whose birth meant "news of great joy for the whole nation," was born "Messiah and Lord" "in the city of David," not Emperor in Rome. The notice of Jesus' birth is brief (2:6-7), yet the theological and political implications of Jesus' birth for Luke are obvious to his audience.

The most important detail in the report of the birth is the place where the babe is placed—in a manger, or feeding trough. The term has both inter- and intra-textual echoes. It recalls God's complaint against Israel in Isaiah 1:3: "An ox knows its owner and a donkey *its master's stall*; but Israel lacks all knowledge, my people has no discernment." The stall, or manger, also evokes the picture of Jesus, lying in a manger, as "food for the world." The theme of food and meals as one of the ways in which Jesus reveals his mission to others runs throughout Luke.

Luke moves rather abruptly from the general notice of an Augustan decree to the Judean countryside (2:8). What modern Christian reader can hear the opening words of this passage and resist being swept back into a sentimental stupor recalling days of childhood Christmases? "Now in this same district there were shepherds out in the fields, keeping watch through the night over their flock." But Luke's original audience would most likely have responded to this text in a much different way. Both the setting and the characters would alert the audience that God had chosen to disclose the birth of the Messiah in a dangerous place to a violence-prone group. Sparsely populated countrysides throughout the Roman Empire were havens for vagabonds and thieves (see also the story of the Good Samaritan in Luke 10). Furthermore, while the image of the shepherd has a positive side and subsequently becomes a dominant image for Jesus and early church leaders, shepherds were often involved in conflict with settled villagers, conflict which usually escalated to violent activities. Josephus reports that a certain Athrongaeus, a shepherd, aspired to Archelaus's throne (see parallel story). Yet even after he "donned the diadem, his raiding expeditions continued long afterwards. Their principal object was to kill Romans and royalists, but no Jew, from whom they had anything to gain, escaped, if he fell into their hands." Josephus concludes his brief section on Athrongaeus by describing this period in Judea's history as "one scene of guerrilla warfare" (*War* 2.65).

With this reality in mind, the angelic chorus's message of "On earth peace to all in whom he delights," delivered to one of the most violent groups in one of the most dangerous places, is remarkable! No less shocking is the reaction of these shepherds who, upon hearing this news, decide among themselves to go to Bethlehem to see for themselves "this thing that has happened, which the Lord has made known to us" (2:15).

Far from a quaint little Christmas story, already the birth of the Messiah, according to Luke, has the power to lift up the lowly, the despised, and the violent (1:52). And these shepherds, whose vocation for the authorial audience at first conjures up an image of a despised and potentially violent group, by their actions—finding the child and "glorifying and praising God"—align themselves with the more positive portrait of "the good shepherd," an image already evoked by the mention of the city of *David*, who was, of course, himself a shepherd before becoming king. The very form of the story reinforces the final positive impression of the shepherds. The story is typical of the Old Testament commissioning story, which Luke has already used (see comments on story 3, "Prophecies of Jesus' Birth").

1. *Appearance of an Angel:* "Suddenly an angel of the Lord appeared to them, and the glory of the Lord shone round them" (2:9*a*).
2. *Reaction:* "They were terrified" (2:9*b*).
3. *Angel's Message:* "... but the angel said, 'Do not be afraid; I bring you good news, news of great joy for the whole nation. Today there has been born to you in the city of David a deliverer—the Messiah, the Lord'" (2:10-11).
4. *Giving of a Sign:* "This will be the sign for you: you will find a baby wrapped in swaddling clothes, and lying in a manger" (2:12).

Of the elements common to these stories, only the objection to the angel's message is missing. Even though the priest, Zechariah, and the mother-to-be of Jesus, Mary, had (like Moses and Gideon and others) initially resisted the divine message, these lowly shepherds resolve immediately to heed the command implicit in the angelic canticle: "You will find a baby wrapped in swaddling clothes, and lying in a manger" (2:12). Thanks to these shepherds (whose reputation might be comparable today to that of an oil rig crew!), not only the ox and the donkey recognize the "manger of their lord," God's people, who these shepherds now represent, have begun to know the manger of their Lord also.

Retelling the Story

The shepherds returned glorifying and praising God for what they had heard and seen. (Luke 2:20)

Timothy fashioned a pillow from his belongings and lay down upon the rocky ground. His face was wrinkled like a piece of fruit that had lain too long in the sun. His bones were stiff and his muscles sore, but at the sound of footsteps in the distance, he touched his staff for assurance, keeping his eyes shut tightly, hoping to fight only if he must. With age and the need for sleep, he was not too sure he would defend himself even if he were attacked. Perhaps his time had come.

As voices grew louder, he realized the intruders were young, but even hungry children could be threatening. Perhaps if they rustled through his pack, he would continue to pretend he was slumbering and let them find the bread he had put away ... but that would be allowing them to steal.

"Do you think that's him?" a small voice whispered.

"Maybe ... or just a dead man," came the reply.

A rough smelly fabric

Josephus tells this story of a shepherd's aspirations to the throne in the first century C.E.: "Now, too, a mere shepherd had the temerity to aspire to the throne. He was called Athrongaeus, and his sole recommendations, to raise such hopes, were vigour of body, a soul contemptuous of death, and four brothers resembling himself. To each of these he entrusted an armed band and employed them as generals and satraps for his raids, while he himself, like a king, handled matters of graver moment. It was now that he donned the diadem, his raiding expeditions ... continued long afterwards. Their principal object was to kill Romans and royalists, but no Jew, from whom they had anything to gain, escaped, if he fell into their hands.... After perpetrating throughout the war many such outrages upon compatriot and foreigner alike, three of them were eventually captured, the eldest by Archelaus, the two next by Gratus and Ptolemy; the fourth made terms with Archelaus and surrendered. Such was the end to which they ultimately came; but at the period of which we are speaking, these men were making the whole of Judaea one scene of guerrilla warfare." (Josephus, *Jewish War*, 2.60-65) (from LCL)

49

brushed Timothy's face, and he could feel a *presence* as one of the children apparently leaned over him, trying to see if his eyes were open. The child's warm breath tickled his whiskers, and he almost sneezed. It was tempting to open his eyes so that he would be staring directly into the face of the child, just for the humor of the yell.

Virgil, the great Roman poet, wrote in his *Fourth Eclogue* of a child born to a virgin who would bring the long awaited "golden age" of peace to the world. He wrote in 40 B.C.E., over a century earlier than Luke's Gospel, and was responding poetically to the event of a peace treaty signed between Octavian (soon to be Augustus Caesar) and Mark Antony that ended a hundred years of civil war in Rome. "Now there has come the last age of which the Cumaean Sibyl sang; a great orderly line of centuries begins anew; now too the Virgin returns; the reign of Saturn returns; a new human generation descends from the high heavens. Upon *the Child* now to be born, under whom the race of iron will cease and a golden race will spring up over the whole world, do you, O chaste Lucina [goddess of childbirth], smile favorably, for your own Apollo is now king. . . . He [the Child] will receive divine life and will see heroes mingling with gods, and will himself be seen by them. And he will rule over a world made peaceful by the virtues of his father." (Brown, *Birth of the Messiah,* 566)

"If he's dead, he's still warm," the first child said, still so close that his breath made Timothy's eyelashes tingle. Perhaps the child wanted him awake. Perhaps they had not come to steal from a weary old man.

Unable to withstand the temptation any longer, Timothy opened his eyes, expecting to hear screams and see the children scatter, but the child hovering over him merely stared back, eyeball to eyeball. "Are you the man?" the child asked.

Timothy moved the boy to one side with some ease, sat up, and looked around at quiet, sad eyes that told stories of hardship. His guess was the children had not been washed since birth—if then.

There were six in total. Without waiting to be asked, he reached for his pack and silently handed them each some bread and cheese, trying to make the portions equal, and took out a bag of wine. He didn't say, "What man?" in answer to the question, but the child continued by saying, "Are you the shepherd?"

"I'm *a* shepherd," he replied. He thought of telling them they should give thanks to God before they ate the bread, but seeing the food disappear and their eagerness to pick up the crumbs, he just watched, thinking they seemed starved for so many things—food, love, knowledge.

"But are you the shepherd who saw the Messiah when he was a child?" the leader asked.

Ah, to be asked the story again. Timothy had told it so many times. Some didn't believe it. Some wanted to hear it again and again as if it were a made-up tale. Others—well—others wanted to pick a fight and chase him off, shouting, "Don't come around here with your ridiculous Messiah stories!"

He didn't answer right away. He made a fire and motioned to the children to gather around him, pulling them close to try and keep them warm. "It was a long time ago," he finally said. "I was much younger than most of you. My father was a shepherd. I do not know where my mother was.... It had been a long day. We had been chased and threatened by a man who said we were grazing the sheep on his land, and we had had a difficult time finding water for our animals. As I lay down on the ground for the night, my bones tired and sore, I thought I could sleep forever, but my father said that I must stay awake and make sure nothing harmed the herd. He fell into a deep sleep and began to snore, leaving nothing in the darkness with me but the sky and the animals. To keep warm and to feel so ... not alone, I nuzzled up to a lamb that was willing to lie still.

"At first I did not think what I was seeing was real. I had been staring at the stars, my eyes going from one to the other, making shapes of them, and I noticed that one seemed larger than the others, and it continued to grow. It came closer as if it had seen me and was coming directly to me. I tell you it was as big as the clouds when it covered the sky, and night suddenly seemed like day. I tried to shake my father from his slumber, but he continued to snore.

"My clothes sparkled as if they were made of gold, and streams of light touched the sheep, giving them a look of royalty. I was so frightened there was a part of me that wished my heart *would* explode, and yet, I was so fascinated by what was going on before me, I wanted it never to end. I trembled, pulling the lamb close. I leaned into the ground, hoping to pull the earth around me for protection. My father finally opened his eyes but said nothing as he looked at the light that was all around us, that star that seemed to have come alive with nearness. Then we saw the angels."

The children were spellbound, their eyes drinking in the words of the ancient shepherd.

"The angel spoke and told us not to be afraid, and the voice was so filled with peace, my heart calmed. She said that a child had been born and that we should go see him.... I like to remember that night of the angel." The children listened, waiting for more.

"My own son does not believe the story," Timothy continued, "but it is true. My son says there is no peace on earth, and perhaps there is not, but I have been prosperous for an old man who was once a hungry child like all of you."

"What is it you make of this story?" asked the child who appeared to be the eldest.

"The star—the angel—the child—gave a poor shepherd boy hope," answered Timothy quietly. "He took that hope and grew in wisdom, and his life became rich with promise. Now he passes that hope on to you ... and so shall it be through the ages." *(Jo-Ann Jennings)*

51

The Beginning of the Gospel

Mark's Gospel begins with the appearance of John the Baptist.

The Story

The beginning of the gospel of Jesus Christ the Son of God. In the prophet Isaiah it stands written:
I am sending my herald ahead of you;
he will prepare your way.
A voice cries in the wilderness,
'Prepare the way for the Lord;
clear a straight path for him.'
John the Baptist appeared in the wilderness proclaiming a baptism in token of repentance, for the forgiveness of sins; and everyone flocked to him from the countryside of Judaea and the city of Jerusalem, and they were baptized by him in the river Jordan, confessing their sins. John was dressed in a rough coat of camel's hair, with a leather belt round his waist, and he fed on locusts and wild honey. He proclaimed: 'After me comes one mightier than I am, whose sandals I am not worthy to stoop down and unfasten. I have baptized you with water; he will baptize you with the Holy Spirit.'

Comments on the Story

Where to begin a story is a critical issue for any storyteller. "Well begun is half-done," the old adage goes, and an audience can quickly become disinterested if the story fizzles in the opening lines. What, then, makes for a good beginning? A good beginning captures the listener's attention, and often foreshadows themes and catchwords to which the storyteller will return again (and perhaps again!). Sometimes the story begins by making reference to another story through an allusion or citation, thus creating an intertextual backdrop against which the current story is to be heard or read.

When we come to the four canonical Gospels, we find that, though they all tell the story of Jesus, each begins in a distinct manner. All the Gospel writers pay considerable attention to the rhetorical effect of their openings. Of the four, Mark has received the most criticism in terms of presenting a well-formed beginning. Indeed, Mark's Gospel has been described by some as a "passion narrative with an extended introduction." Such an assessment, though

52

it rightly highlights the significance of the death of Jesus for Mark, relegates all of the material before chapter 14 to a mere preparatory function. Others, familiar with the infancy narratives of Matthew and Luke, argue that Mark begins *in medias res*, implying that Mark is unconcerned with a proper telling of the Jesus story. Some might argue that Mark is a perfect example of what Lucian of Samosata described as stories that have "bodies without any heads— works lacking an introduction that begin at once with the narrative" (see parallel story).

Closer examination, however, shows that Mark does, indeed, have a rhetorically effective beginning, a "golden helmet," to use Lucian's image, which matches the magnificent "breastplate" that follows. With his very first word (Greek *arche*), Mark, in fact, literally begins with the "beginning." This word can refer to the beginning of a book (as in Diodorus Siculus, 17.1.1; Diogenes Laertius, 3.37) or to a foundation or basis; it may have both connotations here. The phrase "the gospel/good news of Jesus Christ" may mean the good news about Jesus or Jesus' good news. Thus the phrase "the beginning of the gospel of Jesus Christ" is rhetorically rich in ambiguity—the reader is invited into this narrative world to explore these and other potential meanings.

The first sentence in Mark, as a whole, serves as the title of Mark's Gospel—"The Beginning of the Gospel of Jesus Christ, the Son of God." (The title "The Gospel according to Mark," found in most translations, and indeed in most manuscripts of antiquity, was probably added in the second century or later to distinguish Mark from the other Gospels.) The last phrase of the title, "Son of God," is not found in many ancient manuscripts, and scholars are divided on the question of whether or not it belonged to the original text. The phrase is a crucial part of the title, however, whether placed there by the author or a perceptive early reader, as a clue to the rhetorical shape of the Gospel.

Mark's Gospel divides into two rhetorical units. The first half (1:1–8:30) takes place in and around Galilee and revolves around the conflict between Jesus and the religious authorities over the nature of Jesus' authority. The second half (8:22–16:8) records Jesus' journey to and ministry in Jerusalem, culminating with his crucifixion. (Notice that Mark 8:22-30 serves as a literary hinge, both concluding the first half and introducing the second.) The two titles attributed to Jesus in the opening sentence, "Christ" (or "Messiah"—"anointed one") and "Son of God," recur at crucial points in the overall structure of Mark's Gospel. At the end of the first half of the Gospel, Jesus calls his disciples aside at Caesarea Philippi and takes a little Gallup poll about what the people were saying about him: " 'Who do people say I am?' They answered, 'Some say John the Baptist, others Elijah, others one of the prophets.' 'And you,' he asked, 'who do you say I am?' " At this point, for the first time in Mark's narrative since 1:1, the designation "Christ" appears: Peter replied, "You are the Christ" (or "Messiah," 8:29). Though it is clear from the next episode (8:31-33) that Peter does not understand the nature of Jesus' vocation as the "Christ," the placement of the title here at the climax of the first half of the Gospel serves to remind the reader that this story is the good news of Jesus the Christ—the hoped-for anointed one of the line of David.

In an analogous manner, the second title found in Mark 1:1, "Son of God," recurs at the climax of the second rhetorical unit in chapter 15. At the death of Jesus, the Roman centurion confesses, "This man must have been a [or the] son of God" (15:39). Though "unclean spirits" had made this same identification earlier in the story (see 3:11; also 5:7), the centurion (a Gentile) is the first human character to make this confession since the narrator does so in the title to the whole work. From the beginning of the Gospel, then, the storyteller provides clues to the overall rhetorical shape of his story.

According to Mark 1:2-3, the story actually began with Isaiah, long before the Gospel writer took up stylus and papyrus. The Old Testament quotation (actually a conflation of Isa. 40:3 with Exod. 23:20 and Mal. 3:1) speaks of a messenger sent to prepare the way: "a voice cries in the wilderness." The prophecy invites the reader to recall Israel's past, when the people were called upon to prepare themselves to be led by God out of exile in Babylon (during the sixth century B.C.E.), across the desert, and back to the promised land. Against this background of God's past redemptive activity, Mark introduces his story with the claim that God has once again intervened in history.

Like the foretold messenger in the quotation, John is depicted as appearing in the desert (1:4), a desolate and barren place that in Mark is the site of testing: first Jesus is tested in the desert by Satan (1:12-13), and later the disciples' faith is tested when they twice (like the Israelites before them) refuse to believe God can provide bread in a deserted place (see Mark 6:30-44; 8:1-10). John's preaching of repentance, according to Mark, is a ministry intended to "prepare the way for the Lord." This "way" (Greek *hodos*) introduces another key theme in Mark. The word occurs sixteen times in Mark and is variously translated as "way," "path," "journey," and "road." In almost all of these occurrences (14 of 16), the "way" refers to the way of Jesus, which is, ultimately, the way of the cross (see 8:27-31; 9:34; 10:32-34). For Mark, to follow Jesus in discipleship is to follow in that same path of suffering (see 10:46-52).

Verse 6 represents one of a handful of passages containing a physical description of a New Testament character (Jesus is never so described; Paul's appearance is the subject of a passage in the apocryphal *Acts of Paul and Thecla*): "John was dressed in a rough coat of camel's hair, with a leather belt round his waist" (1:6). Why is John's dress and diet of concern to Mark? For an answer, we must turn again to the Old Testament. In 2 Kings 1:7-8, King Ahaziah inquires from his messengers about the identity of a prophet who has foretold Ahaziah's death. The messengers reply that the prophet is "a hairy man, with a leather belt round his waist." Ahaziah declares, "It is Elijah the Tishbite." Mark, then, depicts John the Baptist as dressed in the manner of the Old Testament prophet Elijah. But why? Again we turn to the Old Testament, this time to Malachi 4:5: "Look, I shall send you the prophet Elijah before the great and terrible day of the LORD comes." How widespread in the first century was the expectation of Elijah's appearance before the beginning of the messianic age is unclear. But Mark seems to make several rhetorical moves that he expects his audience to follow. By portraying John the Baptist as an Elijah figure, Mark effectively leads his readers, step by step, toward a striking conclusion. His argument goes like this: (1) John came to prepare the way for the Messiah. (2) John is Elijah *redivivus*. (3) The arrival of Elijah would precede the Day of the Lord. Conclusion: Elijah has come and the Day of the Lord is at hand!

From the title of the Gospel, we have learned that, for Mark, this Messiah/Christ figure is Jesus (1:1). From Mark's narrative beginning, we learn that Elijah has come. The stage is set. All that is left to complete this introduction of Mark's Gospel is for the Messiah to appear. And so he does! "It was at this time that Jesus came from Nazareth in Galilee ..." (1:9). The beginning of the gospel of Jesus Christ, Son of God has begun!

Retelling the Story

> John was dressed in a rough coat of camel's hair, with a leather belt round his waist, and he fed on locusts and wild honey. (Mark 1:6)

Having spent the last few hours of his life with John called the Baptist, I would have to say he was a man driven with duty. He continued to shout even as his hands and ankles were shackled to a nasty wall in the cold of a dungeon. I doubt, having listened to him speak of "the final days of our earth" and the Messiah, that he was ever a child.

I asked him about that.

"John," I said, "one prisoner to another, when did you become a raving madman?" Although he had the reputation of Goliath with his shouting and raving, he was not, to my surprise, even a big fellow. He was just a man with a story to tell, one that he believed in immensely.

I, on the other hand, had never felt that intensely about anything in my life. Before getting in debt and being thrown in prison, I had the three basic needs in life—food, wine, and a wife—in that order

The Baptist was not the least taken aback by my question. "My life has always been about proclaiming the coming of the Messiah," he said.

I noticed that even in chains there was something sturdy and unbending about his nature. Judging by his attitude, had I been in a battle, I would have wanted him on my side. At the same time there was an air about him that said he was a man of peace.

He was a sight to see. We were all smelly and filthy from our lot. Pigs had better quarters, and even those who fed us came and went swiftly to get away from the smell of us drenched in our own scum. But the ever-shouting Baptist came to us disheveled, wearing a rough hide of reddish camel. His dark hair was wild, as if he had spent his entire life in a fierce wind. His skin was leathery where the sun had beat at him with no mercy, and his eyebrows seemed locked in determination. He seemed, unlike so many, to know just what he was about.

I knew at once when I saw him that he was the man of whom I had heard who lived in the wilderness and who was said to eat only honey and locusts. Some said he was the prophet Elijah come back to proclaim the end of the world.

"Are you afraid to die?" I asked the Baptist. All of us feared that the prison would be our end, either from neglect, starvation, or beating—none of which took the Baptist. Even I, who had only been there a few weeks, knew the hacking cough of the dying.

"There is much to proclaim and little time to do it," the Baptist said. "Death slows the spread of the message. I need to stay just ahead of the Messiah to tell the people that he is on his way."

"But you are not afraid to die?" I asked.

"When a man realizes he has been given a duty so great that he is unworthy, has not his time already come?" the Baptist said. "I was baptizing my cousin Jesus, who I thought was just another man, washing him free of his sins, screaming to the crowds that I would wash this man of his sins but that one is coming who would wash him with the Holy Spirit. But as I lifted Jesus out of the water, the Holy Spirit

Lucian, in the second century C.E., in describing how a narrative was supposed to begin, referred to a class of writings that, like Mark, simply started with the narrative: "Again, you may see others writing introductions that are brilliant, dramatic, and excessively long, so that you expect what follows to be marvellous to hear, but for the body of their history they bring on something so tiny and so undistinguished that it resembles a child, some Cupid.... In my opinion the right way to do it is not like this: there must be a general uniformity, a unity of colour, and the body must be in proportion with the head, so that when you get a golden helmet the breastplate is not a silly patchwork of rags or rotten hides with a wicker-work shield and pigskin greaves. You can see plenty of writers like that, who put the head of the Colossus of Rhodes on the body of a dwarf. Then again others produce bodies without any heads—works lacking an introduction that begin at once with the narrative...." (Lucian, *How to Write History*, 23) (from LCL) appeared in the form of a dove, and the heavens parted, and God spoke to him in my arms. I don't think until that time even Jesus himself realized the enormity of what he was about. And what does one do when God speaks? History talks about men who have spoken and wrestled with angels, but to be spoken to by God? We are in awe that it even happened to Abraham and Moses! But think now, could my life ever have more meaning than it did at that moment? I had baptized a man in the water who had no sins. I had baptized the Messiah. I had heard God. I witnessed the Holy Spirit."

When John had finished, I had nothing to say! Somehow when a man has just said he has witnessed the Holy Spirit, it's difficult to have a good comeback. It was certainly not the place to bring up the day I came upon a group of maidens bathing in the Jordan. My cousin Rueben was an important man, but the cousin of the Baptist appeared to belong to God. What could I say? Had I said anything, it would have been, "How 'bout them gladiators?"

The Baptist lay back against the wall, giving into his bondage. He seemed weary. "As burdensome as my life has been," he said, as if talking to himself, "the pressure of telling the world what lies ahead can be nothing as challenging as what Jesus goes through with his mission. He walks swiftly as if there are no minutes to spare, and he tells the people of God's love. He heals them. But for every one who loves him, there is another who wants him dead.... You ask if I am afraid of death? No, but I would like to be able to stay here and

Another version of the story of John the Baptist is found in Josephus: "For Herod had put him [John the Baptist] to death, though he was a good man and had exhorted the Jews to lead righteous lives, to practice justice toward their fellows and piety toward God, and so doing to join in baptism. In his view this was a necessary preliminary if baptism was to be acceptable to God. They must not employ it to gain pardon for whatever sins they committed, but as a consecration of the body implying that the soul was already thoroughly cleansed by right behavior. When others too joined the crowds about him, because they were aroused to the highest degree by his sermons, Herod became alarmed. Eloquence that had so great an effect on mankind might lead to some form of sedition, for it looked as if they would be guided by John in everything that they did. Herod decided therefore that it would be much better to strike first and be rid of him before his work led to an uprising, than to wait for an upheaval, get involved in a difficult situation and see his mistake." (*Antiquities*, 18.116-19 [late first century C.E.]; from Boring-Berger-Colpe, 46, no. 16)

be so convincing in my introduction that Jesus could be spared the pain that I fear lies ahead. He is a man blessed with the love of God and marked with the jealousies of humankind, and he must come to grips with both."

"He must come to grips with both," the Baptist repeated. "How is it possible to be a man of God and also one who eats and drinks? How is it possible to be both godly and a man?"

He was quiet then. There was peace in his eyes when they carried him away to his impending death. He apparently had no trouble coming to grips with what he saw as the truth.

As for me, I prayed for my time in prison to be over so I could go out and find this Jesus myself. I kept thinking, "He must come to grips with both. He is a man, but he is the Messiah... He must come to grips with both." I had no plans to carry on the message of John the Baptist. My intention was just to see things for myself, but I have told the story many times as I'm telling it now. And people listened. *(Jo-Ann Jennings)*

MATTHEW 4:1-11; LUKE 4:1-13

The Temptation

Jesus is tempted by Satan in the desert.

The Story according to Matthew

Jesus was then led by the Spirit into the wilderness, to be tempted by the devil.

For forty days and nights he fasted, and at the end of them he was famished. The tempter approached him and said, 'If you are the Son of God, tell these stones to become bread.' Jesus answered, 'Scripture says, "Man is not to live on bread alone, but on every word that comes from the mouth of God."'

The devil then took him to the Holy City and set him on the parapet of the temple. 'If you are the Son of God,' he said, 'throw yourself down; for scripture says, "He will put his angels in charge of you, and they will support you in their arms, for fear you should strike your foot against a stone."' Jesus answered him, 'Scripture also says, "You are not to put the Lord your God to the test."'

The devil took him next to a very high mountain, and showed him all the kingdoms of the world in their glory. 'All these,' he said, 'I will give you, if you will only fall down and do me homage.' But Jesus said, 'Out of my sight, Satan! Scripture says, "You shall do homage to the Lord your God and worship him alone."'

Then the devil left him; and angels came and attended to his needs.

The Story according to Luke

Full of the Holy Spirit, Jesus returned from the Jordan, and for forty days he wandered in the wilderness, led by the Spirit and tempted by the devil.

During that time he ate nothing, and at the end of it he was famished. The devil said to him, 'If you are the Son of God, tell this stone to become bread.' Jesus answered, 'Scripture says, "Man is not to live on bread alone."'

Next the devil led him to a height and showed him in a flash all the kingdoms of the world. 'All this dominion will I give to you,' he said, 'and the glory that goes with it; for it has been put in my hands and I can give it to anyone I choose. You have only to do homage to me and it will all be yours.' Jesus answered him, 'Scripture says, "You shall do homage to the Lord your God and worship him alone."'

The devil took him to Jerusalem and set him on the parapet of the temple. 'If you are the Son of God,' he said, 'throw yourself down from here; for scripture says, "He will put

59

his angels in charge of you," and again, "They will support you in their arms for fear you should strike your foot against a stone."' Jesus answered him, 'It has been said,

"You are not to put the Lord your God to the test."'

So, having come to the end of all these temptations, the devil departed, biding his time.

Comments on the Story

The temptation of Jesus stands at the beginning of his public ministry in both Matthew and Luke. Both Gospels mention that Jesus was in the desert for forty days, a period reminiscent of Israel's forty years of wandering in the desert. In fact, the content of the tests that Jesus not only endures, but passes, correspond to the tests that Israel faced in the wilderness but failed. Jesus is tempted by his hunger as was Israel (Exod. 16), but whereas Jesus rebukes the temptation with the words "Man is not to live on bread alone," the Israelites simply complain—first about the lack of bread (Exod. 16:3) and then about the lack of variety in their diet (Num. 11:6: "wherever we look there is nothing except this manna"). Jesus is tempted to test God's faithfulness as was Israel (Exod. 17). But whereas Jesus rebuts Satan with the words "You are not to put the Lord your God to the test" (Matt. 4:7; Luke 4:12), when Moses challenged the Israelites ("Why do you test the LORD?" [NRSV]) the people continued to complain against Moses (Exod. 17:2-3). Jesus is also tempted to engage in idolatrous acts by worshiping Satan, but he rebukes Satan with the words "You shall do homage to the Lord your God and worship him alone" (Matt. 4:10; Luke 4:8). Israel, on the other hand, succumbed to the temptation to commit idolatry and fashioned gold in the image of a calf and worshiped it (Exod. 32). For both Matthew and Luke, the specific content of the tests disclose that Jesus *is* Israel, God's son, who is called out of Egypt (see Matt. 2:15) to complete Israel's exodus (see Luke 9:31).

The order of the temptations may be just as important as their specific content. Communication theorists have coined the phrase "recency effect" to refer to the way hearers and readers respond to the last information given about a character or a plot. Often we are able to remember only the last thing a person said or the last deed a character did. Though storytellers may not be familiar with the technical term, they are certainly aware of the phenomenon. How a story ends leaves a lasting impression on the hearer and shapes impressions of the story as a whole. The ending of a story, then, is critical to its overall message. This is true not only of the end of a long story, but also of a short story within a long story.

Recency effect plays a major role in understanding the function of the temptation narrative in both Matthew and Luke. The two storytellers record the same three temptations (often attributed to a common source, "Q"), but they do not present the temptations in the same order. The first temptation is the same in both: Jesus is tempted to turn stones into bread. The order of the next two temptations, however, is reversed.

In Luke, the last temptation occurs on the pinnacle of the temple (Luke 4:9); in Matthew the last temptation occurs on a "very high mountain" (Matt. 4:8). According to the "recency effect," and assuming Matthew and Luke are competent storytellers, the last temptation of Christ in each Gospel may be significant. An examination of the recurrences of the locale in the two Gospels confirms this thesis.

In Luke's Gospel, the temple and synagogue provide the setting for several scenes, including the opening and closing scenes. In every case but the last, the temple is the location of a conflict between God's agents and God's people. For example, in the opening scene (Luke 1:5-23) Zechariah, who the narrator tells us was "upright and devout, blamelessly observing all the commandments and ordinances of the Lord" (1:6), is one of God's people. While in God's sanctuary, the temple, God's agent, an angel of the Lord (vv. 11, 19), appears to him. The conflict begins in 1:18 when Zechariah doubts the angel's prophecy that he and Elizabeth will have a son. The angel rebukes Zechariah, revealing to him that he is none other than Gabriel, who was "sent to speak to you" (1:19). The conflict is resolved when Gabriel strikes Zechariah speechless until Elizabeth gives birth to John. This initial episode provides the type-scene for the other temple and synagogue encounters (4:16-30; 6:6-11; 13:10-17). The tension seems to intensify with each subsequent conflict and reaches a climax in the last temple conflict scene, where the tension is almost unbearable as God's people plot the death of God's agent (19:45-48).

> The baptism and temptation of Jesus can be seen to follow a pattern found in the Old Testament whereby a prophet is confirmed in his prophetic call by means of visionary experiences. See Isaiah 6:1-13, Jeremiah 1:1-19, Ezekiel 1:1–3:11, and especially this close parallel from *2 Baruch* 76:3: "Therefore, go up to the top of this mountain, and all countries of this earth will pass before you, as well as the likeness of the inhabited world, and the top of the mountains, and the depths of the valleys, and the depths of the seas, and the number of rivers, so that you may see that which you leave and whither you go. This will happen after forty days." (Charlesworth, 646)

How does the temptation narrative fit into this pattern? Since the last temptation occurs on the pinnacle of the temple, it both recalls the Zechariah episode and foreshadows the temple scene in Luke 19. Here, God's agent, Jesus, is in direct conflict, not with God's people (as in Luke 1 and 19), but with God's adversary, Satan, on the pinnacle of God's house. The effect of this

61

story is to set the other conflict scenes in a cosmic context and to make clear, at least from the narrator's point of view, that when God's people (Zechariah, the religious authorities) oppose God's agent (Gabriel, Jesus) they are choosing, perhaps unconsciously, to side with God's adversary, Satan.

The last temple scene in Luke depicts a resolution to the conflict. The Gospel concludes with the disciples returning to Jerusalem after the final departure of Jesus, where they "spent all their time in the temple praising God" (24:53). By the end of the Gospel, then, the disciples have become the pious people of God, and there is no conflict between the people of God and the agent of God in God's house. They are obediently, joyously, and continually praising God in the temple.

In Matthew the last temptation occurs on a "very high mountain" (4:8). Again, mountains in Matthew are a setting where significant events take place. This reference to a mountain is the first in Matthew, but there are several others (5:1; 14:23; 15:29; 17:1; 24:3; 28:16). Matthew 5:1 is the introduction to the Sermon on the Mount, where Jesus is depicted as the "new Moses" giving a "new law." Jesus is the Teaching Messiah. In 14:23 he is the Praying Messiah: Jesus "dismissed the crowd" and "went up the hill by himself to pray." In 15:29ff, Jesus received great crowds who brought with them "the lame, blind, dumb, and crippled, and many other sufferers" and "he healed them." Jesus is the Healing Messiah. In 17:1ff, Jesus takes Peter, James, and John "up a high mountain" and is there transfigured "in their presence." He is the Glorified Messiah. In 24:3 he sits upon the mountain called

> In this text from the Talmud, Satan and Abraham debate in a style similar to the temptation story, with each using scripture to buttress his case: "On the way Satan came towards him and said to him, 'If we assay to commute with thee, wilt thou be grieved? . . . Behold, thou hast instructed many, and thou hast strengthened the weak hands. Thy words have upholden him that was falling, and thou hast strengthened the feeble knees. But now it is come upon thee, and thou faintest' (Job 4:2-5). He replied, 'I will walk in my integrity' (Ps 26:2). 'But,' Satan said to him, 'should not thy fear be thy confidence?' (Job 4:6). He retorted, 'Remember, I pray thee, whoever perished, being innocent?' (Job 4:6). Seeing that he would not listen to him, he said to him, 'Now a thing was secretly brought to me (Job 4:12); thus have I heard behind the curtain, "the lamb for a burnt offering but not Isaac for a burnt offering."' He replied, 'It is the penalty of a liar, that should he even tell the truth, he is not listened to.'" (*b. Sanhedrin* 89b [fourth century C.E.?]; from Davies and Allison, 1.352-53)

Olivet and speaks about "the end of the age." He is the Eschatological Messiah. And finally, while Luke ends his Gospel with the disciples in the temple, Matthew ends his Gospel with the disciples going "to the mountain where Jesus had told them to meet him" (28:16), where Jesus gives them the "Great Commission," commanding them to make disciples of the Gentiles/nations. He is the Universal Messiah. Our text, Matthew 4:8, fits perfectly into this pattern. In the last of the temptations of Jesus in Matthew, the devil takes Jesus to a "very high mountain" and offers him "all the kingdoms of the world in their glory" if Jesus will worship him. But Jesus responds, "You shall do homage to the Lord your God and worship him alone" (4:10). Jesus is the Obedient Messiah.

In Nathaniel Hawthorne's *The Scarlet Letter*, the scaffold scenes occur at the beginning, middle, and end. In the first scaffold scene, the sin of Hester Prynne is publicly disclosed and she is thrown into prison. In the second, Hester and Dimmesdale meet in the middle of the night on the scaffold, Dimmesdale confesses what Hester already knows, and the sky (so some say) illuminates in the shape of a giant "A." In the final, climactic scene, the ailing Dimmesdale ascends the scaffold steps during a procession and discloses publicly his relationship with Hester just before he dies. Here the scaffold is the locus of revelation, public and private. So it is with mountains in Matthew; the mountain is the place of revelation. Obedient, teaching, praying, healing, glorified, eschatological, universal—these are characteristics of the Messiah that Matthew reveals in mountain scenes. It all begins with the temptation narrative. The last temptation of Christ in Matthew is the first of a series of disclosures, public and private, about the nature of Jesus' messiahship.

Retelling the Story

> For forty days he wandered in the wilderness, led by the Spirit and tempted by the devil. (Luke 4:1)

Samantha Jordan scrubbed her son in a tub of hot water as the maid lay out quite ordinary clothes.

"He was baptized, and then the Spirit immediately drove him out into the wilderness," the maid mumbled. "He was with the wild beasts, and the angels waited on him."

"What?" asked Charles Thomas Jordan.

"She's mad with scripture today," his mother said softly. "She's convinced if you go to public school, you'll be eaten by a lion. You know there are no lions at school, don't you?"

"I don't know," he said. "There *could* be lions."

Samantha smacked the water playfully in answer to his remark and then became serious.

63

"Your father is an ambassador, representing the United States. Sending you to school is a test of your character, Charlie. Your bodyguard, Jordan, will remain outside the school as inconspicuously as possible, but basically, you'll be on your own to make decisions. You have to learn what it means to be the ambassador's son."

Charlie was alarmed. Was there no way to get out of this?

When he saw Jordan waiting, he looked for the limousine that usually drove them to town.

"We'll walk," said Jordan. "Remember, Charlie, you represent not just your father but your country. This will be a test of your integrity."

Charlie stared far up to the quiet eyes of his protector. "Do I have an integrity?"

Jordan laughed. "It's not something you grow like a beard," he said. "Your parents have integrity. When deciding what to do, think about the decisions they make."

Charlie saw as soon as he entered the schoolroom just how different he was. His toes didn't stick out of his shoes, and he knew to use a tissue when he sneezed. He used textbook Spanish and the other children spoke in an area dialect.

Things went well until the bathroom break.

"If you were to put something sticky in the teacher's chair, we would all like you," he was dared by Raul, the obvious class leader.

"Why would I do that?" Charlie asked. "If I have to do something bad to get you to like me, I am not sure I want you to like me." Had he given the wrong answer?

The *Damascus Document* [ca. 100 B.C.E.], which derived from the Essene Community at Qumran, also spoke of three "snares" of Satan: "During all those years Satan shall be unleashed against Israel, as He spoke by the hand of Isaiah, son of Amoz, saying, *Terror and the pit and the snare are upon you, O inhabitant of the land* (Isa. xxiv, 17). Interpreted, these are the three nets of Satan with which Levi son of Jacob said that he catches Israel by setting them up as three kinds of righteousness. The first is fornication, the second is riches, and the third is profanation of the Temple. Whoever escapes the first is caught in the second, and whoever saves himself from the second is caught in the third (Isa. xxiv, 18)." (4:12-19; Vermes, 100)

When lunchtime came, Charlie was sitting alone when Raul pushed up to him. "If you will hit Rosita, you will have proved your strength," Raul whispered. "You won't get in trouble because you're the ambassador's son."

The possibility of popularity sat right there next to Charlie. If Raul learned to like him, the others would, too. He sighed. "I'll tell you what, Raul. I'd like to share my lunch with you instead."

Decisions had become more difficult.

The playground was covered with rocks and broken glass, but the children ran and wrestled as if in a gymnasium. The merry-go-round was battered and didn't whirl quite right, but the children piled on until it was full, and four of the boys pushed. Charlie tried to be *just one of the kids*, but it was obvious that even if he took his turn at pushing, he was not accepted.

Raul was soon at his side again. "If you will get our lost ball from behind the fence, I will be your very best friend," he said.

The swings in the schoolyard were tall, and a splintery fence stood nearby, hiding an angry dog that growled at the children it could not see as it clawed at the wood on the other side.

"It will be easy," Raul challenged. "You are the ambassador's son, practically a king."

Charlie climbed to the top of the swing pole and stared down at a slobbery, ravenous cur. Did the creatures in this country have anything to eat? There was in truth a ball, however, but not much of one.

"You can do it!" Raul shouted from the ground. "The dog's owners won't let anything happen to you."

Clinging to the pole, Charlie wished his jeans were old and that he had holes in his shoes. He wished he'd had no lunch to share. He wished the kids would let him be their true friend. He could see Jordan in the distance, trusting his decision. He asked himself how his father would get out of this situation and remembered a story of his father's having been the only one to protest a violent undertaking. He looked at the saliva dripping from the dog's mouth and remembered what his father had said once, that there's a difference between courage and being foolhardy. If he got the ball, he would just be showing off.

Slowly he slid down the pole and looked at Raul head-on. "It doesn't matter who my father is," he said. "All I would prove by getting into the yard with that dog is my stupidity."

Charlie felt as if he had passed a test instead of failed it, and then Rosita said, "The ball belongs to the dog. It would have killed you."

That afternoon as they walked home, Jordan said, "You made it."

"I made it barely, but I knew you were there all the time in the distance," Charlie said. *(Jo-Ann Jennings)*

LUKE 4:14-30

The Rejection at Nazareth

Jesus delivers a sermon to a hostile crowd in his hometown.

The Story

Then Jesus, armed with the power of the Spirit, returned to Galilee; and reports about him spread through the whole countryside. He taught in their synagogues and everyone sang his praises.

He came to Nazareth, where he had been brought up, and went to the synagogue on the sabbath day as he regularly did. He stood up to read the lesson and was handed the scroll of the prophet Isaiah. He opened the scroll and found the passage which says,

'The spirit of the Lord is upon me because he has anointed me;
he has sent me to announce good news to the poor,
to proclaim release for prisoners and recovery of sight for the blind;
to let the broken victims go free,
to proclaim the year of the Lord's favour.'

He rolled up the scroll, gave it back to the attendant, and sat down; and all eyes in the synagogue were fixed on him.

He began to address them: 'Today,' he said, 'in your hearing this text has come true.' There was general approval; they were astonished that words of such grace should fall from his lips. 'Is not this Joseph's son?' they asked. Then Jesus said, 'No doubt you will quote to me the proverb, "Physician, heal yourself!" and say, "We have heard of all your doings at Capernaum; do the same here in your own home town." Truly I tell you,' he went on: 'no prophet is recognized in his own country. There were indeed many widows in Israel in Elijah's time, when for three and a half years the skies never opened, and famine lay hard over the whole country; yet it was to none of these that Elijah was sent, but to a widow at Sarepta in the territory of Sidon. Again, in the time of the prophet Elisha there were many lepers in Israel, and not one of them was healed, but only Naaman, the Syrian.' These words roused the whole congregation to fury; they leapt up, drove him out of the town, and took him to the brow of the hill on which it was built, meaning to hurl him over the edge. But he walked straight through the whole crowd, and went away.

Comments on the Story

Luke 4:14-30 presents the inaugural sermon of Jesus in his hometown of Nazareth. The sermon not only introduces the Galilean section of Luke's

66

Gospel (4:14–9:50), it is the "frontispiece" to the entire Gospel. From it we learn about the character of Jesus' ministry from the lips of the Lukan Jesus himself. The passage is framed by double references to the movement of Jesus: in 4:16, Jesus "came to Nazareth" and "went to the synagogue"; in 4:30, Jesus "walked straight through the whole crowd, and went away." In between are two sections, 4:16*b*-22 and 4:23-29, each of which alternates between Jesus' speech and the crowd's reaction to it: A 4:16*b*-21—Jesus' speech; B 4:22—crowd's reaction; A' 4:23-27—Jesus' speech; B' 4:28-29—crowd's reaction.

The first unit, 4:16*b*-21, begins with Jesus' sermon in his hometown synagogue and is in a well-recognized chiastic structure:

> A Jesus stands to read (16*c*)
>   B the scroll is handed to him (17*a*)
>   C he unrolls the scroll (17*b*)
>   D he reads the scripture (18-19)
>   C' he rolls up the scroll (20*a*)
>   B' he hands the scroll back to the attendant (20*b*)
> A' Jesus sits down (20*c*)

In such a structure, the emphasis is on the middle item (4:18-19), which Luke uses to outline the shape of Jesus' ministry. The scripture cited here derives from Isaiah 61:1-2 (with a few Lukan modifications). The authorial audience would have recognized the opening clause ("The spirit of the Lord GOD is upon me") as a reference to Jesus' baptism, where the Spirit descended upon Jesus in the form of a dove (Luke 3:22). Moreover, the reference to being "anointed" would have evoked the term "Messiah," or "Christ," both of which mean "anointed one." Thus, Jesus identifies himself through this scripture with the messianic expectations of his audience.

The construction of the remainder of the citation is obscured in most English translations. The finite verb "he has sent me" controls four infinitives (one before and three after) and the text is best translated as follows:

> "He has sent me
> to preach good news to the poor;
> to proclaim to the captives release and to the blind new sight;
> to send forth the oppressed in release;
> to proclaim the Lord's acceptable year."

The first assignment is to "announce good news." The objects of this good news are the "humble" or "poor" (NRSV). While the term "poor" has primarily economic connotations, like the other designations ("captives," "blind," and "oppressed") it also carries a metaphorical meaning. In Luke's writings, the poor are the economically disadvantaged (see 1:52-53; 6:20-21; 7:22) *and* the spiritually impoverished. The captives are those who have been enslaved because they cannot pay their debts *and* those who are enslaved to sin (Acts 8:22-23). The blind are those who are physically *and* spiritually without sight (Acts 9). The oppressed are those who are subject to unwelcome military forces *and* unwanted demons (Acts 10:38).

The final phrase, "to proclaim the year of the Lord's favour," alludes to Leviticus 25 and the Jubilee year legislation. The Jubilee year (the fiftieth year after seven intervals of seven years) was the "year of release" (Greek Lev. 25:10). It too, in the subsequent Jewish history of interpretation, had both literal and spiritual application.

Here, then, in a nutshell at the beginning of Luke's Gospel is a précis of Jesus' public ministry. The rest of the story unfolds the ways in which Jesus preaches good news, proclaims new sight and forgiveness, and sends forth the oppressed in release. In Luke 4, Jesus declares that the "year of the Lord's favour" has already begun: "Today," he said, "in your hearing this text has come true" (4:21). The emphasis is on the immediacy of the fulfillment; it has occurred "today" (on this word, see also Luke 5:26; 19:5, 9; 23:43).

The audience's response is two-fold. First, the narrator reports that "there was general approval; they were astonished that words of such grace should fall from his lips" (4:22a). Then they ask, "Is not this Joseph's son?" (4:22b). Often this question is taken as a pejorative inquiry (perhaps because of the negative connotations found in the partial parallel to this story in Matthew 13:53-58 and Mark 6:1-6). By what authority does Joseph's son say "words of such grace"? In reality, both responses are positive. In fact, the question "Is not this Joseph's son?" should be taken as an example of the "general approval" (NRSV: "all spoke well of him"). From the point of view of the Nazareth crowd, being from their hometown entails certain social obligations. The "words of such grace" that "fell from his lips" were understood to refer primarily to his audience, members of his own village.

Jesus' first response/aphorism ("Physician, heal yourself!" 4:23a) should be interpreted in light of the second ("We have heard of all your doings at Capernaum; do the same here in your own home town," 4:23b). Jesus understands full well that by referring to him as "Joseph's son," the crowd expects him to show preferential treatment to his own family and village. But he rejects their expectation. "Truly I tell you ... no prophet is recognized in his own country" (4:24; for other versions of this saying, see Mark 6:4; Matt. 13:57; John 4:44). A prophet who, by the nature of his vocation, criticizes the unjust practices of his own people and is not ruled by the self-interests of his community is naturally displeasing to his own hometown or country. Jesus is such a prophet. His ministry of proclaiming good news to the poor is not limited to Israel's poor; he brings good news to ALL poor. His proclamation of release to the indentured and sight to the blind is not just for Israel's slaves or Israel's blind; he proclaims release and sight for ALL who are physically or spiritually enslaved or blind. He declares free ALL who are oppressed by soldier or spirit. This focus on the excluded, however, wins him no friends among his own people.

Jesus cites two examples from Israel's scriptures to prove his point, one about Elijah (1 Kgs. 17:1-24), the other about Elisha (2 Kgs. 5:1-19). In recounting the two stories, Jesus emphasizes that the object of the prophet's miraculous ministry is a Gentile. In Elijah's case, it is the poor widow at Zarephath in Sidon; with Elisha it is Naaman the Syrian official. These stories make it clear that prophets of old did not limit their ministries to the "in-group." They, like Jesus, were no respecter of gender, class, or race.

The radical inclusiveness of Jesus' ministry shocks his audience. They had understood themselves to be the primary beneficiaries of Jesus' message. They could all relate to being poor, captive, blind, or oppressed. They are ready for deliverance, but they are not prepared to share it. When they hear that Jesus intends for his Jubilee ministry to extend to Gentiles, they are "roused to fury" and fulfill Jesus' aphorism that "no prophet is recognized in his own country." "They leapt up, drove him out of the town, and took him to the brow of the hill on which it was built, meaning to hurl him over the edge" (4:29), presumably so they could stone him. The crowd's intentions, however, are thwarted: "But he walked straight through the whole crowd, and went away" (4:30). On this day, Jesus escapes death on a hill in his hometown. His radical ministry of reaching out to those excluded because of race, gender, or economic and social status, however, eventually does lead to his execution on another hill called Calvary in the city of Jerusalem. This story should not be taken to mean that Israel, in Luke's view, is permanently rejected. Stories of positive Jewish response to Jesus' ministry are found throughout the Third Gospel and Acts. But those who respond positively to Jesus' message recognize the inherent inclusiveness of his message. Those who don't hear that message of inclusion or choose to reject it do not respond positively. "No prophet is recognized in his own country."

Retelling the Story

But he walked straight through the whole crowd, and went away. (Luke 4:30)

Principal Sydney Shobe picked up only bits of conversations as she searched the crowd in the high school auditorium... "No, I hadn't heard she was pregnant... Yes, I knew he had broken his leg... He beats his wife, does he?... Have you planted your bulbs yet?... Don't tell me your son is already in high school?... Yes, they cut a small hole in my side, and it just popped right out... No, I haven't tried that. I've heard it tastes like chicken."

It was difficult to interrupt the gossip and get on with the introduction of newly hired high school teachers to the parents of the students.

69

The auditorium was unusually full compared with past years on Parents' Night at the beginning of the school year. That was evident when the cheap cookies with the stale pink and yellow icing and the lukewarm coffee had already disappeared, and people were still pouring in the door.

Principal Shobe thought she would scream if she heard one more person say, "Isn't there any cream?" Of course there was no cream! There was never cream at school events. Sometimes there was the powdered "stuff," but it ran out in a hurry. Didn't anyone know it was loaded with fat? She wondered why the kitchen always chose the cookies shaped like crescents on outhouses that had little prickly multi-colored sugary things on them—or ancient coconut flakes. There had to be two kinds of coconut—the fresh, soft kind used in ordinary places and the hard, brittle kind saved for school functions.

She folded her hands in front of her waist like an opera singer and mentally super-glued a fake smile onto her face—"Hello, Mrs. Barnes. How lovely to see you again this year. We can always count on you, can't we?"— although what she really wanted to do was shout, "No, but it doesn't matter that there's no cream, because there's no coffee left, and even if there were, it was terrible, and it's terrible because the librarian volunteers to make it every year, and we continue to let her! The woman is 90 years old! Why is she still driving when she's a menace on the highway and can't make decent coffee? But have a cookie! Just knock the decorations off, pound them on the table for an hour, and eat the crumbs out of your hand so you don't break your teeth!" But she thought better of it—Did anyone else think old coffee smelled like stinky feet?

Jesus as "savior" in this text can be contrasted with Caesar as savior: "This [Augustus] is the Caesar who calmed the torrential storms on every side, who healed the pestilences common to Greeks and barbarians, pestilences which descending from the south and east and coursed to the west and north sowing the seeds of calamity over the places and waters which lay between. This is he who not only loosed but broke the chains which had shackled and pressed so hard on the habitable world. This is he who exterminated wars both of the open kind and the covert which are brought about by the raids of brigands. This is he who cleared the sea of pirate ships and filled it with merchant vessels. This is he who reclaimed every state to liberty, who led disorder into order and brought gentle manners and harmony to all unsociable and brutish nations. . . . He was also the first and the greatest and the common benefactor." (Philo, *Embassy to Gaius*, 145-49 [15 B.C.E.–50 C.E.]; Boring-Berger-Colpe, 195, no. 270)

The principal knew it was not the coffee or the geriatric coconut flakes that disturbed her. She had flashbacks of a beautiful little girl with coffee-cream-colored skin who had managed to do well in school year after year even though it was probably her very family who had caused someone in the worldwide social services department to come up with a word like *dysfunctional*. Having no role models and very few friends, the child had managed to succeed and with scholarships had forged together a decent life with unbelievable potential. She had decided not to take her talent to where acceptance and the big bucks lay. She wanted to give back to the community that had given her nothing else—but who had hired good teachers and provided a school building.

Principal Shobe knew what Elizabeth Terry had gone through because she had been her friend. What could be worse than having to introduce a friend to a waiting crowd filled with condescending, small-minded people?

"May I please have your attention?" she had to ask several times when the parents and curiosity-seekers finally gathered. They ignored her at first, and she wondered why such meetings didn't allow for a gavel so she could throw it at the audience, but one meeting, and she would be rendered gavel-less with thousands of meetings to go before the school year was over.

The idea that a prophet or philosopher would not be accepted in his own homeland was something of a commonplace in the Greco-Roman world of Jesus' day. Among those who expressed such a sentiment were Dio Chrysostom: "All the philosophers held life to be difficult in the [homeland]" (*Discourses* 47.6; ca. 40 to 112 C.E.); Epictetus: "The philosophers advise us to leave our country; we cannot bear that those who meet us should say, 'Hey-day! such a one is turned philosopher, who was formerly so and so'" (*Discourses* 3.16; ca. 55 to 135 C.E.); and Apollonius of Tyana: "Until now my own country alone ignores me" (*Epistles* 44; first century C.E.). (Davies and Allison, 2.460)

The introduction of the new teachers went well at first, but Principal Shobe's heart would not stop racing. She now had giant wet rings of perspiration in the armpits of her new business suit.

Eight new teachers had been introduced, each with the same overwhelming welcome and applause.

"I am proud to announce our new chemistry teacher," Principal Shobe began. "Many schools have been unable to hire a chemistry teacher this year. They've resorted to just *punting*. We have, however, one of our very own returning graduates who is one of the best teachers in her field. We are the envy of every school in the state."

The quiet was eerie. Was no one breathing?

Principal Shobe's words echoed as rows of parents played possum. This was Exhibit A, Small Town America.

"Elizabeth graduated at the top of her class at the University of Minnesota, and she has been a successful junior college teacher in the Chicago area. We are fortunate to have her ... Elizabeth?"

"Maybe she needs to go back to Chicago!" someone shouted from the back, setting off an explosion of frenzied comments. "She's a Terry!"

"How'd she get hired anyway? Who did she sleep with?"

"We don't need any more Terrys!"

"Her father is the town drunk."

The principal pleaded with her eyes to the chairperson of the board for help, but he was examining the knee of his pants and apparently the most investigated piece of lint in the universe.

"She just flat can't teach here!" someone shouted.

"Well, isn't that the most ridiculous thing I've ever heard," the principal said.

Elizabeth Terry herself stood, straight and slender and confident. Whatever races had been mixed to create her had been combined beautifully with all the proper ingredients. She was not just smart; she was beautiful.

"It must be true that one can't go home," she said. "I would like to stay here and teach your children, but apparently that's not going to work."

She boldly marched down the steps from the stage and down the aisle toward the exit door.

The principal, her friend, watched her with some sadness. "I'm sorry," she shouted. "In fact, I'm going to leave, too!"

Elizabeth Terry stopped and searched the faces in the audience. "Don't be sorry," she said. "I can get another job. This isn't the first time something like this has happened. It happened, in fact, to Jesus when he tried to go home."

She reached out her hand to her childhood friend, and they left together. Like Jesus, they merely walked through the midst of the crowd.

(Jo-Ann Jennings)

The Healing of the Paralytic

Jesus heals a paralytic when he sees the faith of his friends.

The Story

After some days he returned to Capernaum, and news went round that he was at home; and such a crowd collected that there was no room for them even in the space outside the door. While he was proclaiming the message to them, a man was brought who was paralysed. Four men were carrying him, but because of the crowd they could not get him near. So they made an opening in the roof over the place where Jesus was, and when they had broken through they lowered the bed on which the paralysed man was lying. When he saw their faith, Jesus said to the man, 'My son, your sins are forgiven.'

Now there were some scribes sitting there, thinking to themselves, 'How can the fellow talk like that? It is blasphemy! Who but God can forgive sins?' Jesus knew at once what they were thinking, and said to them, 'Why do you harbour such thoughts? Is it easier to say to this paralysed man, "Your sins are forgiven," or to say, "Stand up, take your bed, and walk"? But to convince you that the Son of Man has authority on earth to forgive sins'—he turned to the paralysed man—'I say to you, stand up, take your bed, and go home.' And he got up, and at once took his bed and went out in full view of them all, so that they were astounded and praised God. 'Never before,' they said, 'have we seen anything like this.'

Comments on the Story

This story introduces us to one in a series of minor characters who play a major role in defining discipleship in Mark. We will also encounter a leper (Mark 1), a demoniac (Mark 5), a synagogue leader and a woman with a life-draining flow of blood (Mark 5), a Gentile woman (Mark 7), a blind beggar (Mark 10), a poor widow (Mark 12), an anointing woman (Mark 14), a Roman soldier (Mark 15), a town alderman, and the list goes on. A tin man seeking a heart, a scarecrow in need of a brain, a lion bereft of courage, and a little girl seeking passage home could scarcely form a more incongruous group. These minor characters in general, and the four unnamed friends of this story in particular, display persistent faith, a disregard for personal status and power, and a capacity for sacrificial service.

The scene in Mark 2:1-12 begins with Jesus returning to Capernaum and reports circulating that "he was at home" (2:1). While the specific house is not identified, the authorial audience might reasonably assume that Jesus has returned to the home of Simon Peter in Capernaum (1:29). At any rate, his presence back in Capernaum creates no little stir, and soon "such a crowd collected that there was no room for them even in the space outside the door" (2:2). The stage is set for the appearance of the paralytic and his four friends.

With Jesus preaching literally to a "full house," four men approach the house carrying a paralytic, but "because of the crowd they could not get him near [Jesus]" (2:4). These particular friends, however, are both persistent and resourceful. They remove the roof (literally, "unroof the roof") above him. The house here in Mark was probably a thatched hut, the kind found by archaeologists throughout ancient Capernaum. So the friends simply dug through the matting of reeds, branches, and dried mortar. (Interestingly, Luke "contextualizes" the story for his urban readers by reporting that the friends removed the "tiling" from the roof, evoking the image of a tiled peristyle home more common among the Mediterranean city centers of late antiquity [Luke 5:19].) This kind of relentless faith is characteristic of these minor characters who are models of discipleship in Mark. The woman with the hemorrhage pursues Jesus despite ritual taboos (Mark 5); the Syrophoenician woman refuses to allow Jesus' biting remark about the dogs to deter her (Mark 7); blind Bartimaeus continues to call upon Jesus even when the crowds reprimand him. Likewise, in Mark 2 four friends literally cut a hole in the roof above Jesus' head and "lowered the bed on which the paralysed man was lying" (2:4).

Now the recognition of their faith comes. Once Jesus had presumably cleared his throat and eyes from the dust of this "forced entry," he saw what most others would not have seen. He saw *their* faith, the faith of these persistent friends, not, as one might expect, the paralytic's faith. Their persistence and sacrifice is not self-serving. Rather, it contributes to the healing of their friend.

Jesus' response to this demonstration of faith is, "My son, your sins are forgiven" (2:5). To the authorial audience, it would be most natural to equate the man's physical disability with some previous egregious sin. The Old Testament and post-biblical Judaism give a variety of perspectives on physical suffering. Sometimes physical suffering was understood as divine punishment for sin (Pss. 38:1-3; 41:3-4; 107:17; Isa. 57:17). Sometimes the purpose of physical suffering was understood to serve as *paideia*, moral instruction, for the one stricken (Prov. 3:11-12; Wis. of Sol. 3:4-6; 17:1; Sir. 2:5-6; Pss. of Sol. 18:4-5). Sometimes the physical suffering of one was seen as beneficial to others (Gen. 50:15-21; Isa. 53:2-12; 2 Macc. 7:37-38). Early Christian writings reflect these same three views: suffering as divine punishment (John 5:14; 1 Cor. 11:30; Jas. 5:16);

suffering as moral instruction (Rom. 5:3-4; 1 Cor. 11:32; Jas. 1:2-3); and suffering as beneficial for others (Mark 10:45; Col. 1:24; Gal. 1:3-4).

Clearly, Jesus' words in Mark 2 reflect the first perspective: the man's paralysis is somehow related to divine punishment for sin. A modern audience might find such a notion distasteful. We recognize that physical inactivity combined with overeating can lead to heart disease; and we now know that smoking can cause cancer. We have no rational explanation, however, for how an immoral action of this man in Mark 2 could have led to his paralysis. Even if we did know, we could not be sure that we would make the same equation of sin and suffering that the authorial audience of Mark would have readily made. Nevertheless, we should resist the temptation to dismiss the "antiquated," "prescientific" worldview behind this story. If our postmodern culture has taught us anything in this regard, it is that sometimes our modern, scientific worldview, rather than these ancient texts, needs to be demythologized.

No sooner has Jesus pronounced the paralytic's sins forgiven than the religious authorities bristle at his words—not at the equation of sin and suffering, but at the audacity of Jesus to claim the authority to forgive sins: "Now there were some scribes sitting there, thinking to themselves, 'How can the fellow talk like that? It is blasphemy! Who but God can forgive sins?'" (2:6-7). In their ponderings, the religious leaders are actually reflecting another long-standing tradition: while the sacrificial system presumed that restitution and rituals could gain forgiveness

> Stories about seers and miracle workers in the ancient world often mentioned their ability to know the thoughts of others. Tacitus told of the priest of the oracle of the Clarian Apollo in Colophon "who hears the number and the names of the consultants, but no more, then descends into a cavern, swallows a draught of water from a mysterious spring, and—though ignorant generally of writing and of meter—delivers his response in set verses dealing with the subject each inquirer has in mind" (*Annales* 2.54 [first century C.E.]). Plutarch spoke similarly about the ability of the priestess of the oracle at Delphi to "deliver some oracles on the instant, even before the question is put—for the god whom she serves understands the dumb and hears when no man speaks" (*De garrulitate* 512E [late first–early second century C.E.]). (referenced in Davies and Allison, 2.92)

for the sinful party (see Lev. 17:11), only God could forgive sins. The God of Israel declares: "I shall forgive their wrongdoing, and their sin I shall call to mind no more" (Jer. 31:34; see also Isa. 33:22-24). The charge of blasphemy would not be difficult to make stick since the point of the story is that Jesus, as the anointed one of God, does indeed have the divine authority to forgive sins.

Now, the scribes had been pondering this issue. They must have been startled when Jesus responded to their inner musings: "Is it easier to say to this paralysed man, 'Your sins are forgiven,' or to say, 'Stand up, take your bed, and walk'?" (v. 9). In the prophetic tradition, a prophet was judged (in part) to be "true" or "false" on the basis of whether or not what he predicted actually came to pass. Therefore, it was easier to say, "Your sins are forgiven," since such a statement was not open to human falsification. A declaration of healing, on the other hand, could be readily verified or falsified. Thus Jesus, in typical Jewish fashion, reasons from the greater (harder) to the lesser (easier). If his opponents are able to verify the healing of the paralytic, then they must also accept his "lesser" (i.e., less verifiable) declaration of healing. " 'But to convince you that the Son of Man has authority on earth to forgive sins'—he turned to the paralysed man—'I say to you, stand up, take your bed, and go home' " (2:10-11).

Verification, in fact, occurs instantly: "And he got up, and at once took his bed and went out in full view of them all" (2:12a). The story ends with the \narrator's summary: "they were astounded and praised God" (2:12b). If the reference to "all" here is taken seriously, then Jesus' detractors are apparently convinced of both words: Jesus has the power to heal illnesses and the authority to forgive sins. And all because of four friends who, rather than sitting around trying to guess what sin had been committed to cause such an illness (like Job's friends), had the faith and persistence to bring the paralyzed man to one who could both heal and forgive. No wonder they all could say at the end, "Never before have we seen anything like this" (2:12).

Retelling the Story

"I say to you, stand up, take your bed, and go home." (Mark 2:11)

There is no terror as great as hope.

Today I am a successful weaver. Am I wealthy? Yes, but I share my wealth because I remember when there was not even the terror of hope.

No one knew why I was a paralytic. Some say my mother looked at a dead animal when I was in her womb. The midwife called me the last of the flour in the bowl.

I am fortunate my parents did not put me outside the city wall to be eaten by dogs. I was their youngest, and my sisters cared for me. I never left home except when my brothers carried me to the latest miracle fountain or magic mud bath, traveling often with the same desperate people we had seen before.

I was able to swallow only if my sisters chewed my food. I was as useless as a newborn, except that I continued to grow, became heavy to carry, and required more care. I knew nothing but pain, so that my fingers and limbs became gnarled. I lay awake at night half fearful my family would grow tired of the burden and let me die ... and half afraid they would not.

My oldest brother ran home one day shouting that Jesus was in Capernaum. Jesus had been added to our list of miracle possibilities long ago, a list I hated. How many times in one lifetime could I be disappointed? That's what I meant when I said there is no terror like hope. What if I dared believe, and once again, it did not happen?

What would it be like to stand on my feet? To speak? Was my voice deep like my brothers'? What would it be like to tear my teeth into a piece of meat? I longed so to feel the fuzzy ears of our donkey and the long hair of my sisters. I had lived for sixteen summers, and I longed for a normal life with a wife and with children I could carry on my shoulders.

My family tried to fill me with inspiration as they prepared for the trip. They said Jesus was not like the others.

> The *Prayer of Nabonidus* (first or second century B.C.E.) is another story in the Jewish tradition in which a Jewish healer heals by forgiving sins: "I was afflicted [with an evil ulcer] for seven years ... and an exorcist pardoned my sins. He was a Jew from [among the children of the exile of Judah, and he said], 'Recount this in writing to [glorify and exalt] the name of the [Most High God].'" (Vermes, 329)

He had even brought some from life to death. Was I not in some ways already dead?

The feet of my brothers blistered as they walked in the rock and sand, trying to carry my pallet, and our skin peeled from the heat of the sun. There was never enough water. My body wrenched with pain with every rock we stumbled over, but I could not distress my family with tears. I prayed that a vulture would swoop down and eat away my flesh so they could get on with their lives.

We were not the only ones who expected to see Jesus. We found ourselves somewhere in the vicinity of his doorstep behind hundreds of hopefuls. The dust was rampant, and I could barely breathe. My brothers leaned over me and breathed air in and out of my lungs while people stared. I wanted to say, "Just let me die!"

We could have been there all day in the sun. Would Jesus grow tired of company before he got to me? I lay there frustrated with such thoughts.

Who was I to think I was important enough to be healed by this man?

You can imagine my fear when suddenly my brothers tied cords around my pallet and hoisted me to the roof of the home where Jesus was. They pulled on the cords, taking me above the noise and the smell of filthy bodies. My heart surged! I heard them tear apart the roof. Was I really going to see Jesus? Excitement flowed through me. And then my bed was set down so that it landed next to Jesus, and he smiled, calling me by name. For once there was no terror in my hope.

I knew as soon as I saw his eyes that I was not to be disappointed this time. There was something about the sparkle within them that said, "What are you doing lying there? You have work to do." He told me that my sins were forgiven and that I should get up. The biggest shock of all is that I did.

I spread my arms out like the wings of eagles, and I stooped to feel my knees bend. I hopped around like a crazy chicken, and people laughed, but I didn't care.

"Who are you to say you can forgive a man's sins?" someone shouted at Jesus. "Only God can do that!" Without a thought I started to punch the man right in the mouth, but Jesus caught my arm, holding it gently and said, "Violence isn't the way."

I couldn't have shared this story if I had gone into the fields every day with my brothers, so I learned the trade of my sisters, working magic with colors and dyes, especially blues and reds. The rumors began to spread of my recovery and of my skill with cloth. People came from all around for my work and for my story. I never embellished it. I had truly transformed from a man afraid to hope to a man of means. I danced with my wife, who gave me six children. I felt the fuzzy ears of the donkey and have several donkeys of my own. I touched not only the hair of my sisters but also that of my mother and my own little daughter. I held each of my children on my arm with their tiny head in the palm of my hand. I have lifted them and hugged them and shouted, "Praise God! Praise God!"

I have never stopped being grateful now that I see the world from the eyes of man who is six feet tall.

When I heard that Jesus had been crucified, I cried without humiliation. I wished so that I had been in the crowd that day he was presented to the people so that I could have shouted, "Give us Jesus. Give us Jesus. Give us Jesus."

Since I could not, I can only act as his agent and share my story again and again. *(Jo-Ann Jennings)*

The Stilling of the Storm

Jesus demonstrates his authority over nature and the demonic.

The Story

That day, in the evening, he said to them, 'Let us cross over to the other side of the lake.' So they left the crowd and took him with them in the boat in which he had been sitting; and some other boats went with him. A fierce squall blew up and the waves broke over the boat until it was all but swamped. Now he was in the stern asleep on a cushion; they roused him and said, 'Teacher, we are sinking! Do you not care?' He awoke and rebuked the wind, and said to the sea, 'Silence! Be still!' The wind dropped and there was a dead calm. He said to them, 'Why are you such cowards? Have you no faith even now?' They were awestruck and said to one another, 'Who can this be? Even the wind and the sea obey him.'

So they came to the country of the Gerasenes on the other side of the lake. As he stepped ashore, a man possessed by an unclean spirit came up to him from among the tombs where he had made his home. Nobody could control him any longer; even chains were useless, for he had often been fettered and chained up, but had snapped his chains and broken the fetters. No one was strong enough to master him. Unceasingly, night and day, he would cry aloud among the tombs and on the hillsides and gash himself with stones. When he saw Jesus in the distance, he ran up and flung himself down before him, shouting at the top of his voice, 'What do you want with me, Jesus, son of the Most High God? In God's name do not torment me.' For Jesus was already saying to him, 'Out, unclean spirit, come out of the man!' Jesus asked him, 'What is your name?' 'My name is Legion,' he said, 'there are so many of us.' And he implored Jesus not to send them out of the district. There was a large herd of pigs nearby, feeding on the hillside, and the spirits begged him, 'Send us among the pigs; let us go into them.' He gave them leave; and the unclean spirits came out and went into the pigs; and the herd, of about two thousand, rushed over the edge into the lake and were drowned.

The men in charge of them took to their heels and carried the news to the town and countryside; and the people came out to see what had happened. When they came to Jesus and saw the madman who had been possessed by the legion of demons, sitting there clothed and in his right mind, they were afraid. When eyewitnesses told them what had happened to the madman and what had become of the pigs, they begged Jesus to leave the district. As he was getting into the boat, the man who had been possessed begged to go with him. But Jesus would not let him. 'Go home to your own people,' he said, 'and tell them what the Lord in his mercy has done for you.' The man went off and made known throughout the Decapolis what Jesus had done for him; and everyone was amazed.

Comments on the Story

The original New Testament texts were not divided into chapters and verses. Although the practice of dividing NT books into chapters dates back to at least the fourth century (see Codex Vaticanus, an important manuscript from the fourth century), dividing chapters into verses is usually associated with Stephanus's fourth edition of the New Testament, which was published in 1551.

Unfortunately, the somewhat arbitrary divisions can lead to misunderstanding as the rhetorical shape of the text is changed. Such, I argue, is the case with Mark 4:35–5:20. The impact of the stilling of the storm (4:35-41) can only be fully appreciated when read in light of the story of the Gerasene demoniac (5:1-20). The intrusive chapter division, which separates the two stories in modern versions, discourages such a reading.

The story begins at the end of the day. According to Mark, Jesus has finished a full day of teaching (see Mark 4:1-34). He suggests to his disciples that they cross over to the other side of the Sea of Galilee (4:35), presumably for some rest and relaxation. The disciples spring into action: "they left the crowd and took him with them in the boat in which he had been sitting; and some other boats went with him" (4:36). Two details of this report, peculiar to Mark's Gospel, demand our attention. Beginning at the end, the narrator notes, almost in passing, that "some other boats went with him," a detail suggesting a sizable party. This point becomes interesting in the second of our two stories, the healing of the Gerasene demoniac, and we shall return to it later. The other peculiarity is Mark's notice that the disciples took Jesus with them "in the boat in which he had been sitting" (literally, "in the boat, *just as he was*"). What does this phrase mean? It could simply refer to the fact that they left immediately, and Jesus remained in the boat from which he had been teaching, as the REB implies (see 4:1). But the reference also suggests a kind of familiarity with Jesus on the part of the disciples. They took him "just as he was," because they knew him "just as he was." This smugness of false familiarity is about to be blown away by the storm that approaches!

The authorial audience would have been familiar with the stories of sudden storms on the Sea of Galilee. The storm in Mark 4 is no small event. It is a violent squall, and the boat immediately begins to fill with water. The disciples, who were seasoned fishermen, are filled with fear and amazed to find Jesus asleep in the stern. They mistake his slumber for indifference: "Teacher, we are sinking! Do you not care?" (4:38). This is the first of three unanswered questions in this story (see also 4:40, 41), and each arrests the audience's attention. The fact that the first question is left unanswered increases the tension in the story just prior to its climax. Like the disciples, the audience is eager to learn why Jesus is sleeping during such a crisis. They wait, on the edge of their seats, for Jesus' response, but he never answers the question. In this case, Old Testament echoes suggest a different interpretation of Jesus' sleeping than the one given by the disciples. Sleep in the Old Testament is a symbol of divine sovereignty, as may be seen in Isaiah 51:9-10:

> Awake, awake! Arm of the LORD, put on strength;
> awake as you did in days of old, in ages long past.
> Was it not you who hacked Rahab in pieces
> and ran the dragon through?
> Was it not you who dried up the sea,
> the waters of the great abyss,
> and made the ocean depths a path for the redeemed?

Jesus' sleeping, then, is no less an indication of his divine power than is his calming of the storm. Before addressing the disciples, Jesus "awoke and rebuked the wind, and said to the sea, 'Silence! Be still!' The wind dropped and there was a dead calm" (4:39). The language of Jesus "rebuking" the wind and "silencing" the sea is reminiscent of an exorcism story (see esp. 1:25) and highlights the nature of the miracle. Jesus is not simply manipulating the elements into a more favorable weather pattern; he is engaging demonic powers and demonstrating his authority over them. Here the narrator picks up on a common theme in antiquity, especially in Jewish literature: that the sea is to be equated with chaos and evil. From the beginning, when the spirit of God hovered over the unformed and unfilled waters (Gen. 1:2), "creation" was understood as bringing order to chaos. The passage from Isaiah cited above alludes to this reality, as do other Old Testament texts:

> God, my King from of old,
> whose saving acts are wrought on earth,
> by your power you cleft the sea monster in two
> and broke the sea serpent's heads in the waters;
> you crushed the heads of Leviathan
> and threw him to the sharks for food. (Ps. 74:12-14)

> LORD God of Hosts, who is like you?
> Your strength and faithfulness, LORD, are all around you.
> You rule the raging of the sea,
> calming the turmoil of its waves.
> You crushed and slew the monster Rahab
> and scattered your enemies with your strong arm. (Ps. 89:8-10)

81

Apocalyptic texts, both Jewish and Christian, speak of a future world in which the watery chaos has been finally defeated, variously depicted by the monsters of the sea being devoured at the messianic banquet (2 Bar. 29:4; see also 2 Esd. 6:49-52) or by a simple assertion that "there was no longer any sea" (Rev. 21:1). So Jesus' calming of the sea has both christological and eschatological implications. Jesus has authority over the watery chaos, an authority typically associated with God himself, and his calming of the sea is a foreshadowing of the world to come.

Jesus then turns to his disciples and asks, "Why are you such cowards? Have you no faith even now?" (4:40). The second and third unanswered questions in this story put the disciples in a bad light. Even though they have heard his teaching, they still do not grasp the significance of his miracles. They lack faith in who Jesus is, a point confirmed by their closing question. Still filled with fear, they say to one another, "Who can this be? Even the wind and the sea obey him" (4:41). Those who were so sure that they were taking the familiar Jesus with them, "just as he was," are now revealed to be clueless regarding the true identity of Jesus. He is sovereign over wind and sea; he is Lord over evil and chaos.

As noted above, the story does not end here. The theme of authority continues as Jesus completes his journey and lands in the region of the Gerasenes (5:1). The first half of the story of the Gerasene demoniac (5:1-13) is closely linked with the story of the stilling of the storm. The journey across the Sea of Galilee had begun with several boats full of disciples. The story then focuses on just one boat, the one carrying Jesus. Finally, the narrator notes that when they reach the other shore, only Jesus disembarks. What began as a journey of Jesus with a large number of followers has been reduced to Jesus alone. The narrator makes no further mention of the other boats or the disciples, but the audience might rightly hear this story with those disciples still present in the background. The temptation to fill this gap is great. Did the disciples stay in the boat because they realized where they were and were fearful of facing the dreaded demoniac? Had they discussed the legend of the demoniac during the rest of the trip? Did they feel safer there in the water, the place of chaos, than they did on solid ground with Jesus? We do not know, but it may be helpful to remember that there is an implied audience to this scene, the disciples in the boat, whose reactions to the event remain powerfully unstated. We shall return to those disciples in a moment.

Meanwhile Jesus steps out on the shore. The narrator digresses to give a detailed description of the demoniac's condition. He is physically violent and destructive, socially alienated, and ritually unclean (living as he is among the tombs). After he confronts Jesus, the audience learns an even more startling fact. His name is Legion because the demons within him are countless! There is an ironic reversal of the One and the Many. "Jesus, son of the Most High

82

God" (5:7), began a journey with many followers, the destination of which was an encounter with a man possessed by an unclean spirit. But at the dramatic climax of the encounter, the "many" who were ostensibly on the side of the good have been reduced to one, Jesus, and the one representative of evil, the demoniac, turns out to be a man with "many" demons.

The demons bargain with Jesus to be allowed to enter a herd of swine feeding on an adjacent hillside. This aspect of the story would have been humorous to an authorial audience who was either Jewish or familiar with Jewish dietary law (a familiarity which early Gentile Christians presumably possessed). The unclean swine were an appropriate refuge for the unclean spirits. Jesus grants their request, and immediately "the herd, of about two thousand, rushed over the edge into the lake and were drowned" (5:13).

The authorial audience knows what the unclean spirits do not: Jesus is Lord even of the sea, the place of chaos and evil. The unclean spirits had hoped to escape the authority of Jesus by entering unclean swine and returning to the place of primordial chaos and evil. But, according to Mark, there is nowhere that they can go that lies outside the divine jurisdiction of Jesus. They are the victims of their own ingenuity, and once again the narrator demonstrates the authority of Jesus over the demonic.

> This story about Rabbi Gamaliel, who lived in the late first century C.E., imputes to him the ability to still a storm. "R. Gamaliel too was traveling in a ship, when a huge wave arose to drown him. 'It appears to me,' he reflected, 'that this is on account of none other but R. Eliezer b. Hyrcanus.' Thereupon he arose and exclaimed, 'Sovereign of the Universe! Thou knowest full well that I have not acted for my honor, nor for the honor of my paternal house, but for Thine, so that strife may not multiply in Israel!' At that the raging sea subsided" (*b. Baba Mezia* 59b [ca. first century C.E.]). (Boring-Berger-Colpe, 68, no. 57)

The story of the stilling of the storm easily lends itself to a kind of allegorical reading. The ship or boat is one of the earliest symbols of the Christian church, and the storm a handy metaphor to describe personal or communal calamity. Thus, the ship tossed to and fro by a violent storm is a readily recognizable image of the *ecclesia pressa*, the oppressed church. Indeed, Matthew seems to have pushed the story in this direction with several subtle changes in his account. The story follows a passage about discipleship (Matt. 8:18-22) and begins by noting that when Jesus got into the boat, "his disciples followed" (8:23). The disciples, fearful of the storm, address Jesus: "Save us, Lord; we are sinking!" (8:25). The theological connotations of "save" and "Lord" are obvious. Likewise, the response of Jesus to the disciples is slightly different, and, unlike Mark, the rebuke occurs before the stilling of the storm: "Why are you such cowards? How little faith you have!" (8:26). Jesus' disciples, fearful of the storm raging outside their boat, petition the "Lord" to "save" them. Jesus, in turn, rebukes them for having so little faith. How easily Matthew's community could appropriate this story to their own context, whether of persecution of the church by outside forces or more personal crises of faith. In either case, Jesus has the power and authority to still the storm, rescue the disciples, and bring the boat safely to its destination.

It was said of Apollonius of Tyana that when he boarded a ship, crowds of people came to board with him because "they all regarded Apollonius as one who was master of the tempest and of fire and of perils of all sorts, and so wished to go on board with him, and begged him to allow them to share the voyage with him" (Philostratus, *Life of Apollonius of Tyana* 4.13 [third century C.E.]). Similarly, the sixth century B.C.E. philosopher Pythagoras was said to have "calmed rivers and seas so that his companions might cross over easily" (Iamblichus, *Life of Pythagoras* 135 [late third to early fourth century C.E.]). (Davies and Allison, 2.70)

These two seemingly unrelated stories, the stilling of the storm and the healing of the Gerasene demoniac, underscore the same reality (see also Ps. 65:7: "you calm the seas and their raging waves, and the tumult of the nations"). Jesus has ultimate authority over evil, whether that evil manifests itself in nature, in the life of an individual, or in institutional opposition to the church. By the end of these stories, the audience is hopefully much better prepared to answer the pressing question, "What sort of man is this?"

Retelling the Story

He said to them, "Why are you such cowards? Have you no faith even now?" (Mark 4:40)

The torment of memories.

Andrew sat at the base of the cross, from which the body of Jesus had hung earlier that day. There was nothing left but the cold of the night and a raging storm. Perhaps it would wash away the smell of blood and death.

Andrew's head was bowed as the chilling rainwater crashed onto his body with the weight of the wind and drenched him, reminding him of other times when he had felt this frightened, cold, wet, and unsure of what the next moment would bring. He was so absorbed in the memories and the storm, he was not even concerned that he would be found there and get himself killed for having been a friend of Jesus.

It was a sad lot to be a fisherman's son and be afraid of the water. Andrew had never learned to swim, but even so, he left with his brother at a young age to pull in fish, always concerned that his foot would slip and he would suffocate in the darkness of the very fish he tried to catch. He had nightmares in which strangers had hoisted a net aboard their boat with much struggle only to find his pale blue body among their catch, his fingers sticking through the holes of the binding. They just shrugged and threw him back. Although dead in the dream, his subconscious could feel the splash of being tossed back into the water to drown all over again.

One time when he and Simon were pulling in a particularly large catch, the boat shifted, and the weight of the fish dragged the net back into the water, taking Andrew with it. He flailed unsuccessfully, trying to keep from going beneath the thick

> Once, when Apollonius of Tyana was teaching on the proprieties of the libation, he was interrupted by a youth who "burst out into loud and coarse laughter. . . . And in fact the youth was ... possessed by a devil; for he would laugh at things that no one else laughed at, and then he would fall to weeping for no reason at all. . . . Now when Apollonius gazed on him, the ghost in him began to utter cries of fear and rage ... and the ghost swore that he would leave the young man alone and never take possession of any man again. But Apollonius ... ordered him to quit the young man and show by a visible sign that he had done so. 'I will throw down yonder statue,' said the devil. . . . [And] the statue began by moving gently, and then fell down. . . . But the young man rubbed his eyes as though he had just woke up ... he no longer showed himself licentious, nor did he stare madly about, but he had returned to his own self ..." (Philostratus, *Life of Apollonius of Tyana* 4.20 [third century C.E.]). (Boring-Berger-Colpe, 71-72, no. 61)

quiet of impending death that sloshed around his head. His eyes were open, sound disappeared, and his ears filled with water. A vacuum "thloop" resounded as he went under, as if the sea had sucked him in like a yummy morsel. His foot tangled in the net held him tight like an angry animal, and he had wanted to cry, but the frenzy of trying to stay alive and not being able to breathe fought even that. It was an odd world inside the sea with bits of growing things and creatures, his foot bound tightly.

He was exhausted by the time Simon pulled him back into the boat, and he lay for a while near tears, amazed that he was alive. Simon scolded him and didn't seem to understand the terror of his experience. He had almost died! He never wanted to get back in a boat again, but how could he avoid the necessity of his trade? It was difficult to hide that fear. What a joke if people knew.

He had never expected to be afraid once he was in the company of Jesus. He had seen Jesus perform real miracles.

But there was that one time.

He and his brother Simon, later called Peter, had left behind their fishing nets and followed Jesus, and there had come a time when Andrew had felt true fear.

It had been a busy day. Jesus had asked that they get into a boat and go to the other side of the water to rest. He needed a respite from the crush of the people and was weary. They had all eagerly agreed, as it was difficult to keep up the pace that Jesus kept. He stayed on the move, trying not to miss anyone. They often had to coax him to stop and rest.

Jesus had fallen asleep and seemed comfortable in the boat, as had the others. It had taken Andrew a long time to go to sleep, and he had been the first to waken when the wind came up. The wind was crying out like a woman caught somewhere between this world and the next. There was an uncertainty of things shuddering and wobbling, particularly in the boat, the sounds of lost souls whispering and spirits nipping at life with cold prickly fingers.

The eerie sounds of the wind woke Andrew with a start, and he stood up, shouted, and awoke the others.

The storm was raging now, and his panic spread. "We're going to die!" he shouted. "This must be stopped! I do not want do die in the water."

Having been awakened with such frenzy, some of the other disciples caught fear like a plague and screamed that there had never been a storm as threatening, that they would be thrown into the sea. There would be no hope of their swimming to land in time.

"We must wake Jesus!" someone shouted.

"We must wake Jesus!" echoed repeatedly through the darkness, as the disciples danced nervously around Jesus waiting for him to wake up.

A question, however, came from the puzzled look of the sleeping man whom they awakened.

"What is this all about?" Jesus asked.

"The storm! The storm! There has never been a storm like this! It's going to take us all. This will be our last day, our last hour."

Jesus raised his hand, and the storm quieted. Obviously, he was disgruntled with them and not ready to be awake yet. He curled up and went back to sleep, mumbling something about their lack of faith.

The disciples looked at one another in embarrassment, particularly Andrew, who had started the ruckus. "What is this man that he can make a storm stop?" he had asked. "We have faith—don't we? It was a bad storm... The wind was ..."

Now as Andrew remembered the storm on the sea and Jesus' complacent stopping of the raging water and wind, he was ashamed that he had doubted Jesus that day in his terror Yet he knew he could tell many stories of Jesus, and that would be one of them.

He sobbed then, mourning the loss of his friend and teacher.

(Jo-Ann Jennings)

Jairus's Daughter and a Woman's Faith

Jesus heals two "daughters of faith": an official's daughter and a hemorrhaging woman.

The Story

As soon as Jesus had returned by boat to the other shore, a large crowd gathered round him. While he was by the lakeside, there came a synagogue president named Jairus; and when he saw him, he threw himself down at his feet and pleaded with him. 'My little daughter is at death's door,' he said. 'I beg you to come and lay your hands on her so that her life may be saved.' So Jesus went with him, accompanied by a great crowd which pressed round him.

Among them was a woman who had suffered from haemorrhages for twelve years; and in spite of long treatment by many doctors, on which she had spent all she had, she had become worse rather than better. She had heard about Jesus, and came up behind him in the crowd and touched his cloak; for she said, 'If I touch even his clothes, I shall be healed.' And there and then the flow of blood dried up and she knew in herself that she was cured of her affliction. Aware at once that power had gone out of him, Jesus turned round in the crowd and asked, 'Who touched my clothes?' His disciples said to him, 'You see the crowd pressing round you and yet you ask, "Who touched me?"' But he kept looking around to see who had done it. Then the woman, trembling with fear

because she knew what had happened to her, came and fell at his feet and told him the whole truth. He said to her, 'Daughter, your faith has healed you. Go in peace, free from your affliction.'

While he was still speaking, a message came from the president's house, 'Your daughter has died; why trouble the teacher any more?' But Jesus, overhearing the message as it was delivered, said to the president of the synagogue, 'Do not be afraid; simply have faith.' Then he allowed no one to accompany him except Peter and James and James's brother John. They came to the president's house, where he found a great commotion, with loud crying and wailing. So he went in and said to them, 'Why this crying and commotion? The child is not dead: she is asleep'; and they laughed at him. After turning everyone out, he took the child's father and mother and his own companions into the room where the child was. Taking hold of her hand, he said to her, 'Talitha cum,' which means, 'Get up, my child.' Immediately the girl got up and walked about—she was twelve years old. They were overcome with amazement; but he gave them strict instructions not to let anyone know about it, and told them to give her something to eat.

Comments on the Story

In the stories of Jairus's daughter and a woman's faith, Mark employs a rhetorical technique known as intercalation, a "sandwich" structure in which one story is enveloped, or sandwiched, inside another. Mark uses this technique frequently throughout his narrative (3:20-35; 4:1-20; 6:7-30; 11:12-21; 14:1-11; 14:17-31; 14:53-72; 15:40–16:8). The rhetorical effect is to suggest that the two seemingly unrelated stories are, in fact, best understood when read in light of one another.

The story about Jairus and his daughter begins with a report that Jesus has crossed the Sea of Galilee again, following his encounter with the Gerasene demoniac. Upon landing, he is met by a large crowd, one of whom is Jairus, a leader of the synagogue. The authorial audience would have known from this identification that Jairus was not only a religious leader but also a well-to-do and highly respected member of the community as well. Thus, his actions are a bit startling: "he threw himself down at his [Jesus'] feet and pleaded with him. 'My little daughter is at death's door,' he said. 'I beg you to come and lay your hands on her so that her life may be saved'" (5:22-23). Without comment, Jesus begins to go with him (5:24).

At this point, the first story is interrupted by the story of the woman with the flow of blood (5:24b-34). As Jesus is journeying with Jairus, he was "accompanied by a great crowd which pressed round him" (5:24b). Among this crowd was "a woman who had suffered from haemorrhages for twelve years" (5:25). While the nature of the woman's loss of blood is not detailed (though the audience might readily infer that she has experienced some chronic uterine bleeding that has left her ritually unclean and a social outcast; see Lev. 15:25-33), the narrator does digress to describe her other losses in some detail. She had wasted time, suffering much under many physicians; she had squandered whatever material wealth she had at her disposal, spending all that she had; and despite her best efforts she had lost her health, growing worse, not better. Like the Syrophoenician woman (Mark 7), the woman with the hemorrhage was in despair when she "heard about" Jesus. Since a person with a flow of blood is also shunned by the community (the Mishnaic tractate on menstruation is even entitled *Nidda*, i.e., "banished"), she risks one final loss—public shame—in an effort to restore her health. The narrator underscores her social transgression by reminding the audience that the woman not only came up behind Jesus, but she did so "in the crowd" (5:27). The woman in Mark is not the first to touch Jesus' garment in search of a healing (see also 3:10; 6:56; for other examples of the widespread notion of the healing efficacy of garments, see Acts 5:15 and 19:12). She is, however, the first for whom the narrator records the inner reasoning behind this act: "for she said, 'If I touch even his clothes, I shall be healed'" (Mark 5:28).

The next section in Mark provides an interesting parallel structure. After the woman touched Jesus' cloak, "*there and then* the flow of blood dried up and she *knew in herself* that she was cured of her affliction" (5:29). Jesus likewise was "*aware at once* that power had gone out of him" (5:30). The two events are related chronologically by the phrases "there and then" (Greek *euthus*) and "at once" (Greek *euthus*) and epistemologically by the fact that both Jesus and the woman perceive what has happened in and through their connectedness with their physical selves (no Cartesian split between mind/body here!). Jesus turns and asks the seemingly ridiculous question in light of the pressing crowds, "Who touched my clothes?" (5:30). The disciples, who evidently lack this corporeal basis for knowledge, take the bait and ask what would seem obvious to anyone not privy to this exchange: "You see the crowd pressing round you and yet you ask, 'Who touched me?'" (5:31). The audience, of course, *is* aware of what happened, and this word serves only to contribute further to the distance between disciples and audience, which the narrator is subtly working to establish (see 4:35-41, and later not so subtly in 6:52; 8:14-21; the disciples' reaction to the three passion predictions in chs. 8, 9, and 10; and finally the betrayal, denial, and forsaking of Jesus by the disciples in the passion narrative).

Unperturbed by their question, Jesus wheels around to look at the crowd and "to see who had done it" (5:32). Again, the woman's feelings and actions are detailed: "Then the woman, trembling with fear because she knew what had happened to her, came and fell at his feet and told him the whole truth" (5:33). She who had hoped to "lift" a healing from Jesus is caught red-handed! Jesus' power is at the root of her fear (see also the disciples' reaction to the stilling of the storm in Mark 4:41). She already knows of his power to heal, because she knows what *had happened* to her. She now fears what *might* happen to her if Jesus directs his power to curse, by exposing her only recently cured cultic uncleanness to the crowds. So in a move no less audacious than her original plan of stealing a healing, she turns fully to Jesus with her emotion, her knowledge, her obeisance, and her speech.

Of course, the question lingers: why does Jesus publicly call attention to the woman's action? Since the woman's physical condition had severe implications for her social condition, her healing is not complete until Jesus deals with its social dimension. The unnatural expelling of blood from her body led naturally in Jewish ritual understanding to her expulsion from the social body, the community. Jesus completes her physical healing by re-integrating her into the community. He makes this clear by addressing her in familial language, "daughter." He continues, "Your faith has healed you. Go in peace, free from your affliction" (5:34). Both physical and social status are restored. The reference to her "faith" makes it clear that it is not the magical properties of his clothing that heals her, but rather her act of faith in risking public shame by reaching out to him and by standing up to be identified. That faith made her well. The Greek word for "heal" here (*sozo*) is also the word translated "save." Her faith has made her physically well and theologically placed her in a right relationship with God.

Finally, Jesus comes back to the social dimension of the healing. He tells the woman to "Go in peace, free from your affliction." "Peace" in the ancient world had profound material, social, and political—as well as spiritual—implications. To go in peace was to be re-integrated fully—materially, socially, politically, and spiritually—into the community. Thus, Jesus' final command to be "free from your affliction" referred not only to the physical healing that had just occurred but was an imperative designed to guarantee the social healing that must follow in the life of the community.

The scene then abruptly shifts back to the first story. With Jesus' comforting words addressed to this "daughter of faith" still ringing in his ears, Jairus is confronted by messengers from his household who report rather coldly: "Your daughter has died; why trouble the teacher any more?" (5:35). The delay caused by Jesus' interaction with the woman with the hemorrhage has had catastrophic consequences for Jairus's daughter. Before Jairus can respond, Jesus gently reassures this powerful synagogue ruler: "Do not be afraid; simply have faith" (5:36; see also 6:50). Taking with him only the inner core of the disciples, Peter, James, and John, Jesus proceeds to Jairus's house.

They arrive at a scene of much commotion, where people are loudly "crying and wailing" (5:38). The mourners' remorse is not very profound (they may have been professional mourners rather than family members or friends; see *Mishnah Ketubbot* 4.4). When Jesus asks them why they weep and suggests that the child is not dead, but sleeping (5:39), "they laughed at him" (5:40). Unlike the authorial audience, these mourners had not witnessed the calming of a violent storm or the restoration of a violent demoniac. Jesus rejects them and their cynicism by "turning everyone out" (5:40). To be "outside" in Mark's Gospel is to be put in the place of unbelief and opposition to the ways of God (Mark 3:31; 4:11). Jesus thus puts these mourners "in their place"! He then takes his disciples and the child's parents inside to where the child was. There, he takes her by the hand and whispers, " 'Talitha cum,' which means 'Get up, my child'" (5:41). The scene is intimate and poignant. Immediately the little girl gets up and walks around, much to the amazement of all who have been privileged to witness this event. Jesus tells these witnesses to say nothing about what has happened.

The story has several strange features. Until this point in Mark's Gospel, the authorial audience has been led to expect many individual episodes to end with an aphorism by Jesus—a memorable, pithy saying that summarizes the lesson to be learned from the story. Thus, in the story of the paralytic (Mark 2:1-12), Jesus says, "But to convince you that the Son of Man has authority on earth to forgive sins ..." (2:10); at the conclusion of the call of Levi (2:13-17), Jesus says, "It is not the healthy who need a doctor, but the sick; I did not come to call the virtuous, but sinners" (2:17); at the end of the story of the disciples' plucking heads of grain (2:23-28), Jesus says, "The sabbath was made for man, not man for the sabbath" (2:27 REB; "so the Son of Man is lord even of the sabbath" [2:28]); at the conclusion of the story of the Gerasene demoniac (5:1-20), Jesus says, "Go home to your own people ... and tell them what the Lord in his mercy has done for you" (5:19). The story of Jairus's daughter ends on a rather different note: Jesus "told them to give her something to eat" (5:43). No clever aphorism here, simply a command that the girl's needs not be left unattended. Certainly, the mention of food confirms that the girl is really alive and not a phantom or ghost, but more important, Jesus' attention to detail is consistent with the compassion he displays throughout both stories in Mark 5:21-43. He commends and embraces the woman with the hemorrhage, "Daughter, your faith has healed you," when he could very well have continued her exclusion from the community by condemning her actions. He reassures Jairus when members of his own household callously report that Jairus's daughter is dead.

> "A girl had died just in the hour of her marriage, and the bridegroom was following her bier lamenting ... and the whole of Rome was mourning with him.... Apollonius ... said: 'Put down the bier, for I will stay the tears that you are shedding for this maiden.' And withal he asked what was her name. The crowd accordingly thought that he was about to deliver an oration ... but he did nothing of the kind, but merely touching her and whispering ... at once woke up the maiden from her seeming death; and the girl spoke out loud, and returned to her father's house" (Philostratus, *Life of Apollonius of Tyana* 4.45 [third century C.E.]). (Boring-Berger-Colpe, 203-4, no. 290)

The consistency in Jesus' character is underscored by the other odd feature at the end of Jairus's story. The audience is told in a parenthetical note that the girl was twelve years of age. This detail has spawned a variety of interpretations. Some argue that the mention of age indicates that the girl was old enough to walk around (but this seems a trivial point). Others contend that "twelve years old" indicates that the girl is of marriageable age according to Jewish law (but Jesus is no suitor!). A more likely explanation is found in the rhetorical strategy of intercalation mentioned earlier. The reference to "twelve years" appears to function as a lexical link between the two stories and as a reminder to the audience that they are to be read in light of each other. Twelve years prior, the woman with the hemorrhage became ill and began her descent down the path of disease and affliction toward death. At the same time, a little girl was born to Jairus and his wife and began the journey to life. Twelve years later, both are at the point of destruction when Jesus crosses their paths. His life-giving power restores the woman with the hemorrhage from physical illness and social exile and rescues the little girl from the clutches of death!

The comparison and contrast between the woman and Jairus are even more striking. Jairus and the woman with the hemorrhage function as a bi-polar pair. Jairus is an important male and is named; the woman is left unnamed in the narrative. Jairus is a leader of the synagogue and well connected in his community; the woman is a social outcast and would not be welcome in the synagogue. Jairus is a wealthy householder; the woman is destitute. Jairus approaches Jesus directly, though deferentially; the woman tries to steal a healing from Jesus. Jairus is a member of the religious establishment that as a whole has rejected Jesus; the woman is one of many social outcasts who have thronged to Jesus. Despite these differences, they share several things in common. Both have turned to Jesus in desperation. Both have expressed faith, however partial or incomplete, in Jesus' ability to help them. And both are ultimately rewarded.

In Greco-Roman antiquity, short stories such as these two were often used to communicate moral lessons from the lives of famous men. Such stories were called *chreia* and were brief anecdotes about the words and deeds of a person (see also, e.g., Theon's *Progymnasmata*). The stories of the woman with the hemorrhage and Jairus's daughter would probably have been heard by the authorial audience as *chreia*. Of course, it would have been unusual to have women figure so prominently in the *chreia*, as they do here in Mark, but that is one of the distinctives about early Christian literature and thought. From the stories of these two, one learns the lesson of persistent faith in what appears to be a hopeless situation. One also learns about the gentleness and the authority of Jesus.

The emphasis on Jesus' authority fits well within the immediate context of Mark's Gospel. Just prior to this story, Jesus has demonstrated his authority over nature (Mark 4:35-41) and over demons (5:1-20). Now he demonstrates his authority over disease and death. He is Lord of the winds and the sea, yes, but he is also champion of the outcast and exiled and he is sensitive to the details of life. In each case, Jesus has given them something to eat, something life-sustaining!

Retelling the Story

> Jesus turned round in the crowd and asked, "Who touched my clothes?"
> (Mark 5:30)

The midwife had finally arrived. She had tried to be near in those final days before the birth so that she would not have to be summoned, but there were many in the village who were due, and it was difficult to be everywhere. This particular midwife, called Leah, had quite a reputation for skill and putting her patients at ease, helping them get through the difficult task of childbirth. She said little, and there were none who knew her personal story. She was trusted because of her knowledge and her manner.

Ruth's mother waited by the door, watching for Leah, and their eyes met with recognition when she did arrive, but neither said a word. They could have met anywhere. There was no time to discuss it. Ruth was in terrible pain, something was not right, and it was up to the midwife to decide how to take care of the matter.

"Don't worry. This is a special child," Leah whispered to Ruth as she told her what to do. "You and I both know about miracles. This will be another one."

"I don't know what you're talking about," Ruth said with impatience, "and I don't care."

Leah smiled, used to the tense anger of young, frightened mothers. "There will be a lot of blood, but don't let it frighten you," she said gently. "I'll talk you through this, and I won't leave your side. We'll get this baby turned around so that he can come safely into the world. It will hurt, but you and I are survivors. We'll get through this together. Your husband is not far away. We couldn't get him to go to the fields today. He paces. And your father is with him, stopping people in the street to tell them that the time is near. You're quite the lady of the day."

"Well, I don't feel like the lady of the day," Ruth said. "I've changed my mind. I don't want to do this. Why is this happening to me?"

Although the labor was long and dangerous, Leah kept her promise never to leave the mothers once she arrived to help them. They were her reason for being. Sweat broke out on her forehead as she turned the baby so that it would deliver correctly. She prayed as she worked. "God whom I know so well . . . Jesus with the touch of God . . ."

After the child was born Ruth slept, and when she awoke, the baby had been washed and lay at her side. Leah was there, too. "I have to move on," she said. "I've been summoned, but I wanted to be here when you awoke to see your pretty face one more time and to let you know I'm leaving. I'll be back when I'm needed."

Ruth reached out and grabbed Leah's hand. There was so much to say. They had by this time been to hell and back together while birthing this beautiful child. Finally she said, "I couldn't have done this without you. I know the baby would have died and so would I if you had not been here. Tell me quickly. What did you mean about miracles? Have we met before?"

Leah sighed and shook her head, closing her eyes in prayer and then looking again at the young woman in the bed. "I was living a life much like that of a leper. I was forever unclean, and my flow would not stop. It just came heavier. I was unable to do my work since I had to hide away from the world, unclean. I had been saving what I could for care in my old age, but most of my money was used on physicians who were not helping me. Even had I been able to attend to my mothers in my condition, I would have been little help to them as my body cramped constantly like the labor pains they had. I had almost given up hope, and I had decided I would have to take my own life. What else could I do? I was an outcast, and it seemed like I would be forever if my condition did not improve. With no work, no income, what was my meaning? I have no family.

"With these thoughts I wandered away from the hideaway of women in their time. I was caught up in a crowd and saw that the excitement had to do with a man ahead. Then your father, Jairus, ran through the crowd and grabbed the man by the arm, screaming, 'Come! Come! Come with me! My little girl is near death!' And the man hurried with him, as did the crowd. In the excitement no one noticed that I followed.

"I was able to push my way to the front to see you lying in your mother's arms in front of the doorway where she had taken you to feel the sunshine, hoping for some miracle that would save you. I saw the man reach out and touch your beautiful face, and you opened your eyes and smiled at him.

A menstruating woman was restricted from access to the temple at all levels, as Josephus explained: "It [the temple] had four surrounding courts, each with its special statutory restrictions. The outer court was open to all, foreigners included; women during their impurity were alone refused admission. To the second court all Jews were admitted and, when uncontaminated by any defilement, their wives; to the third male Jews, if clean and purified; to the fourth the priests robed in their priestly vestments. The sanctuary was entered only by the high-priests, clad in the raiment peculiar to themselves." (*Against Apion* 2.103-4 [first century C.E.]) (from LCL)

"Your mother started to cry, and Jairus told the crowd that you had not awakened in days. You sat up, asking for something to eat.

"The crowd was wild with tears and disbelief, and they were pulling at the clothing of the man, Jesus, asking for favors. I reached out just to feel the hem of his robe. My touch was brief, and then I drew my hand away. The flow stopped. I felt the spirit of healing rush through me, and I cried with joy.

"'Who touched me?' Jesus called out.

"I apologized and bowed, backing away, but he said, 'Woman, because of your faith, you are healed.' His strength surged through me. The weariness and depression I had felt for days slipped away. The pain in my head and the eternal cramping disappeared. I left quickly for a blessing and to cleanse so that I could be about my work.

"This child is here because you were healed by Jesus—and so was I. We are miracles, just as this child is."

Leah left then, and Ruth marveled at the sleeping miracle who nursed at her breast.

"You would never have been," she said, "if it had not been for the man who touched me. And your journey into the world was made safe by another he touched." *(Jo-Ann Jennings)*

The Feeding of the Five Thousand

Jesus feeds five thousand with five loaves and two fish.

The Story

The apostles rejoined Jesus and reported to him all that they had done and taught. He said to them, 'Come with me, by yourselves, to some remote place and rest a little.' With many coming and going they had no time even to eat. So they set off by boat privately for a remote place. But many saw them leave and recognized them, and people from all the towns hurried round on foot and arrived there first. When he came ashore and saw a large crowd, his heart went out to them, because they were like sheep without a shepherd; and he began to teach them many things. It was already getting late, and his disciples came to him and said, 'This is a remote place and it is already very late; send the people off to the farms and villages round about, to buy themselves something to eat.' 'Give them something to eat yourselves,' he answered. They replied, 'Are we to go and spend two hundred denarii to provide them with food?' 'How many loaves have you?' he asked. 'Go and see.' They found out and told him, 'Five, and two fish.' He ordered them to make the people sit down in groups on the green grass, and they sat down in rows, in companies of fifty and a hundred. Then, taking the five loaves and the two fish, he looked up to heaven, said the blessing, broke the loaves, and gave them to the disciples to distribute. He also divided the two fish among them. They all ate and were satisfied; and twelve baskets were filled with what was left of the bread and the fish. Those who ate the loaves numbered five thousand men.

Comments on the Story

The feeding of the five thousand is the only miracle to occur in all four Gospels. As such, it is an important window into the nature of Jesus' ministry. Each story has its own particular nuances and emphases. What is distinctive about Mark's story is its attention to the setting of the miracle (a "remote place"), to the character of Jesus as the Good Shepherd, and to the role of the disciples as skeptics. The story in Mark begins with Jesus displaying concern for the needs of the disciples, who had been so busy that they had not even had time to eat. He urges them, "Come with me, by yourselves, to some remote place and rest a little" (6:31). So they got into a boat and went away "privately" to a "remote place" (6:32).

While both Matthew and Luke make reference to this "remote place" where Jesus goes with his disciples (Matt. 14:13, 15; Luke 9:12), the phrase receives special emphasis in Mark, occurring in this story three times (Mark 6:31, 32, 35). The authorial audience will perhaps remember this phrase from earlier in Mark's Gospel, when Jesus "went away to a remote spot and remained there in prayer" (1:35), or a bit later when Jesus, who could no longer openly go into a town, "stayed outside in remote places; yet people kept coming to him from all quarters" (1:45). Add to these references the earlier occurrences of "remote" (*eremos*), and conflicting images of a "remote place" in Mark begin to emerge. John the Baptist is a "voice crying out in the wilderness [*eremos*]" who first appeared "in the wilderness [*eremos*]" (Mark 1:3, 4). Furthermore, at the beginning of his public ministry, Jesus is compelled to go into the desert, where he is tempted by Satan. The deserted place in Mark conjures up a number of images: Is it a place of isolated prayer or a place of encounter between Jesus and the throngs? A place of revelation or place of temptation? Which deserted place has Jesus gone to now?

The place Jesus had picked may have been deserted, but it was not unknown! "But many saw them leave and recognized them, and people from all the towns hurried round on foot and arrived there first" (6:33). When Jesus saw the "large crowd," he was not angry; rather "his heart went out to them, because they were like sheep without a shepherd" (6:34). Here, then, is the first distinctive theme in Mark—Jesus in the character of the shepherd. The image of the shepherd is so firmly rooted in the Christian tradition that it is difficult to think of a shepherd without attaching the adjective "good" in front of it, or indeed without conjuring up images of Jesus as the Good Shepherd. But Mark's authorial audience would not necessarily have made these connections. In the biblical tradition, shepherds were viewed both negatively (Jer. 23:1-2; Ezek. 34:1-10) and positively (Ps. 95:7; Ezek. 34:11-31; Jer. 23:3-4). Jesus' role here is clearly positive and echoes Psalm 23: "The LORD is my shepherd; I lack for nothing." Jesus' first act of compassion is NOT to feed them literal bread, but rather to satisfy their spiritual hunger: "and he began to teach them many things" (6:34*b*).

When the hour grew late, the disciples requested Jesus to send the crowds away: "This is a remote place and it is already very late; send the people off to the farms and villages round about, to buy themselves something to eat" (6:35-36). A second theme begins to emerge here—the remarkable display of the disciples' inability to see Jesus' capacity to provide. They even unwittingly acknowledge that this is a "remote place," with all of its latent possibilities for surprise and epiphany. In the immediate context of this story, Jesus has provided a place of (now interrupted) rest for the disciples and spiritual food for the crowds. Earlier, the disciples had been witness to a number of Jesus' miracles: the healing of the sick and demon-possessed, the raising of the dead, the calming of the sea. Yet it never occurs to them that Jesus might miraculously provide food in this instance.

Jesus' response is rather terse: "Give them something to eat yourselves" (6:37). Here the disciples might have recalled that earlier, when they had been sent out on their mission, Jesus had commanded them not to take anything with them, including bread, but rather to depend on the hospitality of those to whom they ministered (Mark 6:7-13). Now when they are given the opportunity to reverse that role and serve as host to the throng, they choose instead to play the role of accountant. "Are we to go and spend two hundred denarii to provide them with food?" (6:37). Two hundred denarii represents 200 days' wages for a day laborer (Matt. 20:2) and would buy 2,400 loaves, about half a loaf per person (thus *Mishnah Pe'ah* 8:7), so the question does not exhibit pessimism that the resources existed to feed this crowd. Rather, the question displays the lack of faith on the part of the disciples.

The only other time the monetary unit of the denarius is mentioned in the plural in Mark is again on the lips of the disciples. In Mark 14:3-9, the disciples scold the woman who anoints Jesus with a bottle of very costly perfume: "Why this waste? The perfume might have been sold for more than three hundred denarii and the money given to the poor" (14:4-5). In both cases the disciples are quick to calculate the cost of extravagant actions, real or potential, and the note of cynicism is close to the surface: Do you really want us to spend our savings on food for these people?

Rabbi Hanina ben Dosa was such a holy man that, as this story proclaims, God miraculously provided an abundance of bread to protect him from the spying of a nosy neighbor: "Rab Judah said in the name of Rab: Every day a heavenly voice is heard declaring, The whole world draws its sustenance because [of the merit] of Hanina my son, and Hanina my son suffices himself with a *kab* of carobs from one Sabbath eve to another. Every Friday his wife would light the oven and throw twigs into it so as not to be put to shame. She had a bad neighbor who said, I know that these people have nothing, what then is the meaning of all this [smoke]? She went and knocked at the door. [The wife of R. Hanina] feeling humiliated [at this] retired into a room. A miracle happened and [her neighbor] saw the oven filled with loaves of bread and the kneading trough full of dough; she called out to her: You, you, bring your shovel; for your bread is getting charred; and she replied, I just went to fetch it" (*b. Tannith* 24b-25a [Hanina ben Dosa, first century C.E.; text fourth century C.E.]). (Boring-Berger-Colpe, 98, no. 109)

Can you believe this woman wasted this expensive oil in such a foolish act? In both instances Jesus' response has a hint of rebuke for the disciples. In the feeding story Jesus ignores their appeal as trivial and asks, "How many loaves have you? Go and see" (6:38). And to those snorting at the woman, he responds, "You have the poor among you always, and you can help them whenever you like; but you will not always have me" (14:7). The opportunity for extravagant action tolerates no indecision, and it allows no time for counting nickels.

Mark's story about Jesus echoes an Old Testament story about Elisha: "A man came from Baal-shalisha, bringing the man of God some of the new season's bread, twenty barley loaves, and fresh ripe ears of corn. Elisha said, 'Give this to the people to eat.' His attendant protested, 'I cannot set this before a hundred people.' Still he insisted, 'Give it to the people to eat; for this is the word of the LORD: They will eat and there will be some left over.' So he set it before them, and they ate and had some left over, as the LORD had said" (2 Kings 4:42-44).

The disciples do as instructed and report to Jesus that they have five loaves and two fish (6:38). With no further comment, Jesus "ordered them to make the people sit down [Greek: recline] in groups on the green grass" (6:39). The mention of "green" grass is unique to Mark and, while at first glance may seem to be an irrelevant—if startling—detail (where did green grass come from in a "remote place"?), the reference may actually serve to remind the authorial audience of Psalm 23:2 ("He makes me lie down in green pastures") and to underscore the role of Jesus here providing leadership to the shepherdless herd ("*ordered* them to make the people sit down"). The division of the crowds into groups of hundreds and fifties not only made the distribution of bread more orderly (6:40), it also echoed the organization of the people of Israel into more manageable units by Moses (see Exod. 18:25: "He chose capable men from all Israel and appointed them leaders of the people, officers over units of a thousand, of a hundred, of fifty, or of ten.").

The narrative of the blessing and distribution of bread has several Old Testament echoes that fill out the meaning of the story for Mark. First, as the previous reference to Moses suggests, the story has clear allusions to the exodus and the feeding of the Israelites in the desert. The reference to the crowd lacking proper leadership echoes Numbers 27:16-17, where Joshua is appointed to succeed Moses: "Let the LORD ... appoint a man over the community ... so that the community of the LORD may not be like sheep without a shepherd." Now in this story Jesus "succeeds" Moses and Joshua as the "shepherd," and what at first appeared to be an uncoordinated crowd of people becomes the organized "congregation of the Lord." But this successor is even greater than Moses, for Moses could only provide manna and quail for the Israelites in the desert, about which they murmured bitterly ("Remember how in Egypt we had fish for the asking.... Now our appetite is gone; wherever we look there is nothing except this manna"; Num. 11:5-6). Jesus is able to provide the fish that Moses could not and he provides it beyond their satisfaction. And, in the end, the message is driven home to the disciples, for it is they who are entrusted with the task to serve the people (6:41).

The gestures here are remarkably similar to the actions at the Last Supper. Jesus took bread, blessed it, broke it, and gave it to the disciples (6:41; see also Mark 14:22). The banquet of the Messiah is more lavish than Herod's (see Mark 6:6-29)! The life-giving bread blessed, broken, and distributed in the desert prefigures the sustenance found in the bread of the Messiah's body, blessed, broken, and given outside the city of Jerusalem.

Ultimately, then, the story echoes the Old Testament narratives of God as the great provider. The call to God's banquet was issued by the prophet Isaiah: "Listen to me and you will fare well, you will enjoy the fat of the land" (Isa. 55:2). The crowd, numbering five thousand men, is indeed satisfied, and twelve baskets of broken pieces of bread and fish are collected. So one day, when the hour was late and the place was deserted, an aimless herd of sheep became the people of God and a wandering peasant its shepherd.

Retelling the Story

It was already getting late, and his disciples came to him and said, "This is a remote place and it is already very late; send the people off to the farms and villages round about, to buy themselves something to eat." "Give them something to eat yourselves," he answered. (Mark 6:35-37)

Denise blew her nose and wiped her eyes on the hem of her apron. It was silly to cry over a turkey.

She filled the sink with cool water, and then submerged the frozen bird. The package instructions said that soaking the turkey in cool water would speed the defrosting process. Even so, she calculated, she wasn't going to be able to start cooking it until some time tomorrow.

Back in Ohio, Denise's mother had always bought their turkey from Mr. Wellstone's grocery. He saved their family a twenty-pound, fresh bird from the supplier. So Denise had never even seen someone prepare a frozen turkey, much less roast one herself.

While Denise was trying to imagine how she would replicate the Thanksgiving lunches of her childhood, given her late start, Becky ran up to the sink and peered in at the plastic-wrapped turkey. "Mama, I don't like turkey salad."

"Fine, Becky," she said absently. "I wasn't going to make any."

"Mama, I don't much like turkey and rice soup either."

Denise replied, "Well, you ate some last year. What do you want me to do with the leftovers?"

"Mama, on the TV they said that somebody stole the truck of turkeys from the hungry people. I don't like leftover turkey much. And this is one big turkey. Can we give some of our turkey to the hungry peoples?"

Denise turned to face her daughter, whose six-year-old face was covered with earnestness, dotted with freckles. She stood with one hand on her hip, just like Denise herself stood when she was trying to get her way. Denise's voice sounded harsher than she intended. "Becky, what are you talking about?"

Taking a deep breath, the six-year-old began again slowly, as though she were speaking to a child. She tapped her sneaker-clad foot. "Mama, I told you. I just heard on TV that somebody stole all the turkeys from the hungry people. And so I want us to give them some of our turkey. We have too much."

Denise looked into the face of her only child. The sweetness of Becky's eyes always caught her breath. How could she have taken Becky away from their huge extended family? From so many people who loved her?

When the job opening in Atlanta had become available, it had seemed like a gift from God, a chance to spread her wings and prove she could be a good mother, independent of her own family. But two months in a new city without family had tried her strength. And now their first holiday alone was threatened because she had forgotten to buy the turkey until after work tonight.

Denise handed Becky a pilgrim-shaped sugar cookie and said, "Honey, I'm trying to get our Thanksgiving dinner started. Go on back into the living room and watch TV." Becky took the cookie and reluctantly left the kitchen.

Two hours later, as Becky said her prayers, she included, "And God bless the hungry peoples. Send them lots of peanut butter and jelly since they won't have turkey."

Denise finished mixing up the cornbread and spices for the dressing and then started to fold laundry. The nightly news began with the report of the stolen turkeys. "Civil rights leader and Atlanta city councilman Hosea Williams has reported that his 'Feed the Hungry Dinner' is without turkey."

They went on to say that someone had stolen the refrigerator truck holding the hundreds of turkeys intended for Thanksgiving. And though people from all over the city were coming out to donate money for more, it was believed that there would not be enough turkeys available or time to prepare them for Thanksgiving lunch the next day.

Denise stopped matching socks and let her mind play over the wonderful Thanksgivings of her childhood. When Denise's grandmother had lived with them, she had let Denise help make pecan pies and her famous yeast rolls. Thanksgiving was never complete without her Aunt Pearl's dressing and cousin Lynn's sweet potato casserole.

This year was the first she had ever spent without twenty close relatives. She and Becky weren't exactly homeless, thank the Lord, but they were family-less.

In the kitchen Denise poked at the opalescent, submerged bird. Becky was right, it was too big for just the two of them. It wasn't what they needed. Denise picked up the phone and dialed information.

An hour later, Becky stirred in the backseat of the car. She sat up rubbing sleep from her eyes and asked, "Mama, are we there yet?"

"No, honey, but I think we're close." Denise turned on the overhead light and looked again at the directions she had scrawled on the back of an envelope. She had made the third left, but all the warehouses looked alike. It was so dark. And she had never been in this part of town before.

Then up ahead she saw a building with the doors open and light spilling out. As she pulled into the parking lot, a woman came out and waved. As they entered the building, Lucille—the woman in charge—shouted out to the dozens of other volunteers, "Everybody say hello to Denise and her daughter, Becky." Voices rang out, "Hello!"

Lucille introduced Becky to her daughter Deidra, and gave Denise the job of opening huge cans of green beans and kernel corn.

Many hours later, Denise reached under a long metal table and shook Becky and Deidra awake. The two new "bestest" friends came out from

The lavish provision of food in this miracle story is clearly meant to evoke the messianic banquet, a widespread motif in Jewish and Christian literature in which the joys of the end time were symbolized by a great feast. In a list of provisions that includes fish (in the form of the monsters from the sea, Behemoth and Leviathan) and bread ("manna"), *2 Baruch* 29:1-8 describes the abundance of food at the messianic banquet: ". . . when all that which should come to pass in these parts has been accomplished, the Anointed One will begin to be revealed. And Behemoth will reveal itself from its place, and Leviathan will come from the sea. . . . And they will be nourishment for all who are left. The earth will also yield fruits ten thousandfold. And on one vine will be a thousand branches, and one branch will produce a thousand clusters, and one cluster will produce a thousand grapes, and one grape will produce a cor of wine. And those who are hungry will enjoy themselves and they will, moreover, see marvels every day. . . . And it will happen at that time that the treasury of manna will come down again from on high, and they will eat of it in those years because these are they who will have arrived at the consummation of time." (Boring-Berger-Colpe, 249-50, no. 375; Smith, 168-69)

under the table, holding hands. Becky and Deidra asked, "Is it time?"

Denise said, "Yes, just about. Deidra, find your mother. She's filling plates in the kitchen. Rev. Williams is going to say the prayer before everyone eats."

Denise looked around the room at the hundreds of people lined up for plates of turkey, dressing, vegetables, and peanut butter sandwiches. Men, women, families, all together, out of the cold, sharing a meal.

When Rev. Williams finished the prayer, Denise squeezed Lucille's hand and said, "Lucille, let's get the girls together this weekend?"

Lucille smiled and said, "Sure. And I'll give you my recipe for sweet potato casserole. I bet you like it better than your cousin's. The secret is in the sugar, you know. You need two different kinds."

Two different kinds? As Denise looked around at the full tables she thought, "No, there are many more kinds of sweetness here than two."

From that year on, Denise's traditional Thanksgiving dinner included Lucille's sweet potato casserole and a platter of peanut butter and jelly sandwiches. And as much loving company as her heart could hold. *(Pam McGrath)*

The Walking on the Water

Jesus walks on the water and rescues Peter, disclosing his divine nature to the disciples.

The Story

As soon as they had finished, he made the disciples embark and cross to the other side ahead of him, while he dismissed the crowd; then he went up the hill by himself to pray. It had grown late, and he was there alone. The boat was already some distance from the shore, battling with a head wind and a rough sea. Between three and six in the morning he came towards them, walking across the lake. When the disciples saw him walking on the lake they were so shaken that they cried out in terror: 'It is a ghost!' But at once Jesus spoke to them: 'Take heart! It is I; do not be afraid.'

Peter called to him: 'Lord, if it is you, tell me to come to you over the water.' 'Come,' said Jesus. Peter got down out of the boat, and walked over the water towards Jesus. But when he saw the strength of the gale he was afraid; and beginning to sink, he cried, 'Save me, Lord!' Jesus at once reached out and caught hold of him. 'Why did you hesitate?' he said. 'How little faith you have!' Then they climbed into the boat; and the wind dropped. And the men in the boat fell at his feet, exclaiming, 'You must be the Son of God.'

Comments on the Story

The story of Jesus walking on the water is one of the most popular, and arguably least understood, stories from the ministry of Jesus. Its popularity is attested in part by the fact that it is one of the few stories shared in common between the Synoptics and John (see Mark 6:45-52; John 6:16-21). In all three accounts, Matthew, Mark, and John, the walking on water follows on the heels of the feeding of the five thousand. The story is an epiphany, designed to disclose more about the divine character of Jesus. We shall focus on Matthew's version, which includes an episode involving Peter found only in the First Gospel.

The transition from the feeding of the five thousand to this story is abrupt. Jesus "made the disciples embark and cross to the other side ahead of him, while he dismissed the crowd" (Matt. 14:22). The narrator gives no explicit explanation for Jesus' actions. The dismissal of both disciples and crowds becomes clearer in the next verse, which describes Jesus' need to be alone: "then he went up the hill by himself to pray" (14:23). The disaggregation of the disciples from the crowds sets the stage for an epiphany that is limited to the disciples alone.

While Jesus is praying, the disciples are trying to maneuver the boat against the wind (14:24). Jesus finally comes to them during the fourth watch of the night (3:00–6:00 A.M.). The time is significant not only because it is just before dawn and means the disciples had been struggling most of the night, but also because the fourth or "morning watch" was the time God had often chosen to intervene on behalf of his people. "In the morning watch the LORD looked down on the Egyptian army through the pillar of fire and cloud, and he threw them into a panic" (Exod. 14:24). "God is in her midst; she will not be overthrown, and at the break of day he will help her" (Ps. 46:5).

So during the fourth watch, the time of divine benefaction, Jesus comes to the disciples "walking across the lake" (14:25). This activity, too, identifies Jesus with God, since in the Old Testament only God had the authority to tread and trample the sea (or the agent of God; see personified Wisdom in Sir. 24:5-6). "[God] by himself spread out the heavens and trod on the back of the sea monster" (Job 9:8; also Job 38:16; see also comments on the stilling of the storm for more on the sea as a place of chaos and evil). "Your path was through the sea, your way through mighty waters, and none could mark your footsteps" (Ps. 77:19). Whether at creation, when God subdued the chaotic waters, or during the exodus, when God made a path through the Red Sea, divine authority over the waters has beneficial effects for God's creatures. And so it is here, too. Jesus comes to them, walking on the water, to help them reach the other side.

The disciples, missing all these echoes of divine presence and comfort (admittedly more easily heard in the calm after the storm than during it!), react in fear, thinking Jesus is a ghost. Jesus offers them one final opportunity to recognize the significance of his appearance on the sea: "But at once Jesus spoke to them: 'Take heart! It is I; do not be afraid' " (14:27). His words are not only reassuring; they continue the theophany, the disclosure of the divine character of Jesus. In Greek, the words translated "it is I" are actually *ego eimi*, "I am." These words, of course, suggest the exodus story again. When Moses asks God whom he should say has sent him to deliver the Israelites, God replies, "I AM that I am. Tell them that I AM has sent you to them" (Exod. 3:14).

Though the Greek translation of Exodus 3 does not use the phrase *ego eimi,* it does occur as the divine name in other important Old Testament texts (see Isa. 41:4; 46:4; Greek Isaiah 43:25 and 51:12). Of special interest is Isaiah 43:10 (Greek), where Yahweh says: "You are my witnesses, you are my servants chosen by me to know me and put your trust in me and understand that I am the Lord" (literally, "understand that I AM"). Earlier in that same chapter is this reference: "When you pass through water I shall be with you; when you pass through rivers they will not overwhelm you" (Isa. 43:2*a*). In the context of Matthew, these Old Testament allusions help confirm the image being created by Jesus walking on water. He is fulfilling the name promised to him at birth, "Emmanuel" (Matt. 1:23; see also Matt. 28:20). He is "God with them," even through the stormy waters, and his presence will not only comfort ("when you pass through water I shall be with you"), it will preserve them safely ("[it] will not overwhelm you").

In Matthew, Jesus engages in activity reserved for divinity, he walks on water, and he uses words reserved for naming the divine, "I am." In Mark's version, Jesus' deeds and words point also in the direction of a theophany. A phrase peculiar to Mark's Gospel strengthens this reading. Mark 6:48 adds the detail that Jesus "was going to pass by them." At first hearing, the phrase is ambiguous, and indeed, a plethora of interpretations have been offered. Some have suggested that the text reveals a playful or whimsical Jesus who had intended to pass them by until he saw their distress. Others have asserted that Jesus meant to test the disciples' faith. In keeping with the general theophany theme (found in both Matthew and Mark), however, it is best to look again to the Old Testament to understand this phrase. And again, its significance is to be found in theophanic contexts. Two texts in the Greek Old Testament use this very word (*parechomai*) to describe an action of God within the context of an epiphany:

> But Moses prayed, 'Show me your glory.' The LORD answered, 'I shall make all my goodness pass before you, and I shall pronounce in your hearing the name "LORD".... The LORD said, 'Here is a place beside me. Take your stand on the rock and, when my glory passes by, I shall put you in a crevice of the rock and cover you with my hand until I have passed by.' (Exod. 33:18-22)

Later, in 1 Kings, the epiphany to Elijah also uses this language: God told Elijah, "'Go and stand on the mount before the LORD.' The LORD was *passing by* ..." (1 Kgs. 19:11). So Jesus had intended to pass his disciples by; that is, he intended to reveal his divine glory. Now we know a little more about his reasons for withdrawing to pray and for wanting his disciples to be separate from the crowds. This event was designed to be an epiphany, but had to be interrupted while Jesus reassured his disciples. In a sense, the transfiguration completes this theophany (Matt. 17:1-8; Mark 9:2-8; Luke 9:28-36). Interestingly, in that episode, the same two Old Testament figures who were privy to the "passing by" of Yahweh, Moses and Elijah, were also present for Jesus' transfiguration. What appears to have been an ambiguous phrase in Mark actually turns out to be an amplification of the theophany theme also developed in Matthew.

Both Mark and John conclude just after this saying by noting that Jesus got into the boat with the disciples, but Matthew's story continues in a different direction. Peter responds to Jesus' statement ("Take heart! It is I; do not be afraid"): "Lord, if it is you, tell me to come to you over the water" (14:28). Though it is possible to translate the first part of the sentence as "Lord, *since* it is you"—as an assertion—given the other places in Matthew where this construction occurs, it is better to understand it as expressing some doubt on Peter's part. Satan says, "*If* you are the Son of God" (Matt. 4:3, 6). After beating him, Jesus' accusers ask, "Now, Messiah, *if* you are a prophet, tell us who hit you" (26:67). Later, as Jesus hung dying on the cross, those who passed by derided him: "*If* you really are the Son of God, save yourself and come down from the cross" (27:40). In every case, the speakers are skeptical of Jesus' identity. And Peter's comment should probably be read along these lines as well.

Among the Greeks, Poseidon, the god of the sea, and those related to him were said to have the ability to walk on the sea. "Hesiod says that he [Orion] was the son of Euryale, the daughter of Minos, and of Poseidon, and that there was given him as a gift the power of walking upon the waves as though upon land" (Eratosthenes, Fragment 182 [from Hesiod, *Astronomy* 4; 700 B.C.E.]). "[H]ave you not heard that Xerxes, the king of the Persians, made of the dry land a sea by cutting through the loftiest of the mountains and separating Athos from the mainland, and that he led his infantry through the sea, riding upon a chariot just like Poseidon in Homer's description?" (Dio Chrysostom, *The Third Discourse on Kingship*, 30 [40–120 C.E.]). (Boring-Berger-Colpe, 99, nos.111-12)

Jesus does, indeed, invite Peter to join him on the water, thus confirming his identity as "Lord" (14:29). Peter complies: "Peter got down out of the boat, and walked over the water towards Jesus. But when he saw the strength of the gale he was afraid; and beginning to sink, he cried, 'Save me, Lord!'" (14:29-30). There are some positive aspects to Peter's actions: the often impetuous Peter waits until bidden by Jesus to come out onto the water (contrast 26:35); Peter has enough faith to get out of the boat when commanded to do so; Peter drops the conditional "Lord, if it is you" for the more positive (and time-saving!) "Save me, Lord!" But given the general flow of the story, it is difficult to imagine that the Matthean narrator is holding Peter up as a model of discipleship for the authorial audience to imitate. After all, we have already seen that God alone has the power to tread on the sea, and to share in Jesus' healing ministry (as in 10:8) is quite different from wanting to share in his divine status. And if the boat were recognized as an early symbol for the church, it certainly makes sense to see that Jesus has come to help the boat through this storm. But what benefit is there for Peter to leave the boat?

Reading Peter's actions as understandable but not commendable may also shed some light on Jesus' response: "Jesus at once reached out and caught hold of him. 'Why did you hesitate?' he said. 'How little faith you have!' " (14:31). As we have seen, Peter's doubt came *before* he left the boat, not after. He began to sink because of his "fear" of the wind. His doubt manifested itself when, even after seeing Jesus' divine action of walking on the water and hearing him pronounce his divine name (I am), Peter could still say, "Lord, if it is you ..." and demand a private confirmation of Jesus' identity. The epiphany was not enough for Peter!

What then is the proper response to this theophany? Certainly not to want to intrude and become part of the epiphany as Peter does (and as Peter will also later do at the transfiguration; see 17:4). No, the proper response to a theophany is worship and confession. After Jesus and Peter got into the boat, "the wind dropped. And the men in the boat fell at his feet, exclaiming, 'You must be the Son of God'" (Matt. 14:33). The disciples are finally able to find an answer to their earlier question, also posed on a boat during a storm, "Who can this be? Even the wind and the sea obey him" (Mark 4:41; see also Matt. 8:27). The answer in both cases is: "Take heart, I AM!"

Retelling the Story

> Jesus at once reached out and caught hold of him. "Why did you hesitate?" he said. "How little faith you have!" (Matthew 14:31)

The lilac and plum paisley silk scarf slipped through my fingers as I called to mind the face of my mother. I became unaware of the sounds of the Christmas crowds around me. Mother's pixie hair swirled as she swung the scarf about her shoulders. Her eyes danced with the wonder of a three-year-old ogling examples of Santa's generosity. She giggled. Then, in delight she raised the silk to her cheek and felt its smooth embrace. When the image was gone, again I heard the tidal wave of other shoppers.

The visual images of my mother, children, and friends opening their gifts determine what I buy. I imagine the person's face, voice, excitement. And if, in my imagining, they love the gift, I buy it.

Visual images are also how I take my grandmother with me everywhere I travel. For forty years of my life, she was my hero, confidante, and champion. Unfortunately, her desire to travel was never satisfied before her death at ninety. So, when I stood on the steps of the Acropolis, I imagined her petite, stooped frame next to me. I could almost see her raise her hand, brush back her silver curls, and shake her head with wonder at the magnificence of such a place. "Would you look at that," she would say. In my mind, we shared the beauty of a place built over two thousand years ago.

Imagining has always kept me connected to those I love. So when my daughter was twelve and a psychologist told me that she couldn't visualize, I was stunned. Was it possible to live without making pictures in your head?

The next day, I asked my daughter to go for a walk around our neighborhood. I said, "You want to play a game?" She squinted her eyes, suspecting a trick. "No, really. I mean it. Let's play a game," I begged.

I took her silence as consent and started, "OK, let's make up a story together. Let's start with the smoke." The smell of smoke was thick on the backside of the neighborhood. Someone was burning leaves, and the smoke hung in the young pines that separated the streets. "Let's imagine the burning fire and then build a story around it. Let's start with the colors in the fire. Why don't you imagine the colors? What are they?"

My daughter didn't miss a step, but I felt her hesitate. Then she answered, "I don't know."

I hurried ahead, "The colors. You know, how flames go from blue to orange. Why don't you imagine the flames? Tell me what colors you see."

"I don't know," she responded more forcefully, but still in a monotone.

"Well, let's imagine the wood. Are the logs big and fat and green? Or are they old pine? You know how different woods smell different when they burn? Why don't you imagine what the smell is and then imagine which wood could be burning?"

"I don't know," she answered with an edge of frustration.

"OK, OK. How about sound? Can you hear any sounds coming from the fire? Crackling? Or the singeing, hissing sound of water escaping the logs? Can you hear anything?" Now I was pleading.

My daughter stopped walking, looked me in the eye and said, "I don't know." Then she started to move again. Looking away she added, "I don't want to play this anymore."

The tension between us lingered in the air like the smoke. I hurried to catch up and grabbed her hand. She allowed me to take it, even though we both knew I had been pushing too hard.

We walked a block further before I said, "I'm sorry." She squeezed my hand, then dropped it as she replied, "It's OK."

But we both knew it wasn't. We had hit an impasse. A place where we were never going to connect. It felt at this moment like a chasm.

When I'm afraid, I sometimes imagine different biblical characters or family members. Then by holding tight to their images in my mind I imagine them standing all around me, supporting me. How was my daughter going to pull the memories of those she loved close enough for comfort?

110

We walked a while in silence. Then I apologized again, "I really am sorry. I love making pictures in my head, but not more than I love you. Help me understand? Tell me something that you're proud that you know. Please."

She didn't look at me, but she quietly offered, "Well, I can name the whole periodic table." She glanced over at my stunned face and laughed a satisfied, "Hah."

"Wow. All the elements? How can you remember that? I forget our zip code all the time. I can never remember numbers, dates, or my own address," I said.

She looked up to make sure I was sincere, not patronizing her. When she saw my true amazement and pride in her, she laughed. We both took a deep breath. I heard myself ask again the question I had been asking. Though this time the tone shifted and I said, "Why *don't* you imagine the colors of the flame?"

An epiphany by the god Serapis that brings rescue from a storm at sea is recounted in a prayer by Aelius Aristides: "O ruler of the most beautiful of all cities, on which you look down as it yearly celebrates the festival in your honour, O light shared by all which lately shone so brightly upon us: then, as the sea began to roar and towered on all sides, and nothing could be seen but the threat of doom and our destruction seemed certain, at that moment you lifted your hands to prevent it, you lightened the veiled sky and let us see land and enabled us to land, so against our expectation that ourselves refused to believe it as we set foot on dry land" (*Hymn to Serapis*, 33 [second century C.E.]). (Theissen, 101)

My daughter's eyes danced as she countered, "Why don't *you* know where we live?"   *(Pam McGrath)*

The Syrophoenician Woman

Jesus meets a Gentile woman who challenges him and convinces him to heal her daughter.

The Story

He moved on from there into the territory of Tyre. He found a house to stay in, and would have liked to remain unrecognized, but that was impossible. Almost at once a woman whose small daughter was possessed by an unclean spirit heard of him and came and fell at his feet. (The woman was a Gentile, a Phoenician of Syria by nationality.) She begged him to drive the demon out of her daughter. He said to her, 'Let the children be satisfied first; it is not right to take the children's bread and throw it to the dogs.' 'Sir,' she replied, 'even the dogs under the table eat the children's scraps.' He said to her, 'For saying that, go, and you will find the demon has left your daughter.' And when she returned home, she found the child lying in bed; the demon had left her.

Comments on the Story

She stands as one of the most enigmatic figures in the New Testament. An unnamed woman, a Gentile of Syrophoenician origin, presumably residing in the vicinity of Tyre. She comes to Jesus on behalf of her small daughter, ready to do battle to secure her wellness—fierce, determined, armed with only her wit and ability to think quickly on her feet. In the end, this child advocate gets what she has come for and Jesus is left all the wiser for the encounter.

The Markan scene is set with Jesus entering a house in Tyre, presumably for some respite. The narrator tells us that Jesus "would have liked to remain unrecognized" (7:24). His hopes for solitude and anonymity are soon dashed, since by this point in Mark's story, for Jesus to escape notice "was impossible" (7:24b). A woman whose daughter had an unclean spirit heard about him and came immediately to the house where he was temporarily residing. Only after noting she is the mother of a spirit-possessed child and that she has literally thrown herself at Jesus' feet does the narrator reveal that she is a Gentile, and more specifically a Syrophoenician.

The fact that this scene occurs in the vicinity of Tyre may be significant. Tyre had long been known as a bitter enemy of Israel (see Jer. 47:4; Joel 3:4;

112

Zech. 9:2), a reputation that continued into the time of Jesus and beyond (see Josephus, *Against Apion*, 1.70). Tyre accumulated at least some of its material wealth by exploiting the rural Galilean areas (see Acts 12:20). So here in this story, boundaries are blurred. On the one hand, a female typically understood as powerless in a patriarchal society begs a male for a favor. On the other hand, a Gentile Tyrian, member of an exploiting privileged class, asks a Galilean Jew to cast the demon out of her daughter.

Perhaps this social context of male/female, Jew/Gentile, Tyrian/Galilean partially explains the sharpness of Jesus' response. He replies to her request, "Let the children be satisfied first; it is not right to take the children's bread and throw it to the dogs" (7:27). Certainly the notion of salvation history, "the Jew first, but the Greek also" (Rom. 1:16) lies behind this saying. Closer to the surface, however, is Jesus' insult in calling this woman a dog, at the root of which lies the Jewish prejudice that Gentiles were, by nature, unclean (see *Tosefta Zavim* 2:1; *Mishnah Pesahim* 8:8). The harsh tone of Jesus' response, at one level, does not fit our stained-glass image of Jesus, but it is not altogether out of character of one who at various times referred to the person(s) with whom he was speaking as "hypocrites," "an evil generation," "a brood of vipers," "white-washed tombs," "foxes," "foolish of heart and slow to learn," and here, "dogs"!

What may be even more surprising, then, is the woman's response. First, unlike his sometimes dim-witted disciples (see, e.g., 7:14-18), the woman immediately understands the impact of Jesus' statement: Israel comes first, and the time for Gentiles is not yet. Still, she does not storm off, insulted at being compared to an unclean street dog. She does not counterattack Jesus with one of the many epithets available in the Gentile arsenal to launch against Jews. Rather, she responds humbly, quickly, and wittily, building on Jesus' aphorism: " 'Sir,' she replied, 'even the dogs under the table eat the children's scraps' " (7:28). She shows respect ("Sir") where he has not ("dogs"). She accepts his basic premise that the central focus of his ministry must be Israel. But she forces the issue of whether or not Gentiles deserve at least some crumbs from Israel's table. In essence, she refuses to take "no" for an answer. She is willing to become a despised dog in order to secure for her daughter a crumb of healing.

The exchange, however, seems to have implications far beyond this specific request for a healing. To be sure, Jesus has ventured into Gentile territory before, crossing the Sea of Galilee into the Decapolis in the area of the Gerasenes (see Mark 5:1-20). Jesus heals a demoniac there and is asked to leave. Before he does so, he directs the healed demoniac to "Go home to your own people and tell them what the Lord in his mercy has done for you" (5:19). But now Jesus is being asked to be more intentional about his ministry, to recognize that its benefits, even when focused on Israel, most naturally spill over to the non-Jews as well.

113

And so Jesus responds in two ways. First, he commends the wisdom of the woman's saying and delivers the healing she so desperately seeks: "For saying that, go, and you will find the demon has left your daughter." Second, after his encounter with the wise woman of Tyre, Jesus immediately returns to the Gentile area of the Decapolis and heals a deaf man. Even more poignant is that following this miracle, presumably still in the general area of the Gentile Decapolis, Jesus feeds four thousand. The previous feeding story, that of the five thousand, had clearly occurred in Jewish territory. But now Jesus, with the lessons learned from the Syrophoenician woman still fresh in his mind, does not simply give the crumbs to the Gentiles as was requested; he gives them the entire loaves! The "crumbs"—seven basketfuls—are collected as evidence of the extent of Jesus' ministry. Jesus has learned his lesson well!

In ancient artistic depictions of banquets, dogs are often shown under the table, where they would be readily accessible to eat any crumbs that fell to the floor. References to the dogs taking only the crumbs then became a motif for rhetoricians and storytellers, as seen in this example: "It was a lazy fellow and malignant who . . . remarked that he had recorded well enough . . . the opinions and ideas of his hero, but that in collecting such trifles as these he reminded him of dogs who . . . eat the fragments which fall from a feast" (Philostratus, *Life of Apollonius of Tyana*, 1.19 [third century C.E.]). (Boring-Berger-Colpe, 104, no. 119; Smith, 28 n. 59)

The idea that Jesus learns from this encounter has troubled readers from the very beginning. The author of Matthew, presumably one of Mark's earliest readers, was bothered enough to make several significant changes to the story. In Mark, the audience is told only that the Syrophoenician woman had heard of Jesus, but in Matthew, the woman (now a Canaanite) is portrayed as having much more explicit knowledge of Jesus. The word *kurios* can be translated as either "Lord" or simply "sir." In Mark, *kurios* seems to carry this connotation of respect—"Yes, sir,"—but is lacking any explicit christological content. In Matthew, however, the woman's initial address to Jesus sounds like a stereotypical Christian confession: "Son of David! Have pity on me" (Matt. 15:22). Later she beseeches him again, "Help me, sir" (Matt. 15:25). The combination of "Lord/sir" (*kurios*) with "Son of David," and in the context of the verbs "have mercy" and "help," give the last occurrence of "Lord" in Matthew a theological overtone missing in Mark, even though the sentences are essentially the same: "'True, sir,' she answered, 'and yet the dogs eat the scraps that fall from their master's table'" (Matt. 15:27; see Mark 7:28). This interpretation is supported by the fact that the word translated "master's" is also *kurios* (a term missing from Mark's version). The woman accepts the identification as a "dog" and in her response suggests that Jesus is Lord of both beast and bread. No such subtleties are found in the Markan text.

Even more striking is Jesus' response to the woman recorded in Matthew: "What faith you have!" Here Jesus commends the woman for taking a stance of faith. The commendation seems to include not only her pithy saying about the crumbs but also her previous appeals, with their high Christology, as well. The audience rightfully hears the Matthean story as one of deepening faith. In Matthew, the woman's daughter is healed because this woman is a believer in Jesus as Lord, Son of David, healer, helper, and dispenser of mercy. To be sure, in Mark the woman believes Jesus can heal her daughter; why else would she come to him? But wistful thinking in a desperate situation (so Mark) is hardly comparable to the journey of faith described in Matthew. The healing in Matthew comes as a direct result of the Canaanite woman's faith in Jesus; in the Matthean context, the story functions as a conversion narrative. The woman's faith perspective in Mark, however, seems irrelevant; she is commended for what she said (7:29; *touton ton logon*, literally "this word").

If there is "conversion"—that is, a radical re-orientation of perspective—in Mark, it is Jesus, not the woman, who experiences such re-orientation. Jesus is educated by this woman to understand that the implications of his vocational calling extend beyond the boundaries of Judaism. As disturbing as this might initially seem, in fact, more often than not, clarity in religious vocation comes through just such dialogue with others in a faith community. Our biases and prejudices are exposed when we are in intimate dialogue with those "not like us"—like Jesus, the Jewish healer and itinerant preacher, and this well-to-do(?) Gentile woman from Tyre. Though accidental, stumbling steps outside Jewish boundaries had been attempted before (see Mark 5), for the Markan Jesus, the "Gentile mission" is born in this exchange with a remarkable woman whose wit, ingenuity, and resilience converted Jesus to a larger frame of reference.

Retelling the Story

He said to her, "For saying that, go, and you will find the demon has left your daughter." (Mark 7:29)

Imagine this: Your three girls are small—six, eight, and ten. The most difficult thing you do all week is get your family "holy" for church on Sunday mornings.

At 6:30 A.M., when you reach to knock the ringing clock off the nightstand, there next to your bed is your six-year-old with her hand stuck into a box of Fruit Loops. (She only eats the yellow ones.)

You drag yourself out of bed, stumble into the kitchen, make coffee, retrieve the pregnant newspaper overflowing with tempting sale ads, and wonder why holiness needs to come so early in the day.

After scanning the glossy ads for "necessary" discounted items and drinking two cups of coffee, you feel competent enough to begin the process of holiness. And so you pray. You pray that this Sunday might be different from the last. You pray that you will not lose your temper and that your family can all find seats together in church. You pray that you can remember why you do this every week and how lucky you are to have three healthy children.

Then the fun begins.

Coaxing three little girls out of Strawberry Shortcake nighties and into dresses, tights, and patent leather, as well as coordinating hairbows, while "Tom and Jerry" cartoons shriek from the TV set, is hard labor before 9 A.M.

But, finally, you manage to find two shoes for each child and to get everyone into the car. This is when you begin your regime of continuous repetitive prayer. It is also when they begin to whine, "Mama, she's on my dress. Tell her to get off my dress." "Mama, she's looking at me again. You told her not to look at me last night." "Mama, I forgot the church money envelope. I know I said that if you'd let me carry the envelope I wouldn't forget it again. But I had to go to the bathroom and I left it on the sink." This is always followed by, "Mama, I forgot to go to the bathroom. Can we stop at the market so I can go to the bathroom? They have donuts."

This is not a good time for you to be distracted by the confusion in the back seat. Because by now you have reached the church and the church parking lot holds exactly half of the necessary parking places.

And so you begin the long process of circling the lot, waiting for someone to leave from the first service, so you can have their spot.

Then, just when you have almost given up, a woman climbs into her car right in front of you! You are going to be able to park and not be too late to get a seat. Suddenly the man driving the car ahead of you begins to try and force you, and the thirty cars behind you, to back up so he can have that parking place that you and he both know God meant to be yours.

Here's a tip. Don't mouth ugly words at him. Because during the service, when you turn to the person behind you and offer them the "Handshake of Peace," he will be sitting right there. And he has already seen your lips moving with no words coming out. He will not believe you were saying, "Peace be with you."

Finally, everyone makes it from the car into the sanctuary. You all find seats. (Today, all together!) The choir begins to sing and you can feel your stomach start to settle for the first time since climbing from the shower nearly two hours earlier. This is when you notice how sweet the heads of your girls are bowed in prayer. How lucky you are to have such angels entrusted into your care. The gratitude overflows your heart and wets your cheeks.

Unfortunately, it's also about the time the little one starts kicking the pew in front of you and a woman with tight, red, painted lips turns and stares. She stares first at them and then at you. She whispers in a strained voice, "Aren't they sweet." Which you both know is code for "Can't you control your children? Mine behaved more appropriately."

Luckily, this is about the time the children are called down to the altar for the children's sermon. (Obviously, the timing of the sermon has been determined by a saint or a mother.) They rush up to sit on the stairs and show off their ruffled dresses. And then they are off to Sunday school and you get to settle back and listen to God's word.

After church, you collect the girls, who are full of cookies, and climb back into the car. You're going out to lunch. You might as well, this is the best your family's going to look all week. But before you can even get out of the parking lot the girls are yelling in the back seat.

You hear yourself say, "I can't believe you are behaving like this. How can you be so unkind to each other?

> Stories about ancient women often depicted them as tricksters, a type of ancient character who gets his or her way by utilizing trickery or deceit. Because of the marginal status women occupied in their culture, trickery would often be perceived as the only option open to them. Examples of women as tricksters can be found in the Bible, especially in Genesis, as seen in these examples: Sarah (Gen. 12:10-20), Rebekah (Gen. 27), Rachel (Gen. 31:19, 33-35), and Tamar (Gen. 38). Such biblical characters, like the Syrophoenician woman, are often rewarded by God for rising above their marginal status through cleverness. (Newsom and Ringe, 15-16)

You just left church. We have been in God's house. I can't believe you would behave this way."

The car gets quiet. Then your youngest child says, "In Sunday school they said that God loves us no matter what we do. Mama, don't you love us like that?"

You turn and see three innocent faces turned toward you. Wide blue eyes wait for an answer. Suddenly, the grace of being a mother floods over you. And you realize that the huge, overpowering love you feel for these three children is small in comparison to the love of God for all of us. How can you have forgotten how many times Jesus has forgiven you the same mistakes—over and over. These are your daughters who have been entrusted to you to educate. They are teaching you so much. You answer, "I'm sorry, I lost my temper. Of course I love you. I love you just as you are."

And then it's happened. The miracle. They have done it again. Your children have shown you how to be holy. *(Pam McGrath)*

The Confession at Caesarea Philippi

Peter confesses that Jesus is the "Christ," then misunderstands Jesus'
messianic vocation.

The Story

Jesus and his disciples set out for the villages of Caesarea Philippi, and on the way he asked his disciples, 'Who do people say I am?' They answered, 'Some say John the Baptist, others Elijah, others one of the prophets.' 'And you,' he asked, 'who do you say I am?' Peter replied: 'You are the Messiah.' Then he gave them strict orders not to tell anyone about him; and he began to teach them that the Son of Man had to endure great suffering, and to be rejected by the elders, chief priests, and scribes; to be put to death, and to rise again three days afterwards. He spoke about it plainly. At this Peter took hold of him and began to rebuke him. But Jesus, turning and looking at his disciples, rebuked Peter. 'Out of my sight, Satan!' he said. 'You think as men think, not as God thinks.'

Then he called the people to him, as well as his disciples, and said to them, 'Anyone who wants to be a follower of mine must renounce self; he must take up his cross and follow me. Whoever wants to save his life will lose it, but whoever loses his life for my sake and for the gospel's will save it. What does anyone gain by winning the whole world at the cost of his life? What can he give to buy his life back? If anyone is ashamed of me and my words in this wicked and godless age, the Son of Man will be ashamed of him, when he comes in the glory of his Father with the holy angels.'

Comments on the Story

The confession at Caesarea Philippi serves as the literary hinge for the Gospel of Mark. Like a revolving door, it is both the conclusion to the first half of Mark's Gospel and the introduction to the second half. Mark 1–8 is set in the vicinity of Galilee and focuses on Jesus as God's Son who has authority to heal, teach, and forgive sins. His major opponents are the religious authorities. Peter's confession that Jesus is the Son of God is a fitting climax to the first half and reaffirms the identity of Jesus first made explicit by the narrator in Mark 1:1 (see comments on Mark 1:1-8). This text also serves as the introduction to the second half of the Gospel, which is set in and around Jerusalem and

118

addresses the question, "Why did Jesus come?" The conflict is now with the disciples over Jesus' understanding of his vocation as Messiah. Since the lectionary text extends to include the first of the so-called passion predictions, our comments will focus on the connections of Mark 8:27-30 with what immediately follows in 8:31-38 and especially with the journey of Jesus and his disciples to Jerusalem recorded in Mark 8–10.

The scene begins with Jesus traveling with his disciples to the villages near Caesarea Philippi. Along the way, he takes a little Gallup poll regarding his identity: "Who do people say I am?" The disciples oblige and answer: "Some say John the Baptist, others Elijah, others one of the prophets" (8:28). The reader is well aware of these speculations. The response of the disciples in Caesarea Philippi echoes the beginning of the story of the death of John the Baptist: "Now King Herod heard of Jesus, for his fame had spread, and people were saying, 'John the Baptist has been raised from the dead, and that is why these miraculous powers are at work in him.' Others said, 'It is Elijah.' Others again, 'He is a prophet like one of the prophets of old.' But when Herod heard of it, he said, 'This is John, whom I beheaded, raised from the dead'" (Mark 6:14-16). John the baptizer, Elijah, and the prophets of old provide an explanation for "these miraculous powers" in Jesus that enable him to engage in acts of power.

The power and authority of the prophetic tradition is clearly in mind when Jesus asks the disciples, "Who do you say I am?" and Peter responds, "You are the Messiah" (8:29). Peter's notion of Messiah is presumably very traditional: the Messiah is a political figure who will wield power and authority, liberate the Jewish people from Roman occupation, and reestablish the Davidic dynasty. So while Peter gives the right answer, "You are the Messiah," he does not have the proper understanding of the Messiah's role, that is, he does not yet comprehend *Jesus'* understanding of the Messiah's role. For that reason, Jesus "gave them strict orders not to tell anyone about him" (8:30). Better to say nothing about Jesus than to disseminate half-truths.

Jesus then begins to instruct the disciples regarding his own understanding of his vocation: "the Son of Man had to endure great suffering, and to be rejected by the elders, chief priests, and scribes; to be put to death, and to rise again three days afterwards" (8:31). This saying is the first of three so-called passion predictions, and the pattern for each of the three is the same. First, Jesus explains that suffering and rejection are inherent in his vocation. Then it comes to light that the disciples, or some representative(s) of them, have totally misunderstood this message. And, finally, Jesus offers further instruction about true discipleship.

In this first passion prediction, Jesus predicts his suffering and rejection (8:31) and Peter responds by taking him aside and rebuking him (8:32*b*)! Peter obviously understands that the circumlocution "Son of Man" refers to Jesus and that his view of Jesus' vocation does not square with that of Jesus. Fresh from having risen to the head of the class with his "You are the Messiah" answer, Peter takes Jesus aside privately to chasten and reprove him for his egregious mistake. But Peter is the one who ends up being rebuked! And Jesus does not leave it as a private matter. Rather, "turning and looking at his disciples, [he] rebuked Peter. 'Out of my sight, Satan!' he said. 'You think as men think, not as God thinks'" (8:33). Peter's moment of glory turns instantly into a nightmare! Peter, the "rock" (*petros*) of the apostles, at this moment looks more like a "rockhead." He cannot understand the profound implications of Jesus' ministry, which includes a call to obedience even in the face of suffering. Jesus completes the pattern by offering further instructions about discipleship in the familiar saying about his followers taking up their cross to follow him (8:34-38).

Peter, however, is not the only one to misunderstand. In the second passion prediction, recorded in Mark 9:31-32, Jesus tells his disciples, "The Son of Man is now to be handed over into the power of men, and they will kill him; and three days after being killed he will rise again" (9:31). The narrator then reports: "But they did not understand what he said, and were afraid to ask" (9:32). The extent of their lack of understanding is evident in the next section, where Jesus asks them, "'What were you arguing about on the way?' They were silent, because on the way they had been discussing which of them was the greatest" (9:33b-34). Jesus is talking with them of his impending suffering and they are disputing with one another about which of them was the greatest! Jesus responds by proclaiming that "If anyone wants to be first, he must make himself last of all and servant of all" (9:35).

Unfortunately, the disciples still do not learn the lesson, and whatever sym-

> In ancient biographies of heroes, it was common to speculate about the hero's hidden, extraordinary identity, as seen in this example from the biography of Pythagoras, the philosopher: "[The followers of Pythagoras] reckoned Pythagoras henceforth among the gods, as a beneficent guardian spirit . . . and most benevolent to humanity. Some spread a report that he was the Pythian Apollo, others that he was Apollo from the Hyperboreans, others that he was Paean, others that he was one of the spirits . . . dwelling in the moon. Still others reported that he was one of the Olympian gods, claiming that he appeared in human form to those then alive for the benefit and improvement of the mortal way of life, in order that he might give mortal nature a saving spark of well-being and philosophy" (Iamblichus, *Life of Pythagoras* 6.30 [fourth century C.E.]). (Boring-Berger-Colpe, 176, no. 240)

pathies the authorial audience may have had for the disciples' inability to hear this admittedly very difficult word about the suffering dimensions of Jesus' vocation have long since evaporated by the time we reach the third passion prediction in Mark 10. "[H]e took the Twelve aside and began to tell them what was to happen to him. 'We are now going up to Jerusalem,' he said, 'and the Son of Man will be handed over to the chief priests and the scribes; they will condemn him to death and hand him over to the Gentiles. He will be mocked and spat upon, and flogged and killed; and three days afterwards, he will rise again'" (10:32b-34). This prediction, the most detailed of the three, once again meets with the disciples' complete failure to comprehend. James and John come to Jesus asking him to grant whatever they request (10:35). Jesus is quick to respond with a question of his own before granting such a blanket request: "What is it you want me to do for you?" (10:36). Their response is outlandish! "Allow us to sit with you in your glory, one at your right hand and the other at your left" (10:37). Perhaps James and John had heard only the end of his saying, which speaks of his vindication ("and three days afterwards, he will rise again"); or perhaps they had heard nothing at all.

Just after Jesus describes in painstaking detail the torture that lay in his immediate future, two of his disciples are seeking corner offices in his corporate kingdom! Jesus tells them that they do not know what they are asking. He then tells them that they shall indeed drink the bitter cup of death that he shall drink and be baptized with the baptism of suffering with which he is to be baptized—both images are allusions to their own martyrdom. His concluding remark ("to sit on my right or on my left is not for me to grant; that honour is for those to whom it has already been assigned"; 10:40) is often overlooked, but it is an important element in understanding the irony that pervades Mark's passion account. James and John, who along with Peter form the inner core of Jesus' disciples, ask to sit on Jesus' right and left in his glory, but Jesus tells them those places are already spoken for. Of whom does Jesus speak? The audience will learn later that Jesus does indeed have companions sitting on his right and on his left. But the occasion is not the stereotypical coronation of a king; the occasion is the crucifixion of Jesus! "Two robbers were crucified with him, one on his right and the other on his left" (15:27). Ironically, in Mark, the crucifixion is a kind of coronation of a king whose body had been anointed beforehand for burial (14:3-9). And in order to enter into the glory of this king, one must sit on the splintery crosses to his left and his right, places of ironic honor reserved "for those to whom it has already been assigned."

The shame of self-aggrandizement is not limited to James and John: "When the other ten heard this, they were indignant with James and John" (10:41). Earlier in the Gospel, the authorial audience might have been inclined to give this verse a more charitable reading; perhaps the disciples are angry at the insolence of James and John. How dare they make such a preposterous request of Jesus, a man on his way to Jerusalem to suffer and die! But by now the audience is left with only one way to read this text. The ten are indignant because James and John had jumped the gun. Each of the remaining ten had intended to make the same request of Jesus; they were simply waiting for the right moment.

The portrayal of the disciples' increasing ignorance occurs in the context of Jesus' journey to Jerusalem. That story is framed by two healings, in both cases of blind men. In the first (8:22-26), which immediately precedes the confession at Caesarea Philippi, a blind man is so blind that he requires an unprecedented second touch by Jesus. In the second (10:46-52), blind Bartimaeus persists in his cries to the Son of David until Jesus heals him. These stories may be about more than just healing; they may contain implications for discipleship. The disciples, like the first blind man, are so spiritually blind to Jesus' vocation that they will require a second (and third) touch in order to be able to see what Jesus is about. He speaks to them intimately and openly about his own impending pain, but they cannot assimilate such talk. Such blindness is difficult to heal. Like the outsiders Jesus mentions in Mark 4, the disciples "look and look, but see nothing; they ... listen and listen, but understand nothing." Will Jesus be able to restore their sight and make them insiders again?

This story, of course, is not just about the twelve. It concerns the audience as well. What about us? Do we mouth the words "You are Messiah" with no clue as to the vocation of Jesus and his followers? Do we still see but fail to perceive? Do we still hear but not understand? Can our blind eyes finally be opened, too?

Retelling the Story

But Jesus, turning and looking at his disciples, rebuked Peter. "Out of my sight, Satan!" he said. "You think as men think, not as God thinks." (Mark 8:33)

I called her on the phone and said, "Grandma, guess what? I'm going to tell stories at another church. They're going to pay me to tell Bible stories. Can you believe it? I really do think I've found my gift."

My grandmother had been telling me since childhood that "God gives everyone a gift." I had been looking for mine everywhere. Until I found storytelling, I had been convinced that my gift was going to be something mundane like ironing. I just knew that I was going to end up being "the best sleeve presser in history."

She said, "Well good, honey. I'm so glad. What are you going to do?"

"I'm going to tell them my favorite story, Shadrach, Meshach, and Abednego. And I think I'll link it up with a personal story about being in church with you and Papa," I said.

There was a pause in the conversation. I could feel her take in a breath before she asked, "Where will you be?"

122

"At the Presbyterian church on Clairmont. You know the one near Mama's house?" I replied.

Grandma said, "No, honey, where will you be in the church?"

I heard a shift in her tone, but I didn't understand what it meant. Like a five-year-old who has been asked to do something she doesn't understand, I repeated her question. "Where will I be?"

Grandma responded like she was speaking to that child. Slowly and in a slightly incredulous tone she said, "Well, surely you won't be on the altar."

I didn't answer.

Once, when I was playing kickball, my classmate kicked the ball right at me from three feet away. The red rubber ball caught me in the stomach and I felt all the air swoosh out of my lungs. Suddenly, I doubled over gasping for air, unable to catch my breath. Tears sprang to my eyes before I could stop them and I sat down on the blacktop, stunned. That day on the playground was the first time I had the wind knocked out of me.

> Philo, who interpreted Jewish heroes according to Greco-Roman categories, speculated about the true nature of Moses: "His associates and everyone else, considered earnestly what the mind which dwelt in his body like an image in its shrine could be, whether it was human or divine or a mixture of both" (Philo, *Life of Moses* 2.17 [first century C.E.]). (Boring-Berger-Colpe, 176, no. 240)

This time, as I struggled to catch my breath, I heard myself say, "What? I don't know. I don't know where I'll be standing."

My grandma, the person who had loved me unconditionally for over thirty-five years, replied, "Hummph."

Grandma is famous for her "hummphs." She has one for every situation. Positively, a "hummph" can be used as praise, like when you finally succeed at rolling out smooth biscuits. Or it can replace a wink and a raised eyebrow, like when you brag about beating your cousins at cards. Negatively, a "hummph" can represent a statement of disbelief, almost an "I don't think so." Or it can stand in for a reprimand of "You should know better."

Grandma and I both knew the meaning of that one. I made an excuse to get away and hung up the phone.

I felt her "hummph" settle in my stomach. That "hummph" lay in my stomach, causing me indigestion for years. Oh, I knew she loved me. And in fact, she listened to my stories on tape over and over before she died. But I have often wished I had been brave enough to say, "Don't take away my excitement. I know you don't believe in a woman on the altar. But Grandma, you're the one who convinced me my gift was from God. Shouldn't I use it in God's house for God work?"

I imagine that she winks and smiles and says, "Hummph." *(Pam McGrath)*

The Transfiguration

Jesus' divine nature is revealed in a transfiguration that foreshadows the resurrection.

The Story according to Matthew

Six days later Jesus took Peter, James, and John the brother of James, and led them up a high mountain by themselves. And in their presence he was transfigured; his face shone like the sun, and his clothes became a brilliant white. And they saw Moses and Elijah appear, talking with him. Then Peter spoke: 'Lord,' he said, 'it is good that we are here. Would you like me to make three shelters here, one for you, one for Moses, and one for Elijah?' While he was still speaking, a bright cloud suddenly cast its shadow over them, and a voice called from the cloud: 'This is my beloved Son, in whom I take delight; listen to him.' At the sound of the voice the disciples fell on their faces in terror. Then Jesus came up to them, touched them, and said, 'Stand up; do not be afraid.' And when they raised their eyes there was no one but Jesus to be seen.

The Story according to Mark

Six days later Jesus took Peter, James, and John with him and led them up a high mountain by themselves. And in their presence he was transfigured; his clothes became dazzling white, with a whiteness no bleacher on earth could equal. They saw Elijah appear and Moses with him, talking with Jesus. Then Peter spoke: 'Rabbi,' he said, 'it is good that we are here! Shall we make three shelters, one for you, one for Moses, and one for Elijah?' For he did not know what to say; they were so terrified. Then a cloud appeared, casting its shadow over them, and out of the cloud came a voice: 'This is my beloved Son; listen to him.' And suddenly, when they looked around, only Jesus was with them; there was no longer anyone else to be seen.

The Story according to Luke

About a week after this he took Peter, John, and James and went up a mountain to pray. And while he was praying the appearance of his face changed and his clothes became dazzling white. Suddenly there were two men talking with him—Moses and Elijah—who appeared in glory and spoke of his departure, the destiny he was to fulfil in Jerusalem. Peter and his companions had been overcome by sleep; but when they awoke, they saw his glory and the two men who stood beside him. As these two were moving away from Jesus, Peter said to him, 'Master, it is good that we are here. Shall we make three shelters, one for you, one for Moses, and one for Elijah?' but he spoke without knowing what he was saying. As he spoke there came a cloud which cast its shadow over them; they were afraid as they entered the cloud, and from it a voice spoke: 'This is my Son, my Chosen; listen to him.' After the voice had spoken, Jesus was seen to be alone. The disciples kept silence and did not at that time say a word to anyone of what they had seen.

Comments on the Story

The transfiguration figures importantly in all three Synoptic Gospels. All three agree that it is the moment in which "the wick of Jesus' divinity is turned up" as a foreshadowing of Jesus' resurrection, but each evangelist emphasizes different aspects of the event. The modern storyteller will do well to appreciate both the repetition and the variation found in the three performances of this one event. First, we will note the similarities.

Matthew and Mark agree in noting that the transfiguration occurred "six days later" (Matt. 17:1; Mark 9:2). Six days after what? Luke provides the answer, though he asserts eight days, not six, have passed "after these sayings" (Luke 9:28 NRSV). "These sayings" in all three Gospels have to do with the disciples taking up their crosses and following Jesus. Thus, in all three Synoptics there is an intimate connection between the suffering Jesus and his followers will endure and the glory revealed in the transfiguration. All three accounts also draw heavily on the Jewish scriptures to narrate the transfiguration. In all three Gospels, the parallels between Jesus and Moses are highlighted:

1. Jesus takes three disciples up the mountain; Moses goes with three named persons (and seventy others) up Mt. Sinai (Exod. 24:1, 9).
2. Jesus is transfigured, his face shines (Matthew and Luke), and his clothes become dazzling white; Moses' skin shines when he comes down from the mountain (Exod. 34:29).
3. In both stories, God's voice is heard from an overshadowing cloud (Exod. 24:15-18).

Moses, however, is not the only one to appear with Jesus at his transfiguration; Elijah is there as well. Both are eschatological figures and are associated with the end times. "A prophet like Moses" was expected to arise and liberate Israel (see Deut. 18:15). Before "the great and terrible day of the LORD," Elijah would appear (Mal. 4:5-6; see comments on Mark 1:1-8). All three Gospels suggest that, with the appearance of Elijah and Moses, the transfiguration is a foreshadowing of the end time; the kingdom of God is at hand and Jesus will reign supreme. But all three also agree that Jesus' glory is inseparable from his suffering; there is no easy triumphalism here.

The differences in emphasis in the three stories are instructive also. For Mark, there is a focus on the disciples. The transfiguration is one of three "private epiphanies" where Peter, James, and John are privy to special insights into the character of Jesus: the raising of Jairus's daughter, later Jesus' prayer at Gethsemane, and here at the transfiguration. In this light, Mark's focus on Peter's response is understandable: " 'Rabbi,' he said, 'it is good that we are here! Shall we make three shelters, one for you, one for Moses, and one for Elijah?' " (9:5). Interestingly, here in Mark, Peter reverts to the title "Rabbi," even though he had just previously pronounced that Jesus was none other than the Messiah (Mark 8:29). Contrast this with Matthew and Luke, where at the transfiguration Peter addresses Jesus as "Lord" (Matt. 17:4) and "Master" (Luke 9:33) respectively. Thus, Mark's additional harsh note that "he did not know what to say; they were so terrified" (9:6) underscores that despite the privileges this inner circle of disciples enjoyed, their understanding is no deeper than the rest of the disciples at this point, and in fact, all three will be singled out for their lack of understanding regarding Jesus (Mark 10:35-41; 14:53-54, 66-72).

The structure of Matthew suggests that he was more interested in the divine voice from heaven. Several interpreters have noticed a chiastic structure in this passage:

> A Narrative introduction (17:1)
>   B Jesus is transfigured (17:2-3)
>   C Peter's response (17:4)
>   D The divine voice (17:5)
>   C' The disciples' response (17:6)
>   B' Jesus speaks (17:7)
> A' Narrative conclusion (17:8)

The emphasis in this literary structure falls on the center of the chiasm, the divine voice that decrees: "This is my beloved Son, in whom I take delight; listen to him" (Matt. 17:5). In the Matthean account of the transfiguration, God not only repeats his assertion about Jesus' identity, first given at Jesus' baptism (Matt. 3:17), God's voice joins the chorus of other characters who make the same assertion: Satan (4:3, 6), the demons (8:29), the disciples (14:33), Peter (16:16), and the centurion (27:54). The focus in Matthew's account is clearly on Jesus' identity as God's son.

Luke, on the other hand, emphasizes what Moses, Elijah, and Jesus were talking about. Luke begins the section on Moses and Elijah with the words "suddenly there were two men" (9:30). This phrase occurs verbatim in two other places in Luke/Acts. First, in Luke's account of the empty tomb, we read: "While they [the women] stood utterly at a loss, suddenly two men in dazzling garments were at their side" (Luke 24:4). Again, in the account of the ascension in Acts, we read: "They were gazing intently into the sky as he went, and all at once there stood beside them two men robed in white" (Acts 1:10). While it is not necessary to identify these two men in the later accounts as Moses and Elijah, the verbal link between the three passages in Luke is striking. At the three moments in the Lukan narratives where the divine status of Jesus is most obvious—the transfiguration, the resurrection, and the ascension—two men appear to discuss the significance of the event. In the empty tomb and ascension accounts the two men speak of the event's meaning in direct discourse. The empty tomb is a reminder of Jesus' words that on the third day he would rise (Luke 24:6-7). The ascension is a foreshadowing of the way in which Jesus would return at the parousia (Acts 1:11). The meaning of the transfiguration is given in indirect discourse, but is no less

> For Philo, as a Jewish writer, describing someone as having a "transfigured" visage was a way of indicating divine election. "Thus whenever he [Abraham] was possessed, everything in him changed to something better, eyes, complexion, stature, carriage, movements, voice. For the divine spirit which was breathed upon him from on high made its lodging in his soul, and invested his body with singular beauty, his voice with persuasiveness, and his hearers with understanding" (Philo, *On the Virtues*, 217 [early first century C.E.]). (Boring-Berger-Colpe, 109, no. 128)

significant for Luke: "Suddenly there were two men talking with him—Moses and Elijah—who appeared in glory and spoke of his departure, the destiny he was to fulfil in Jerusalem" (Luke 9:30-31). The Greek word for "departure" here is *exodus* and connotes again the story of Moses, in this case, as deliverer of the Israelite slaves from Egyptian bondage. This word, standing near the beginning of the travel narrative and as a summary of it, encourages the authorial audience to read the travel narrative as the story of Jesus, "the prophet like Moses" (see also Acts 3:22; 7:37), who embarks on another "exodus," this time to deliver all people from the bondage of sin. The verbal link of "suddenly two men" combines with the narrator's second description of Jesus' journey to Jerusalem as the "time when he was to be taken up" (9:51) to suggest that this journey is not completed until the ascension in Acts 1. Jesus' exodus includes the entire death/resurrection/ascension transit, and only then can repentance and forgiveness of sins be preached to all nations (thus 24:47).

These three accounts variously emphasize the identity of Jesus as God's son, the response of the disciples, and the content and function of the discussion

between Jesus and Moses and Elijah. By attending to the repetition and variations of these three accounts of the transfiguration, the storyteller can assist the
modern audience in probing the meaning of this most remarkable event in the
Synoptic Gospels—the transfiguration of Jesus.

Retelling the Story

And in their presence he was transfigured; his clothes became dazzling
white, with a whiteness no bleacher on earth could equal. (Mark 9:2*b*-3)

Jessica jerked the wheel to the right. The little car slid into the apartment
complex's parking lot. She shoved the stick shift into neutral and cut the
engine.

Lynn said, "What are you doing? We have got to go back to school. It's
hard enough to skip out for lunch without getting caught. We have to be back
before the fourth period bell. Let's go!"

Jessica let her head drop against the steering wheel. "I can't go, Lynn. I hate
it there." She let out a deep sigh, "The truth is, I hate it everywhere."

Lynn patted Jessica's shoulder and said, "We aren't going back today, are
we?" Jessica opened the car door and yelled, "Come on!" as she ran to the
playground of the apartment complex.

Lynn shouted, "It's raining. We'll get all wet."

"Yeah. So? Come on, Lynn! It feels great." Jessica sat down on a swing and
started pumping her feet. Pulling with all her strength. She soared higher and
higher, reaching for the wet, cloudy sky.

"Oh, why not?" Lynn got out of the car and joined her. They propelled
themselves forward and back. Lynn's hair dripped in her eyes. The cold rain
running down the chain wrinkled her fingers. And her shirt became plastered to
her back while her toes squished against her socks.

Jessica laughed and sang, "Jeremiah was a bullfrog. Was a good friend of
mine." She grinned and giggled. "Isn't this great?"

All of a sudden, Jessica stopped. Her feet dragged through the mud until she
stopped dead still. "Lynn! I'm happy. A minute ago I was miserable. Now I
feel great. What's the difference?"

"You're all wet now," Lynn laughed.

"No. Listen. The difference is, I decided to get out of the car and play," Jessica said. She grabbed the chain of Lynn's swing and stared into her eyes.

Lynn said, "Jessica, you're weirding me out. Maybe we should go."

Jessica answered, "Don't get spooked on me, Lynn. Listen, this is important. In the last few minutes, my life didn't change. My mama is still sick. My
boyfriend is still dating my next-door neighbor. I'm still working full time and
going to a high school I hate. So what changed?" Jessica waited for Lynn to

answer. When she didn't, Jessica went on. "I decided to be happy. I decided to stop the car and swing in the rain. Maybe that's the only difference." Her voice dropped, and she went back to swinging. Slowly this time. "Lynn, there are lots of people with better lives than me. And lots with worse. So what if happiness isn't really about what's happening to me?"

Jessica beamed. She lay back in the swing and glided through the air. The rain dripped off the end of her nose and she shook herself like a wet poodle. Her voice low and strong, she said, "Maybe it's something I get to decide."

The two young women swung for a while in silence. Jessica said, "Come on. I've got to go change. I have to go to work."

Jessica stood up from the swing; she looked so tall. Her head and shoulders were straight. She looked sturdy and confident.

The next day, when Lynn saw Jessica in the school hall, she was laughing. She still stood tall with her shoulders relaxed. Her smile was wide and soft. Lynn said, "Hey Jessica. How you doing?"

Jessica grinned and said, "Swingin'."

> For Plutarch, a Greek writer, a shining visage was an indication that one was of divine lineage and destined for greatness. In his story of the birth of Servius, he recounts how Servius's mother, Ocrisia, had been impregnated by Vulcan, the god of fire. "At any rate, it resulted in the birth of Servius, and, while he was still a child, his head shone with a radiance very like the gleam of lightning. But Antias and his school say not so, but relate that when Servius's wife Gegania lay dying, in the presence of his mother he fell into a sleep from dejection and grief; and as he slept, his face was seen by the women to be surrounded by the gleam of fire. This was a token of his birth from fire and an excellent sign pointing to his unexpected accession to the kingship" (*De fortuna Romanorum*, 10 [late first to early second century C.E.]). (Boring-Berger-Colpe, 107-8, no. 126)

Lynn stared into the now glowing face of her friend.

Jessica said, "No more whining about the rain, Lynn. I'm making my own sunshine." Still a little surprised, Lynn said, "Yeah, I can see."

And she could.   *(Pam McGrath)*

The Healing of Bartimaeus

Jesus heals Bartimaeus on the way to Jerusalem.

The Story

They came to Jericho; and as he was leaving the town, with his disciples and a large crowd, Bartimaeus (that is, son of Timaeus), a blind beggar, was seated at the roadside. Hearing that it was Jesus of Nazareth, he began to shout, 'Son of David, Jesus, have pity on me!' Many of the people told him to hold his tongue; but he shouted all the more, 'Son of David, have pity on me.' Jesus stopped and said, 'Call him'; so they called the blind man: 'Take heart,' they said. 'Get up; he is calling you.' At that he threw off his cloak, jumped to his feet, and came to Jesus. Jesus said to him, 'What do you want me to do for you?' 'Rabbi,' the blind man answered, 'I want my sight back.' Jesus said to him, 'Go; your faith has healed you.' And at once he recovered his sight and followed him on the road.

Comments on the Story

Mark 10:46-52 is a brief but moving drama that highlights the blind beggar Bartimaeus's dogged determination to see Jesus. He withstands the ridicule and opposition of the crowd; he responds immediately to Jesus' summons for an audience; his dialogue is clipped and pointed: "David's son, pity me!" "Rabbi, I want my sight back." And he continues to follow Jesus along the way, even after the healing is complete. Nonetheless, despite this straightforward depiction of Bartimaeus as the blind beggar who does what he does best—he begs for a healing—this text has generated a great deal of disagreement among its interpreters. It is a (post modern assumption that texts have multiple meanings, but the episode of blind Bartimaeus challenges a facile embrace of this view since its two major streams of interpretation are at fundamental odds with each other.

At least since Augustine, the story of Bartimaeus has been read as a story primarily about discipleship, about following Jesus (*The Harmony of the Gospels*, 2.265), and there is much to commend this particular interpretation. Some have noted that the very placement of the story after the third passion

130

prediction, at the end of the journey to Jerusalem, and the fact that Bartimaeus is the last one healed in Mark's Gospel require that the story receive special attention. And certain of the details do merit further consideration. After all, as Augustine noted, very few of the recipients of healing in Mark's Gospel are named (see Jairus in Mark 5:22-23), and Bartimaeus's name, "son of Timaeus" (Greek: "honorable"), may have ironical tones since Bartimaeus's actions and words are anything but honorable. In addition to the elements associated with a healing story (see below), this story contains some peculiar aspects. Jesus "calls" Bartimaeus (10:49), an act typically associated with calls to discipleship (see also 1:16-20; 2:14; 10:17-22). Next, Mark adds the curious detail (absent in Matthew and Luke) that Bartimaeus "threw off his cloak" as he arose to meet Jesus, a detail some have taken as part of a larger motif in Mark in which the "old garment" is taken to represent that which must be left behind to follow Jesus in discipleship. After all, Jesus earlier claims that one should not attempt to patch an old garment with a new (unshrunken) cloth (Mark 2:21), and later warns that in the eschatological crisis, one going back to get his garment risks destruction (Mark 13:16). And in the story immediately following this one, others throw their garments on the colt for Jesus and "carpeted the road with their cloaks," preparing for his entry into Jerusalem (11:7-8).

> By stating that Bartimaeus "was seated at the roadside," the storyteller creates a picture image of him as a social outsider. The stigma associated with this position is illustrated in this rabbinic prayer: "I give thanks to Thee, O Lord my God, that Thou has set my portion with those who sit in the Beth ha-Midrash and Thou has not set my portion with those who sit in street corners. . ." (*b. Berakhot* 28b [ca. fourth century C.E.]). (Davies and Allison, 3.106, n. 16)

Bartimaeus calls Jesus "son of David," joining Peter (8:29) as the only other human character in Mark (as opposed to the demons) who announces Jesus' divine identity, and though the crowds rebuke Bartimaeus (10:48), Jesus does not. Jesus' question to Bartimaeus, "What do you want me to do for you?" echoes the question he had earlier posed to the disciples James and John (10:36). Moreover, Jesus' pronouncement "Your faith has healed/saved [Greek *sozo*] you" and the story's ending with Bartimaeus "following him on the road" are phrases usually loaded with theological import in Mark. *Sozo* may refer to physical or spiritual healing or both. In Mark, following Jesus is what disciples are called to do (Mark 1:18, 20; 2:14; 6:1; 8:34; 10:21, 28; 14:54). Similarly, the use of the word "road" or "way" (*hodos*) in Mark often carries connotations beyond mere reference to the "road" and points to the "way" of Jesus, which in Mark is the "way" of suffering.

The cumulative effect of these details combines with the rhetorical effect of the ending of the story, "and followed him on the road," to convince many that Bartimaeus is not only an example of persistent faith but also a model for discipleship.

Not all agree with this interpretation that emphasizes the symbolic value of Bartimaeus for discipleship, arguing rather that the story of Bartimaeus is one primarily of healing, and references to discipleship are either incidental or overdrawn. The inclusion of Bartimaeus's name does not necessarily mean this is a call story since some healing stories identify the patient (see Mark 5:22-24, 35-43; 1:29-31) and some call stories do not (Mark 10:17-22). Though Jesus does "call" Bartimaeus, the word used here (*phoneo*) is not the one (*kaleo*) typically used in call stories (see Mark 1:20); further, Jesus does not call Bartimaeus himself, but does so through intermediaries (contra call stories in Mark 1:29-31; 10:17-22). The reference to "throwing off his cloak" need not be taken as representing leaving one's occupation or possessions to follow Jesus, but rather as part of the narrator's characterization of Bartimaeus's persistent determination. The reference fits into a literary pattern of $ABC/A^1B^2C^3$ where Bartimaeus's actions correspond to the words of those instructed by Jesus to summon him.

A Take heart;	A^1 at that he threw off his cloak
B Get up,	B^2 he jumped to his feet
C he is calling you	C^3 and came to Jesus

The act of "throwing off his cloak" in this pattern corresponds to the imperative "Take heart," and should therefore be viewed as an act of courage, not necessarily part of some larger discipleship motif.

Jesus' question to Bartimaeus, "What do you want me to do for you?" though previously addressed to disciples was uttered in a context that shows James and John acting in a most "undisciple-like" way. While the audience of Mark has been privy to Jesus' teaching in private about his understanding of his vocation over against the messianic expectations of the disciples and others (see Mark 8:27-33), it is not altogether clear that Bartimaeus himself understands the full import of referring to Jesus as "son of David." In fact, far from invoking the popular political understanding of a Davidic messiah (which Jesus has just rejected in chapter 8), Bartimaeus may simply be appealing to Jesus as a potential benefactor of merciful healing. Thus Jesus' silence should not necessarily be taken as an endorsement of Bartimaeus's statement. This point is reinforced by the next scene, where the crowds' unreflective exuberant proclamation, "Blessed is the kingdom of our father David which is coming!" can hardly be viewed as endorsed by the narrator. Nor is it necessary to view Jesus' words, "your faith has healed you," as referring to any deep understanding on Bartimaeus's part about Jesus' identity and mission. In Mark's healing stories, these references to "faith" are almost always in terms of faith adequate for healing, i.e., "trust in an action," not "belief about who Jesus is" (see Mark 2:5, "when he saw their faith"; Mark 5:34, "your faith has healed you").

132

Finally, while it is true that the term "follow" in Mark may often be used of disciples following Jesus on the way to the cross, it is not always used this way. Most significantly, the term does not seem to be used that way in the following episode of the so-called triumphal entry, where the "many" are divided into two groups, "those in front" and "those behind [those who followed]" (11:9). Likewise the term *hodos*, while at times pregnant with theological meaning for the "way of the cross," does not always have this usage in Mark (see 2:23; 6:8). Most importantly, it does not seem to have this sense in the immediate context, where at the beginning of the story Bartimaeus is found "seated at the roadside" (*hodos*, 10:46). Furthermore, in the next scene, the term *hodos* seems to carry its ordinary meaning in the notice that "many spread their garments on the road" (*hodos*, 11:8).

Most telling in support of reading the Bartimaeus story as a healing story is the fact that Bartimaeus's following Jesus appears to be in direct disobedience to Jesus' command. Jesus tells Bartimaeus to "Go your way [Greek *hupage*]"; but Bartimaeus disregards this imperative and follows him instead. With this action, Bartimaeus joins not the band of disciples who follow Jesus when invited or commanded to do so, but rather the collection of those healed by Jesus who subsequently disobey him. Despite being told to say nothing to anyone, the leper proclaims freely (Mark 1:40-45); when the demoniac is told to go home, he proclaims throughout the ten cities (Mark 5:20); when told to be quiet, the former deaf-mute and those who witness the healing insist on proclaiming (Mark 7:36); likewise, when Jesus tells Bartimaeus to go off, he follows Jesus on the way. Bartimaeus, who seeks out Jesus as a potential benefactor, continues to follow him, not in a master/disciple relationship, but in an effort to continue a patron-client arrangement that has been beneficial to him. Thus, one can make an equally compelling case that this story is a highly dramatic healing story with, at best, only opaque references to discipleship.

The storyteller in this instance is faced with an interesting dilemma. There are two compelling retellings of this story, one that emphasizes the physical healing of Bartimaeus, and one that attaches a second level of meaning, making Bartimaeus's story the paradigm of discipleship in Mark. It might be interesting to tell the story *both* ways to the same audience! In either case, Bartimaeus's persistence remains the focus of the story and the story of that determination deserves being heard again and again.

Retelling the Story

Jesus said to him, "What do you want me to do for you?" (Mark 10:51)

Betty stopped washing the breakfast dishes and turned down the radio. Did she hear something? She leaned forward and looked out the window over the sink.

Standing on her front stoop was a man holding a bouquet of balloons. Betty stood staring and muttered to herself, "What in the world?" As the man reached for the doorbell, he turned toward Betty. He looked familiar. Did she know him? He looked like ... like ... like that guy from the clearinghouse sweepstakes. Oh, my Lord. It was the sweepstakes man!

Betty ran to the front door and threw it open. "Did I win? Aren't you the man from TV?" she squealed.

The man smiled and said, "Betty, don't you recognize me?" Betty's hand flew to her mouth. The answer came from her heart, not her head. She heard herself say, "God?" As soon as the name was out of her mouth she knew it was true. God said, "Yes, Betty. I'm here to give you something. Tell me, what would you like from me?"

> The appeal to Jesus as "Son of David" echoes a story in *Testament of Solomon* 20:1-2 (first–second century C.E.): "Now it happened that one of the artisans, a dignified man, threw himself down before me, saying, 'King Solomon, Son of David, have mercy on me, an elderly man.' I said to him, 'Tell me, old man, what you want.' He replied, 'I beg you, King. I have a son, my only son, and every day he does terribly violent things to me, striking me in the face and head and threatening to send me to a terrible death. Because he did this, I came forward [to request] a favor—that you will avenge me." (Boring-Berger-Colpe 122-23, no. 155)

Betty was stunned. She said, "What do I want from you? I thought I was supposed to want whatever you wanted me to want." God chuckled and said, "Well, that works too. But let's try something new. Just for today, what can I do for you?"

Betty wrapped her arms around her body to hold herself up. What did she want? From God? Anything at all? She shifted her weight and said, "I don't know. I know what Jimmy would want. He'd say, 'Honey, choose money. Get enough money so I can retire. Get enough so we can buy a boat, maybe an RV. And enough so we can spend winters in Florida.'"

God asked, "So that's what you want? Money?"

Betty said quickly, "No. No. That isn't what I really want. Wait. Wait. Let me think." Betty started to chew her nails. God waited.

Then she said, "I don't know. I know what I used to want. When I was a young girl I wanted to be a famous movie star. I wanted to go live in California and wear fancy clothes. I sing a little, you know." She looked up into God's kind eyes. "Oh, I guess you do know."

God smiled. He said, "So you want to be a famous movie star? That's what you want from me?"

"No. Wait. Wait." Betty started to sweat. The heat spread up her neck and her face flamed. She whined, "Wait. I don't know what I want. I know what I should want. I should want my children to be safe and healthy. I should want them to find partners to love and to give me lots of grandchildren. And I do want that. But. . ."

"So you want health and happiness for your children. Is that what you're asking for?" God said.

"Yes. No. I mean yes, it's what I want, but it's not what I want. I mean what I want for me. I mean ... I don't know what I mean." And Betty started to cry. A deep sob shook her body and she clung to the screen door for support.

God reached out and touched her shoulder. "It's OK, Betty. I tell you what, why don't we go inside and have a nice cup of tea. We'll sit together while you think. Then you can tell me what you want." *(Pam McGrath)*

LUKE 19:1-10

Zacchaeus

Salvation comes to Zacchaeus, a short, rich, but generous tax collector.

The Story

Entering Jericho he made his way through the city. There was a man there named Zacchaeus; he was superintendent of taxes and very rich. He was eager to see what Jesus looked like; but, being a little man, he could not see him for the crowd. So he ran on ahead and climbed a sycamore tree in order to see him, for he was to pass that way. When Jesus came to the place, he looked up and said, 'Zacchaeus, be quick and come down, for I must stay at your house today.' He climbed down as quickly as he could and welcomed him gladly. At this there was a general murmur of disapproval. 'He has gone in to be the guest of a sinner,' they said. But Zacchaeus stood there and said to the Lord, 'Here and now, sir, I give half my possessions to charity; and if I have defrauded anyone, I will repay him four times over.' Jesus said to him, 'Today salvation has come to this house—for this man too is a son of Abraham. The Son of Man has come to seek and to save what is lost.'

Comments on the Story

The children's song about Zacchaeus remains popular in Sunday schools across our country. The ditty, as I learned it as a child, runs like this:

> Zacchaeus was a wee little man
> And a wee little man was he;
> He climbed up in the sycamore tree
> for the Lord he wanted to see.
> And as the Lord came walking by,
> he looked up in the tree.
> And he said:
> "Zacchaeus, you come down,
> for I'm going to your house today."

136

The song no doubt continues in popularity because it provides young children with an entry point into the biblical story. Zacchaeus, though an adult, was, after all, a "wee little man." However commendable it is to find such points of contact for children with a story that is predominantly "for adults," a focus on Zacchaeus's child-like size may obscure the rhetorical intent of the story.

We are given an unusual amount of information about Zacchaeus. The narrator tells us his occupation and his social status, and provides a physical description as well. The authorial audience would have heard each of these pieces of information as a negative characterization. Zacchaeus holds the position of tax collector, a much-despised occupation in Judea (*Mishnah Teharot* 7:6) and, indeed, throughout the Roman Empire (Plutarch, *Moralia*, 518E). Tax collectors were despised for two reasons. First, they were viewed as traitors to their native land and co-conspirators with the Romans, collecting taxes for which the Romans had no real entitlement. Second, there was a widespread suspicion, confirmed over and over again by experience, that dishonesty was a common practice among tax collectors. Tax collectors overcharged their clients and pocketed the excess for themselves.

The internal evidence of Luke's Gospel confirms this negative characterization of tax collectors found in other first-century witnesses. John the Baptist instructs those tax collectors who come to him, "Exact no more than the assessment" (Luke 3:13). Repeatedly in Luke, tax collectors are coupled with the generic category of "sinners" to describe those who stand outside the people of God and are in need of repentance (5:27-31; 7:34; 15:1; 18:10, 13).

In reality, those like Levi (Luke 5), who sat in tollbooths collecting taxes, may have suffered the verbal and physical abuse that naturally came with the occupation without necessarily enjoying the spoils of the office. Such was clearly not the case, however, with Zacchaeus. As a "*superintendent* of taxes" (this is the only occurrence of this term in the NT) Zacchaeus enjoyed even greater wealth at the expense of his countrymen.

The authorial audience, then, is not surprised to learn that Zacchaeus is rich, and they would have most likely concluded that he had gained his wealth at the expense of others. Luke regularly portrays the "rich" in a negative light. Jesus includes the rich in the list of "woes" of Luke 6 (v. 24). Three of Jesus' parables include a character who is described as "rich," and in each case the character is depicted negatively (Luke 12:16-21; 16:1-3; 18:18-30). Zacchaeus's wealth, then, would have been heard as a negative quality that served as an impediment to his salvation.

The third description of Zacchaeus, his physical stature, is rarely given more than a passing comment by interpreters and is certainly never viewed as a negative characteristic. The New Testament rarely provides physical descriptions of its characters. So why mention the fact that Zacchaeus is "a little man" (Greek *mikros helikia*)? The simplest explanation is that the mention of his

137

physical stature was necessary to explain why he ran ahead of the crowd and climbed a tree in order to see Jesus. An exploration of physical smallness in antiquity, however, might suggest other, more intriguing explanations.

Those who suffered from pathological shortness in antiquity were routinely marginalized. While short stature did not *necessarily* detract from a person's standing, it was certainly not viewed as a virtue. Persons with physical disabilities, as in modern times, were often the objects of scornful jokes, and shortness was a particularly favorite target in the Greco-Roman world. Athenaeus reported that the poet Philetas of Cos was so small and thin that "he had to wear on his feet balls made of lead to keep him from being upset by the wind!" (12.552*b*). The poet Lucilius wrote (11.89): "Short Hermogenes, whenever he drops anything on the ground, pulls it down with a spear" (i.e., he's so short that he cannot even reach objects at ground level). Other literary evidence suggests that dwarfs were especially sought after as dancers at parties because their ungainly and awkward movements were the object of ribald mockery. Lucian gives a vivid account of a clown named Satyrion, a "small, ugly fellow" who "danced by bending himself up double and twisting about so as to appear more ridiculous" (*Symposium* 18).

The prevalent prejudice against physical deformity in antiquity, including shortness, suggests that the authorial audience would have viewed Zacchaeus as a laughable and perhaps despicable character. And given the emphasis on the visual ungainliness of the dancing dwarf in literature (and art), Zacchaeus's "running" ahead of the crowd (Luke 19:4), far more than suggesting "shamelessness" (see the running father in Luke 15), is cruelly comical.

Our inquiry may also shed light on the note that Zacchaeus climbed a tree in order to see Jesus. A very popular myth that dates back to Homer's time concerned two brothers, the Cercopes, whose name became synonymous with robbers and cheats (see, for example, Plutarch, *Moralia* 60c; Diodorus Siculus 4.31.7; Ovid, *Metamorphoses* 14.88). When the Cercopes attempted to steal Heracles's weapons as he slept, Heracles woke up, caught the thieves, and hung them like animals, upside down, facing one another, on a stick. Ovid reported that Jupiter was so exasperated with the Cercopes that he transformed them into apes (*Metamorphoses* 14.90-100).

This story was widespread in the ancient world. An audience familiar with the "ape-like," pathologically short, thieving Cercopes may have heard faint echoes of this story and thus found immensely entertaining the image of Zacchaeus the tax-collecting thief, scurrying ape-like up and down a sycamore tree.

Finally, the crowd's comment that Jesus has "gone in to be the guest of a sinner" (19:7) may also carry additional meaning in light of the ancients' interest in physical deformity. Zacchaeus was regarded as a sinner not only because he cheated people in his role as chief tax collector, but also because his physical disability indicated some serious past sin. Congenital birth defects and even infant mortality were associated with sinfulness in Jewish (2 Sam. 12:15b-23), Christian (John 9:2), and Greek texts (Hesiod, *Works and Days*, 1.235). Thus Luke's authorial audience may have heard a double entendre in the crowd's pronouncement of Zacchaeus's sinfulness: he was born a sinner (as divine punishment), and he lived as a sinner.

Luke and his audience also lived in a world in which it was commonplace to associate outer physical characteristics with inner qualities—a practice known as "physiognomics." Physiognomics played an important role in Jewish, Christian, and Greek texts. While much attention was paid to the eyes or facial details, physical stature was also of keen interest to writers in antiquity. Smallness in physical stature was generally seen as reflective of "smallness in spirit." Pseudo-Aristotle claimed: "These are the marks of a small-minded person. He is small-limbed, small and round, dry, with small eyes and a small face, like a Corinthian or Leucadian" (808a.30). So the authorial audience, upon hearing that Zacchaeus was "a little man," might naturally infer that he was a "small-minded" person. But what does small-mindedness suggest? According to Aristotle, "He that rates himself too high is vain but he that rates himself too low is small-spirited" (*Eudemian Ethics*, 1233a.16-20). Zacchaeus, the short man, could be seen as "selling himself short" by working in a despised occupation. For Chrysostom, "small-mindedness" was related to "pet-

"A very small witness once came forward. 'May I examine him?' said Philippus. The president of the Court, who was in a hurry, answered, 'Only if you are short.' 'You will not complain,' returned Philippus, 'for I shall be just as short as that man is.' Quite comical; but there on the tribunal sat Lucius Aurifex, and he was even tinier than the witness: all the laughter was directed against Lucius, and the joke seemed merely buffoonish" (Cicero, *De Oratore*, 2.60.245). Note that Cicero did not discourage jesting based on physical appearance, but simply that certain restraint be practiced: "In ugliness too and in physical blemishes there is good enough matter for jesting, but here as elsewhere the limits of licence are the main question." (*De Oratore*, 2.58.239 [first century B.C.E.]) (from LCL)

tiness" (*Hom. Matt.* 10.1) or "greediness" (*Hom. Rom.* 18.7). Again, Zacchaeus could certainly qualify for that definition of "small-mindedness," accumulating wealth at the expense of his own countrymen. Consequently, Zacchaeus's small stature could have been interpreted as reflective of a small-mindedness that accounts both for his occupation (he has "rated himself too low") and his greed.

Luke has spared no insulting image to paint Zacchaeus as a pathetic, even despicable character. The image of a traitorous, small-minded, greedy, physically deformed tax collector sprinting in an ungainly manner ahead of the crowd and climbing a sycamore tree like a small animal is derisive and mocking. But as much as Luke leans on this stereotypical trope, his intention is to make the reversal in the conclusion of the story that much more poignant.

The story of Zacchaeus is a double quest story. Zacchaeus seeks Jesus, and like the woman with the hemorrhage (Luke 8:43-48) and the blind man beside the road (Luke 18:35-43), he is willing to risk and endure social estrangement to achieve his goal. But Jesus is also on a quest: "The Son of Man has come to seek and to save what is lost" (19:10). On his way into Jericho, he stops beneath the sycamore tree and informs Zacchaeus: "be quick and come down, for I must stay at your house today" (19:5). Zacchaeus immediately complies and welcomes Jesus to his home. His quest to see Jesus has met with success, and the story reaches its climax with Zacchaeus's confession to the Lord. He stands (Does the ridicule continue? "Go ahead, Zacchaeus, stand up." "I AM standing up!") and announces, "Here and now, sir, I give half my possessions to charity; and if I have defrauded anyone, I will repay him four times over" (19:8).

Zacchaeus's promise of restitution is evidence for Luke of his repentance and conversion. Indeed, Zacchaeus's response indicates what one might expect of a penitent tax collector who returns home, justified by God (see 18:14). Zacchaeus's conversion is confirmed by Jesus' response: "Today salvation has come to this house—for this man too is a son of Abraham" (19:9). This aphorism picks up several Lukan themes. First, the salvation that Jesus offers is immediate: "*Today* salvation has come to this house" (cf. Luke 4:21; 23:43). Second, the salvation that Jesus offers is therapeutic. To be sure, Zacchaeus does not grow in physical stature, but the stranglehold of physiognomic determinacy is broken. Just because Zacchaeus is small in stature does not mean he must be small in spirit. Here the text echoes the words of Yahweh to Samuel: "Pay no attention to his outward appearance and stature, for I have rejected him. The LORD does not see as a mortal sees; mortals see only appearances but the LORD sees into the heart" (1 Sam. 16:7). The heart of Zacchaeus, once two sizes too small, grew three sizes that day! Finally, the salvation Jesus offers is inclusive. Jesus calls Zacchaeus a "son of Abraham." Like the Ethiopian eunuch (Acts 8), Zacchaeus was probably prohibited from full participation in the temple cult because of his physical disability. Leviticus states: "No man among your descendants for all time who has any physical defect is to come and present the food of his God. No man with a defect is to come, whether a blind man, a lame man, a man *stunted* or overgrown, a man deformed in foot or hand, or with misshapen brows or a film over his eye or a discharge from it, a man who has a scab or eruption or has had a testicle ruptured" (21:17-20). Jesus declares that Zacchaeus, too, is included in the Abrahamic covenant, and Jesus' quest for Zacchaeus is completed.

In today's culture we would classify Zacchaeus as "handicapped," or as a person with "special needs." As a "wee little man," he was physically and socially marginalized in his society. By recounting a cycle of salvation that moves from ridicule to repentance, however, the Gospel storyteller reminds us that, in God's eyes, all of us have "special needs." Perhaps this is a "children's" story after all. Fortunately, for all of us children, "the Son of Man has come to seek and to save what is lost" (19:10).

Retelling the Story

But Zacchaeus stood there and said to the Lord, "Here and now, sir, I give half my possessions to charity; and if I have defrauded anyone, I will repay him four times over." Jesus said to him, "Today salvation has come to this house—for this man too is a son of Abraham." (Luke 19:8-9)

When Mr. Sanders turned the corner onto 15th Street, he heard the music—although he scarcely considered the banging of upturned, empty, plastic paint drums, metal garbage cans, and hollow construction pipes to be music. A crowd was gathered around the street performer. People tapped their feet and swayed rhythmically to the drumming. Some came forward and tossed money into a cardboard box, pre-salted with singles. Mr. Sanders turned up the collar on his cashmere coat against the wind and noise and crossed the street.

As Mr. Sanders turned the corner onto Pryor Street, he paused to look up at the gleaming skyscraper that loomed over the block. The corners of his mouth twitched into what was almost a smile. He loved to turn this corner and see her, his building: thirty floors of steel and glass, reflecting the surrounding city and his own success.

Focused on getting upstairs to his board meeting, Mr. Sanders stumbled over the outstretched foot of the old man sitting on the sidewalk. An angry hiss escaped his lips as he turned to look into the unshaved face of the homeless man. Mr. Sanders braced himself, expecting the old man to hold out an empty tin can or to beg for spare change. Instead, the old man's yellowed eyes smiled and his mouth opened into a grin. There, stuck between stained teeth, was a white stick—a lollypop stick.

The old man held out his hand and offered Mr. Sanders a cellophane-wrapped red lollypop. Surprised, Mr. Sanders found himself taking the lollypop and looking more closely into the old man's face. The old man nodded his head as though in answer, tilted his head back against the brick of the building he leaned against, and closed his eyes. Mr. Sanders just stood there. Then he slowly turned and started back toward his building. As he walked, he looked down at the lollypop.

He hadn't seen a red lollypop in years. He was surprised they even still made them. He tore the clear wrapping off and stuck the cherry candy into his mouth.

141

Memories of clear jars holding penny candy on long dark wood shelves flooded his mind. The lollypop colored his tongue bright red as he rolled it around in his mouth, as he had done some forty years before. He pulled the lollypop out and held it up to the light. The world took on a red glow, coloring the street, the people, and his building. He popped it back into his mouth and smiled.

Luke tells the Zacchaeus story in a manner designed to echo the famous story of Abraham's hospitality to divine strangers at Mamre (Gen. 18), a story which was often referenced as an example story. Zacchaeus is singled out for his hospitality and is judged by Jesus to be a "son of Abraham." In the Genesis story, Abraham responds with enthusiasm to the strangers; here Zacchaeus runs and climbs a tree to see Jesus, then welcomes him "gladly." In Genesis, Abraham's hospitality is contrasted with the inhospitality of Sodom; here Zacchaeus's hospitality is contrasted with the "murmur of disapproval" from Jesus' detractors. Just as Abraham was rewarded for his hospitality with the promise of an heir, so also Zacchaeus was rewarded with salvation.

Thirty minutes later Mr. Sanders pushed through the heavy mahogany door of the conference room. The eight waiting executives sat up and flipped open the folders spread around the long table. "Sorry to be late," Mr. Sanders said casually. "Let's get started."

The man on Mr. Sanders's right cleared his throat and began. "We are progressing on schedule. The last of the residents will be bought out and moved from the twelve blocks between Lynwood and Allen by the end of the year. Our contact on the zoning board assures me we will have no problems."

Mr. Sanders interrupted, "Did you know there's a lake back in the woods behind the old grocery on Allen?"

Surprised, the young man looked up from his notes and hesitated. Then he said, "Yes, sir. Bear Lake. The lake will be drained and the spring diverted for use as irrigation for landscaping around the complex."

The young man searched his notes and prepared to continue, but before he could begin Mr. Sanders interrupted. "My father and I used to fish that lake. Did you know that, Jason?"

The young man took off his glasses and looked into the eyes of his boss. Confused, he answered, "No, sir. I didn't know."

"We fished down there most Sunday afternoons in the spring and fall. Anything we caught, my mother would dredge in cornmeal and fry." Mr. Sanders asked, "You fish, Jason?"

"No, sir. My father didn't fish. He golfed."

Mr. Sanders nodded his head. Then he said, "Jason, you should take your boy fishing. You have a son don't you?"

"Yes, sir. Jason, Jr. He's eight."

Mr. Sanders stood up and walked over to the large-scale model of the factory complex that covered one-third of the table. He stood, hands in pockets, staring at it for a few minutes.

Then he said, "Jason, I've decided to make a few changes in the plans."

Jason said, "What? Change? What change?"

Mr. Sanders put his hand on the young man's shoulder, easing him back into his chair. "Don't get upset, Jason. It's bad for your digestion. We're going to relocate the factory complex." Addressing two of the others he said, "Harrison, tomorrow you and Wilson get with our realtors. Find me another piece of property."

All the executives sat stunned. They had never seen Mr. Sanders act so ... irrationally. Slowly, Mr. Sanders looked around the table into the faces of his employees. When he got to Jason he smiled and said, "Jason, take the rest of the day off. Go fishing with your boy. That's an order." Mr. Sanders chuckled and pulled a handful of brightly colored lollypops out of his suitcoat pocket. He tossed them on the conference table and said, "Here. Enjoy yourselves."

Out on the street, Mr. Sanders stopped in front of the sleeping man on the sidewalk. He unfolded a new quilt and covered the homeless man's legs. When the old man opened his eyes, Mr. Sanders handed him a bag of lollypops. Together they tore the cellophane from red lollypops and stuck them in their mouths. Wordlessly, the old man nodded, leaned his head back, and closed his eyes. Mr. Sanders smiled and headed toward the sound of drumming coming from 15th Street.   *(Pam McGrath)*

The Triumphal Entry

Jesus enters the city of Jerusalem in a royal procession.

The Story

With that Jesus set out on the ascent to Jerusalem. As he approached Bethphage and Bethany at the hill called Olivet, he sent off two of the disciples, telling them: 'Go into the village opposite; as you enter it you will find tethered there a colt which no one has yet ridden. Untie it and bring it here. If anyone asks why you are untying it, say, "The Master needs it."' The two went on their errand and found everything just as he had told them. As they were untying the colt, its owners asked, 'Why are you untying that colt?' They answered, 'The Master needs it.'

So they brought the colt to Jesus, and threw their cloaks on it for Jesus to mount. As he went along people laid their cloaks on the road. And when he reached the descent from the mount of Olives, the whole company of his disciples in their joy began to sing aloud the praises of God for all the great things they had seen:
'Blessed is he who comes as king in the name of the Lord!
Peace in heaven, glory in highest heaven!'
Some Pharisees in the crowd said to him, 'Teacher, restrain your disciples.' He answered, 'I tell you, if my disciples are silent the stones will shout aloud.'

Comments on the Story

The point of view from which a story is told is an important rhetorical strategy for any storyteller and can fundamentally shape the plot of any tale. When narrating, for example, the story of an epic battle, it makes a great difference whether the tale is told from the point of view of the conquerors or the conquered. Good storytellers are able to entice their audience, often unbeknownst to the hearers themselves, to adopt the point of view of the narrator. The same is true of the Gospel narrators, and the strategy of point of view is no more important than it is in the telling of the story of Jesus' last visit to Jerusalem. From the point of view of the pilgrims participating in this event in the Gospels, the Roman *triumphus* (the triumphal procession of a victorious

Roman general) seems to provide the most direct or useful background material for a proper understanding of this story; hence the story is often referred to as "the triumphal entry."

To be sure, the Gospel accounts make it clear that the multitudes were acclaiming Jesus as the "coming" king in a way not dissimilar to the cries of the masses in a Roman *triumphus*. Nonetheless, from the writers' point of view, the background to Jesus' entry into Jerusalem is to be found not in the secular accounts of the conquering generals, but rather mostly in Jewish literature, especially the Septuagint. So to understand the point of view of the Gospel narrators (and presumably also that of the protagonist, Jesus), we must examine another rhetorical strategy, intertextuality, that is, the embedding of one text by citation or allusion into another. We will focus on Luke's version of the story and limit our comments to the last four verses, which record the entry itself, after Jesus has ordered his disciples to make preparations in the first section (19:28-36).

> "Then he himself [Romulus], girding his raiment about him and wreathing his flowing locks with laurel . . . began a triumphal march, leading off in a paean of victory which his whole army sang . . . being received by the citizens with joyful amazement. This procession was the origin and model of all subsequent triumphs." (Plutarch, *Romulus*, 16.6 [late first–early second century C.E.]) (from LCL)

Three intertextual elements of Luke's version of Jesus' entry into Jerusalem indicate the evangelist's intent to depict the multitude's conviction that they were celebrating the arrival of a king into the holy city: the spreading of garments along the path; the quotation from Psalm 118; and the use of a colt by Jesus. An examination of the Old Testament texts to which these events allude will demonstrate how the pilgrims accompanying Jesus interpreted his entry into Jerusalem as the foreshadowing of the triumphal procession of a conquering hero into the city of destiny, Jerusalem.

The spreading of garments before a royal figure (Luke 19:36) reflects the nationalistic zeal on the part of the crowds. For example, when it was revealed that Jehu had been anointed to be king over Israel (2 Kgs. 9:4-13), the people responded by taking their garments and placing them before the new king-designate while shouting, "Jehu is king" (2 Kgs. 9:13; see also the similar function of palm fronds in John).

In addition to the spreading of garments along Jesus' path into Jerusalem, the crowd also joined together in singing part of Psalm 118. According to *Mishnah Sukkah* 4.5, Psalm 118 belonged to the Feast of Tabernacles, although it played a prominent role in the liturgy of the Feasts of Passover and Dedication. It concludes the Hallel psalms (113–118) and has the distinction of being the most quoted psalm in the New Testament. The part of the psalm (v. 26) quoted by the crowds at Jesus' entry was originally a reference either to the king as he approached the temple to worship God, or, more likely, to any pilgrim who comes to the temple (see 2 Sam. 6:18). In the Gospels, however, the phrase "he who is to come" is understood as a title for Jesus (Luke 7:19//Matt. 11:3; Luke 13:35//Matt. 23:39); thus, the psalm was invested with messianic meaning by the Gospel writers.

That the disciples in Luke conceived Jesus' entry into the city as a "royal entry" is evident in the addition of the title "king" to the quotation from the psalm (compare Matt. 21:9; Mark 11:9). The Lukan "multitudes" were not proclaiming that the "kingdom of David" was coming (so Mark); rather, they were voicing in chorus-like fashion that the king himself had come to visit the holy city. For those characters viewing the scene in Luke, the festive atmosphere surrounding the arrival of Jesus was not unlike that of the triumphal procession of a Roman general fresh from victory (see Plutarch, *Lives*, 16.6; Josephus, *Jewish Wars*, 7.5.5) or the royal arrival of a newly appointed king (see 2 Sam. 6:1-5). To be sure, the celebration was neither as extravagant nor elaborate as a *triumphus*; nevertheless, the pilgrims traveling with Jesus, along with others who had come out of the city to greet him (see Luke 19:39), believed his entry into Jerusalem marked the arrival of their conquering king. That this fundamental misunderstanding of the significance of Jesus' entry included, in Luke, "the whole company of his disciples" rather than simply the crowd milling about makes the misapprehension that much more tragic.

> "When the time of Cato's military service came to an end, he was sent on his way, not with blessings, as is common, nor yet with praises, but with tears and insatiable embraces, the soldiers casting their mantles down for him to walk upon, and kissing his hands, things which the Romans of that day rarely did, and only to a few of their imperators" (Plutarch, *Cato the Younger*, 12 [late first–early second century C.E.]). (Boring-Berger-Colpe, 123, no. 156)

Jesus had perhaps contributed to their misunderstanding by entering Jerusalem mounted on a young colt and evoking the messianic prophecy in Zechariah 9:9: "See, your king is coming to you, his cause won, his victory gained, humble and mounted on a donkey, on a colt, the foal of a donkey." Luke records that the colt was one on which no one had "yet ridden" (19:30). From the point of view of the crowds gathered there, this action was indicative of Jesus' royal and messianic status, since a true king would not choose an animal previously ridden, both to avoid possible contamination and to preserve his royal dignity. In fact, according to *Mishnah Sanhedrin* 2.5, no commoner was permitted to ride an animal once a king had ridden it.

146

No matter how much evidence the crowds could marshal in defense of their view of Jesus as a political leader entering occupied Jerusalem to conquer its oppressors, from the point of view of the Lukan narrator this interpretation was at least half-wrong. And the Lukan point of view mirrored Jesus' point of view. Jesus was a king, but not the kind of king the crowds so desperately desired. Beginning the last week of his earthly ministry, Jesus entered the city of Jerusalem with all the apparent trappings of a royal entry. Branches and garments were strewn in his path, psalms were sung to his glory, and a colt provided for his transport. But Jesus was willing to accept this royal procession only if the crowds were willing to accept his definition of "king," a term he would define by his example during that last week.

The people, including his disciples, wanted a nationalistic, messianic, militaristic king who would save them from their oppressors and restore political freedom at whatever cost. Jesus, on the other hand, saw his reign not as nationalistic, but universal. His mission included proclaiming release to the captives, but also recovery of sight to the blind and good news to the poor (Luke 4:18-19). His crown was a crown of thorns; his throne a splintery cross. His exaltation did not come in riding a horse-drawn chariot amidst the cheers of family and friends; rather, he found his glory in being raised up on a cross amidst the jeers of the masses. Through his death and resurrection this one who refused to be an earthly king made his royal entry by way of a cross and empty tomb. For this kind of king, even if all others would fall silent, the very stones themselves would cry out (Luke 19:40)!

Retelling the Story

"Blessed is he who comes as king in the name of the Lord! Peace in heaven, glory in highest heaven!" (Luke 19:38)

Sheriff Larry leaned through the cruiser window and listened to the scanner. When he straightened up, he continued talking to Patsy. "I'm sorry, but I can't let you leave. Not even to go to the next exit. Whenever there's a death it's treated like a homicide. You'll have to wait until the state patrol comes and takes your statement. Sorry."

Patsy didn't respond. She needed to go to the restroom and she wanted to get inside somewhere. It was cold on the side of the highway—besides, she was still shaking. The car that had rolled over and landed in front of her had almost hit her. And then she had seen the driver die. She might be unhurt, but she was shaky. She just wanted to go home.

Patsy looked up at Sheriff Larry. He was a solid man. His shoulders and waist were the same width. The flashing blue lights sparked off the badge on his hat. He looked immovable.

Resigned, Patsy leaned back against the passenger door of the sheriff's car. She noticed on the passenger seat a stuffed teddy bear wearing a hat like the sheriff's. Patsy smiled and asked, "Your partner?" Sheriff Larry said, "We give them to kids to hold on to. The department actually issues us one when we start the job. 'Course that first one is gone in no time. You can't take the bear back from a scared child. That must be my three-hundredth bear."

Patsy said, "Why do you do this job?" She could not imagine choosing to be around all this fear and sadness. To say nothing of the danger. "How do you face this every day?"

Sheriff Larry stuck his hands down into the pockets of his jacket. He was staring off down the highway. Then he said, "I quit for a while. I got a job as a manager over at the Wal-Mart. The pay was better. But one night my son was in a car wreck. I heard about it on the police scanner. Jumped in my truck and flew to the site. I didn't even bother to put on my shoes."

Patsy didn't say anything. She waited.

He went on, "He was ok. But the next week I said to my wife, 'Out on that highway I realized where I belong. I've got to go back to law enforcement.' So I did."

When she was sure he was done, Patsy said lightly, "What did your wife say? Managing a store is a lot safer than sheriff-ing."

Sheriff Larry scanned her face, deciding. "My wife said, 'We all knew it wouldn't last. You were born to law enforcement.' Guess it's true."

Patsy looked from his face, glowing in the blue lights, to the teddy bear. She breathed warm air on her cold fingers. "I'm glad. We need someone like you."

After the state trooper took down her statement, Patsy asked Sheriff Larry for his address. She thought she'd send him a box of teddy bears. As he was giving her his card, the police radio yawped his name. He said, "Nice to meet you, Patsy. I'm sorry you had to go through this. I've got another call; I have to go."

In one motion, he slid into the cruiser next to the teddy bear, put the car in gear and pulled away. Patsy watched until he disappeared down the highway. Tears flooded her eyes. Without thinking, she heard herself say, "Blessed is the one who comes in the name of the Lord." *(Pam McGrath)*

The Last Supper

Jesus shares a last meal of bread and wine with his friends.

The Story

In the evening he came to the house with the Twelve. As they sat at supper Jesus said, 'Truly I tell you: one of you will betray me—one who is eating with me.' At this they were distressed; and one by one they said to him, 'Surely you do not mean me?' 'It is one of the Twelve,' he said, 'who is dipping into the bowl with me. The Son of Man is going the way appointed for him in the scriptures; but alas for that man by whom the Son of Man is betrayed! It would be better for that man if he had never been born.'

During supper he took bread, and having said the blessing he broke it and gave it to them, with the words: 'Take this; this is my body.' Then he took a cup, and having offered thanks to God he gave it to them; and they all drank from it. And he said to them, 'This is my blood, the blood of the covenant, shed for many. Truly I tell you: never again shall I drink from the fruit of the vine until that day when I drink it new in the kingdom of God.'

Comments on the Story

The image of the Last Supper for many contemporary audiences has been profoundly shaped by subsequent visual interpretations. One thinks especially of the Renaissance work by Leonardo da Vinci (the much publicized and recently restored *Last Supper* in Milan). Or perhaps the more contemporary twentieth-century depiction by Salvador Dali (*Sacrament of the Last Supper*, 1962, National Gallery, Washington, D.C.). While these efforts of "visual exegesis" are often profound, even inspiring, at times they may obfuscate what the synoptic storytellers are themselves trying to communicate. After all, they too are "literary artists" and we would do well to appreciate each *objet d'art* on its own merit. The comments that follow focus on Mark's story and attempt to take this account of the Last Supper on its terms, with an eye toward understanding the impact the overall whole makes on the authorial audience.

The scene begins with Jesus taking his place at table with the twelve

(14:17). As they eat, Jesus makes a startling announcement: "Truly I tell you: one of you will betray me—one who is eating with me" (14:18). The disciples are distraught. Each one begins to ask Jesus if he is the betrayer. The question in Greek expects a negative answer and is best translated something like, "It isn't I, is it?" The question reflects more an attempt at self-justification than soul-searching. Jesus' answer is tantalizingly ambiguous: "It is one of the Twelve who is dipping into the bowl with me" (Mark 14:20). The fact that the betrayer is one who is eating bread with Jesus only adds to the horror of the pronouncement, since betraying someone who had shared bread with you was unthinkable for Jews (Ps. 41:9). Jesus pronounces a harsh woe upon the perpetrator: ". . . alas for that man by whom the Son of Man is betrayed! It would be better for that man if he had never been born" (14:21).

With those words casting an ominous shadow across an already dark evening, Mark records the details of Jesus' last meal with his disciples, what has come to be known as the "Institution of the Lord's Supper." The well-known symbols of bread broken and wine poured are powerfully evocative symbols of Jesus' impending violent death, of a body broken and blood shed. There is no good reason to suggest that the disciples comprehend the significance of these symbols. After all, the symbolism of the bread and cup, so carefully developed within Mark's narrative, has eluded the disciples' grasp throughout Jesus' public ministry.

Bread, for Mark, is a symbol for Jesus' identity as the source of life. Twice Jesus feeds the multitude in the desert, and both times the disciples are skeptical. In the first account (6:35-44), Jesus tells the disciples, "You give them something to eat." They reply incredulously, "Are we to go and buy two hundred denarii worth of bread, and give it to them to eat?" (6:37 NRSV). While their unbelief is surely understandable in this first story, their actions in the second feeding story seem inexcusable. In this second account (8:1-10), Jesus again suggests that the hungry crowds be fed. The disciples respond as though they had never witnessed Jesus feed five thousand men (plus women and children?) with only five loaves and two fish: "How can anyone provide these people with bread in this remote place?" (Mark 8:4). Between these two stories, bread, eating, and/or food are mentioned a number of times in the episodes of the traditions of the elders (7:1-23) and the Syrophoenician woman (7:24-30).

The theme of "bread" climaxes in the story of the "one loaf" in Mark 8:14-21. After Jesus and the disciples get into a boat to cross to the other side of the Sea of Galilee, the narrator casually mentions that the disciples had forgotten to bring bread (8:14). While Jesus tells them to beware of the leaven of the Pharisees and Herod, they are discussing the fact that they have no bread (8:15-16). Exasperated, Jesus asks them, "Why are you talking about having no bread? Do you still not perceive or understand? Are your hearts hardened?" (8:17 NRSV). With these words, Jesus is suggesting that the disciples are beginning to act more like the "outsiders" mentioned in Mark 4:11-12, to whom "everything comes by way of parables, so that ... they may look and look, but see nothing; they may listen and listen, but understand nothing; otherwise they might turn to God and be forgiven."

Jesus then rehearses for the disciples the salient facts of the two feeding stories. One can only imagine the gestures and voice inflection that accompany this little exchange! "When I broke the five loaves among five thousand, how many basketfuls of pieces did you pick up?" "Twelve," they said [with a shrug of the shoulders?]. "And how many when I broke the seven loaves among four thousand?" "Seven," they answered [now slightly annoyed?]. He said to them, "Do you still not understand?" (8:19-21). That question very nearly leaps off the page right at the audience. The unspoken answer is, of course, they do not understand, and neither do we! Otherwise, they (and we) would have realized that there is no need to worry about the bread. They (and we) would have known that the "one loaf" in the boat with them was not a stray bun that someone had absentmindedly tossed into the boat at the last minute. The "one loaf" is none other than Jesus himself! This story is Mark's rather clever and subtle way of making the same point that John does much more straightforwardly (notice their role reversals here!): Jesus is the "bread of life"!

And so now at the Last Supper, Jesus takes bread once again, blesses it, breaks it, and gives it to them, with these simple words: "Take this; this is my body" (14:22). Perhaps now they will finally understand! But, of course, they do not, and Jesus knows that they do not. A little while later, he follows his prediction of betrayal with the prediction that all of them will forsake him and flee and one of them will deny him three times (14:27-31).

Likewise Jesus gives them the cup, and while they are still swilling it in their mouths he asserts (contra Matthew and Luke, who report that he gives the words of institution before they drink): "This is my blood." Given the Jewish aversion to blood, this saying must have been hard to swallow! Harder still, when combined with the following words that the blood is "shed for many" (14:24). If the disciples do not understand the symbolism of bread for Jesus' identity, it is unlikely that they understand yet the sacrificial nature of his mission, despite his previous reference to it (see 10:45). Otherwise James and John would not have given such a glib response as "We are able" when asked by Jesus if they were able to drink the cup that he must drink. To be sure, many of them would indeed follow in his path of suffering, but such understanding must wait until some point on the other side of the resurrection (see Mark 16:5-7).

On the night before his death, Jesus sat down with his friends. He took bread and blessed it, broke it, and gave it to them, saying, "This is my body." He took a cup of wine, gave thanks, gave it to them, and after they all drank of it, said, "This is my blood of the covenant, poured out for many." Do you not yet understand?

Mark's description of the Last Supper is meant to create an image in the reader's mind based on meal customs of the day. Jesus and his disciples are taking part in a reclining banquet—the Greek term in verse 18 means "while they were reclining." Greeks, Romans, and Jews all reclined at their meals, at least the formal ones, and dining rooms were designed accordingly. Couches were arranged around a room so that the diners could recline on their left elbows and eat with their right hands. They often shared the same tables, and even the same dishes, as Jesus and Judas do here. The Greek banquet was divided into two courses, and those two courses seem to be indicated here. The first course was the eating course proper, or the *deipnon* ("supper"); so also here Jesus first gives thanks for the bread. The second course was the symposium, during which the wine was mixed with water and shared among the diners; so also here Jesus gives thanks for the wine and passes it around for all to share. The traditional Jewish blessing for the bread was: "Blessed art thou, O Lord our God, king of the universe, who bringest forth bread from the earth," and the traditional Jewish blessing over the wine was: "Blessed art Thou, O Lord, our God, King of the universe, Creator of the fruit of the vine" (*m. Berakhot* 6.1). The Greeks, on the other hand, offered their wine libation to Dionysus, the god of wine. (Smith, pp. 25-31, 146)

Retelling the Story

During supper he took bread, and having said the blessing he broke it and gave it to them, with the words: "Take this; this is my body." (Mark 14:22)

Jenny ran into the house and straight to her great-grandmother. Grandma Harris was sitting on the right-hand side of the sofa, in the sunshine. She hugged Jenny and then patted the seat next to her for Jenny to sit down. Once Jenny was settled and the pleasantries of "How are you?" were over she said to her husband, "Jim, hand me down the doll."

Great-grandpa Harris went to the "whatnot" shelf and brought the little six-inch plastic doll to his wife. He placed it in her outstretched hands. Grandma Harris fingered the doll's braided hair, tiny beaded necklace, and fringed leather dress. Then she carefully placed the delicate plastic doll in Jenny's six-year-old hands.

Grandma Harris had been blind since half a dozen years before Jenny was born. She recognized things now by sound and touch. Sometimes she'd say to Jenny, "Honey, come here and let me see how you've grown." Jenny knew that meant Grandma Harris would touch the top of her head to measure her height. And with a feather-light touch she would run her fingers across Jenny's face, trying to see with her hands. Jenny liked sitting next to Grandma Harris on the sofa in the sunshine. And Jenny liked being the only one who got to hold Grandma Harris's special doll.

When the doll came off the shelf, Jenny knew her great-grandma was going to tell her stories. She told Jenny stories of animals that talked and behaved like people.

Finally Grandma Harris said, "Jim, you can come put the doll back up." Jenny knew then it was time to go back home.

Six years later, Grandma Harris died. Jenny was sad, but Grandma Harris hadn't been able to tell her stories for the past four years. After the stroke, Grandma Harris had mostly sat still and quiet.

After the funeral, Jenny's mother brought her home a package. She said, "Grandma Harris wanted you to have this." Jenny opened the box to discover that Grandma Harris had left her the little doll dressed as an Indian princess. The doll stayed on her bedroom shelf until she went away to college. Then it was wrapped up and stored away with her childhood memories in a cedar chest.

When Jenny's own grandmother, Grandma Harris's daughter, turned eighty-five, Jenny decided to interview her on video. Jenny loved Grandma Williamson like a mother. She couldn't imagine what she'd do when her grandma died. Jenny knew that she didn't want to lose all the family stories along with her grandma. Jenny set up the video camera in the living room of Grandma Williamson's house. Then they had tea and sweet potato pie, just to try and forget being nervous about the filming.

Jenny asked Grandma Williamson about her days as a young girl, her brothers and sisters, and about her own grandma. Grandma Williamson told Jenny about her father's mother and father. Jenny said, "But what about Grandma Harris's parents? Didn't you know them?"

Grandma Williamson said, "No. I never knew them."

Jenny asked, "Did they both die before you were born?"

Grandma Williamson hesitated. "No. But they never had anything to do with us."

"Why not?"

"Because they didn't want to have anything to do with Great-grandma, that's why. And when Great-grandpa married her, his own family stopped speaking to him. Her family did the same. We children never knew much about our grandparents on that side."

Jenny said, "Why have I never heard this? Why did they stop speaking?"

Grandma Williamson looked away. "Things were different then, Jenny. When Great-grandpa and ma married things were different."

"What things were different?"

"Great-grandpa went against his family and married her." She hesitated, then said, "He married her even though she was Indian."

Shocked, Jenny said, "Who was? Your great-grandma? You mean Grandma Harris's mama? Why didn't I know that?"

Grandma Williamson stirred her tea, though the sugar was long dissolved. "Well, it wasn't something people talked about."

Jenny remembered sitting in the sun with her great-grandmother. She remembered listening to her stories of the talking animals. She remembered holding on to the treasured doll. The doll wearing a fringed leather dress and beads. Jenny said, "So, Grandma Harris's mother was an Indian? And she never knew her own grandparents?"

Grandma Williamson nodded her head. "Yes, she always wanted to be a grandmother herself, since she never had one. She loved your mama. Then when you were born, she was thrilled. She thought you were the sweetest child she ever knew. You sat so quiet next to her, listening to all her stories." Then Grandma Williamson said, "Honey, I'm tired. Let's do some more of this another time?" Reluctantly, Jenny turned off the video and packed up.

> When Jesus speaks of drinking wine anew "in the kingdom of God," he is invoking the image of the messianic banquet, or the banquet of the afterlife at which the messiah would preside. This image is found scattered throughout Jewish literature. Isaiah 25:6-8 speaks of "a feast of rich food, a feast of well-aged wines, of rich food filled with marrow, of well-aged wines strained clear" [NRSV] that "the LORD of hosts" will provide at the end time.
> *I Enoch* 62:12-14 talks about the end of time, when the rulers of the earth will be judged and "the righteous and elect ones . . . shall eat and rest and rise with that Son of Man forever and ever." (Smith, 168-69)

That night Jenny hunted through the basement until she found her mother's old cedar chest. Inside, wrapped in crinkled tissue, she found the little Indian doll. Jenny fingered its braids and beads. Then she took it upstairs and showed it to her husband. "I can't imagine what that was like. Can you imagine losing your family? Nobody speaking to you? Not having a grandmother? Grandma Harris never had one. All she had was a silly, plastic doll."

Tears rolled down Jenny's cheeks. "I wonder if her mama gave it to her? I never asked where it came from. Maybe the stories she told me were from her mama? I wish I had known. I would have paid more attention."

Jenny sobbed. Her husband hugged her. Jenny held tight to the little plastic doll. She said, "If only I had known how important it was. Before she was gone." *(Pam McGrath)*

Jesus Taken Captive

Jesus is arrested and all his disciples flee and forsake him.

The Story according to Matthew

He was still speaking when Judas, one of the Twelve, appeared, and with him a great crowd armed with swords and cudgels, sent by the chief priests and the elders of the nation. The traitor had given them this sign: 'The one I kiss is your man; seize him.' Going straight up to Jesus, he said, 'Hail, Rabbi!' and kissed him. Jesus replied, 'Friend, do what you are here to do.' Then they came forward, seized Jesus, and held him fast.

At that moment one of those with Jesus reached for his sword and drew it, and struck the high priest's servant, cutting off his ear. But Jesus said to him, 'Put up your sword. All who take the sword die by the sword. Do you suppose that I cannot appeal for help to my Father, and at once be sent more than twelve legions of angels? But how then would the scriptures be fulfilled, which say that this must happen?'

Then Jesus spoke to the crowd: 'Do you take me for a bandit, that you have come out with swords and cudgels to arrest me? Day after day I sat teaching in the temple, and you did not lay hands on me. But this has all happened to fulfil what the prophets wrote.'

Then the disciples all deserted him and ran away.

The Story according to Mark

He was still speaking when Judas, one of the Twelve, appeared, and with him a crowd armed with swords and cudgels, sent by the chief priests, scribes, and elders. Now the traitor had agreed with them on a signal: 'The one I kiss is your man; seize him and get him safely away.' When he reached the spot, he went straight up to him and said, 'Rabbi,' and kissed him. Then they seized him and held him fast.

One of the bystanders drew his sword, and struck the high priest's servant, cutting off his ear. Then Jesus spoke: 'Do you take me for a robber, that you have come out with swords and cudgels to arrest me? Day after day I have been among you teaching in the temple, and you did not lay hands on me. But let the scriptures be fulfilled.' Then the disciples all deserted him and ran away.

Among those who had followed Jesus was a young man with nothing on but a linen cloth. They tried to seize him; but he slipped out of the linen cloth and ran away naked.

The Story according to Luke

While he was still speaking a crowd appeared with the man called Judas, one of the Twelve, at their head. He came up to Jesus to kiss him; but Jesus said, 'Judas, would you betray the Son of Man with a kiss?'

When his followers saw what was coming, they said, 'Lord, shall we use our swords?' And one of them struck at the high priest's servant, cutting off his right ear. But Jesus answered, 'Stop! No more of that!' Then he touched the man's ear and healed him.

Turning to the chief priests, the temple guards, and the elders, who had come to seize him, he said, 'Do you take me for a robber, that you have come out with swords and cudgels? Day after day, I have been with you in the temple, and you did not raise a hand against me. But this is your hour—when darkness reigns.'

Comments on the Story

The arrest of Jesus in the garden of Gethsemane (so called by Matthew and Mark) is told in essentially the same way in all three Gospels. Some interesting variations emerge in each retelling and in this analysis we will pursue the general plot, stopping from time to time to note when one of the synoptic storytellers adds a slight twist to the storyline.

All three versions agree that while Jesus is still speaking with the disciples about their lack of preparation for the impending events, Judas arrived with a crowd (Matt. 26:47; Mark 14:43; Luke 22:47), many of whom were bearing swords and clubs (so Matthew and Mark). In each of the accounts, Judas approaches to kiss Jesus, the prearranged "sign" to indicate which of the men was to be arrested. In both Matthew and Mark, Judas prefaces his kiss with a simple salutation: "Hail, Rabbi!" (Matt. 26:49); "Rabbi" (Mark 14:45). Judas delivers the ill-fated kiss in Matthew and Mark, but in Luke Jesus addresses him before Judas actually kisses Jesus: "Judas, would you betray the Son of Man with a kiss?" (Luke 22:48). This slight change in Luke allows Jesus to take the initiative in the encounter with the high priests.

The address of Jesus in Matthew is slightly different. Whereas the Lukan Jesus calls Judas by name and asks him a question, in Matthew Jesus says simply, "Friend, do what you are here to do" (26:50). The word "friend" is rather rare in Matthew, occurring only four times (11:19; 20:13; 22:12; and here). The first three occurrences are used with a negative context. In anticipating objections to his ministry, Jesus comments: "... they say, 'Look at him! A glutton and a drinker, a friend of tax-collectors and sinners!' " (11:19). Twice Jesus uses the word in parables. In both cases, the word introduces a reproach. In the parable of the laborers, the householder responds to one of the laborers

156

who had worked all day and were complaining that everyone had received the same wages: "My friend, I am not being unfair to you. You agreed on the usual wage for the day, did you not?" (20:13). In the parable of the wedding guest, the king confronts the man who did not have the proper attire: " 'My friend,' said the king, 'how do you come to be here without wedding clothes?' But he had nothing to say. The king then said to his attendants, 'Bind him hand and foot; fling him out into the dark, the place of wailing and grinding of teeth'" (22:12-13). For Matthew's authorial audience, when Jesus addresses Judas as "friend" there is no doubt that the words that follow are meant as rebuke and judgment: "do what you are here to do."

In both Matthew and Mark, Jesus is immediately arrested, though in Luke this action is delayed until after the next scene. In all three Gospel accounts, one of Jesus' followers suddenly draws a sword and cuts off the ear of the high priest's servant (in John, we are told the names of those involved: Peter is the assailant, Malchus the victim). Luke adds the interesting detail that it was the right ear of the slave. Older interpreters have taken this as evidence of the author's medical interest and additional proof that the author was none other than Luke the Beloved Physician. A more convincing reading, however, is that the right ear is mentioned to imply that the slave has been struck from behind. After all, assuming that the assailant was right-handed (a rather widespread assumption in antiquity, given the negative connotations that accompanied left-handedness), it would have been difficult to cut off the slave's ear while facing him without also slicing his nose. This interpretation receives support from the logion in Matthew's Sermon on the Mount, where Jesus says, "If anyone slaps you on the right cheek, turn and offer him the other also" (Matt. 5:39). Being struck on the right cheek (again presuming a right-handed assailant) implies being struck with the back of the hand, a gesture which in Judaism added insult to injury (*Mishnah Bava Qamma* 8:6). Thus Luke, by including the detail of the right ear, implies that the slave was hit from behind in what was not only an act of violence but of cowardice as well.

The immediate response of Jesus varies in all three accounts. In Matthew, Jesus reprimands the offending disciple: "Put up your sword. All who take the sword die by the sword" (Matt. 26:52). He then launches into a brief, but bold speech: "Do you suppose that I cannot appeal for help to my Father, and at once be sent more than twelve legions of angels? But how then would the scriptures be fulfilled, which say that this must happen?" (26:53-54). In Luke, Jesus' approach is altogether different. He says simply, "Stop! No more of that!" touches the slave's ear, and heals him (22:51), making this the only miracle Jesus performs in the passion narrative. The Markan Jesus seems to ignore this incident altogether and goes straight into his next speech, found (with minor variations) also in Matthew and Luke (Matt. 26:55-56*a*; Luke 22:52-53): "'Do you take me for a robber, that you have come out with swords and cudgels to arrest me? Day after day I have been among you teaching in the temple, and you did not lay hands on me. But let the scriptures be fulfilled'" (Mark 14:48-49).

Luke ends his version here (in an effort to soften the negative picture of the disciples?), but both Matthew and Mark add the stark note: "Then the disciples all deserted him and ran away" (Matt. 26:56b; Mark 14:50). Jesus had anticipated the disciples' desertion (Matt. 26:31; Mark 14:27), but his prediction does not lessen the starkly negative picture of the disciples fleeing from Jesus at his moment of greatest need. Mark goes on to add a very curious detail to his story that highlights the disciples' failure. If Matthew and Luke were aware of Mark, they fastidiously avoid any reference to it: "Among those who had followed Jesus was a young man with nothing on but a linen cloth. They tried to seize him; but he slipped out of the linen cloth and ran away naked" (Mark 14:51-52). Of course, it is hard to resist the humorous mental image of a naked man fleeing from the scene (the one-liners roll easily—the first streaker in the New Testament? Was he wearing a tear-away jersey? Did he fail to hold his end up?).

> Jewish tradition spoke of three kinds of kisses: "In general kissing leads to immorality: there are however three exceptions, namely kissing someone to honour that person (Samuel kissing Saul, 1 Sam 10.5), or kissing upon seeing someone after a long absence (Aaron kissed Moses, Exod 4.27) and the farewell kiss as when Orpah kissed Naomi (Ruth 1.14)" (*Genesis Rabbah* 70 [45b]). (Klassen, 126)

Even the serious attempts at interpretation fail to convince. Some have argued that the detail represents Mark's insertion of a personal experience into the account; in other words, he is the young man who stumbled into the garden at the moment of the arrest, and the verses represent his "signature" to verify the account. Others think the young man symbolizes the resurrection of Jesus, who, like the young man, leaves his garments behind in the empty tomb (see John 20:6) as he eludes his captors. Still others suggest that an implicit reference to early Christian baptismal practices is to be seen in the shedding of garments. None of these views is compelling, however.

The text, nonetheless, does give several clues for the construction of a coherent reading. First, note that the young man is "following Jesus" (14:51). As we have suggested before, the use of the word "follow" in Mark often refers to "following Jesus," e.g., with regard to disciples (see Mark 1:18, 20; 2:14; 6:1; 8:34; 10:21, 28; 14:54). Thus, the young man and his actions here are to be understood as representing the disciples. How low have the disciples sunk? The young man shows us. He literally leaves everything to get away from Jesus. This action not only vividly dramatizes the action of the disciples in the garden (they "all deserted him and ran away"), it stands in sharp contrast to the initial depiction of the disciples who left everything to follow him (Mark 1:16-20). The young man, then, symbolizes the degenerating story of the disciples in Mark, from their courageous following of Jesus to their cowardly flight from him.

Mark's story of the young man and the disciples does not end here, however. The word "young man" (Greek *neaniskos*) occurs once more in Mark, at the account of the empty tomb (Mark 16:1-8). There the women discover that the tomb is not altogether empty. The evangelists disagree on the number of messengers in the tomb (Matthew/Mark—one; Luke/John—two), but Matthew, Luke, and John do agree in identifying the messenger/s in the tomb as "angel/s" (even Luke, who initially calls them "two men," later has one of the characters refer to them as angels; Luke 24:23). Mark, on the other hand, simply identifies the messenger as a "young man," a *neaniskos*! It is not too far-fetched to imagine that the authorial audience, upon (re-)hearing this word applied to the messenger in the empty tomb, would make a connection with the earlier reference to the young man who fled in the garden. If the young man, naked and fleeing, represented the failure of the disciples then, here he is clothed in a white robe and seated on the right side of the tomb (Mark 16:5), representing the impending post-resurrection rehabilitation of the disciples. He tells the women to tell Jesus' disciples and Peter that he (Jesus) is "going ahead of you into Galilee," presumably to be reconciled with them. In Mark's Gospel, then, the message of rehabilitation for the disciples is given by none other than one who himself has been rehabilitated and restored. He who had fled Jesus has presumably met him, and the restored disciple has been entrusted with the hopeful message of restoration for the rest of the disciples. This Jesus ultimately cannot be taken captive, either by the powers of human establishment or by the power of death!

Retelling the Story

Among those who had followed Jesus was a young man with nothing on but a linen cloth. They tried to seize him; but he slipped out of the linen cloth and ran away naked. (Mark 14:51-52)

Marybeth stood in the doorway of the diner, looking down the street at the flashing lights. She said, "Hey, Pete. Something's going on over by the courthouse. I just saw an ambulance pull away."

Pete, the cook, stuck his head out the pass-through from the kitchen and hollered, "What is it?"

Marybeth said, "I don't really know. Here comes Gail. Maybe she knows."

Marybeth stepped back to let Gail in. Gail walked to the counter and plopped down on her usual stool. Marybeth followed, picking up the coffee pot

159

as she slid behind the counter and pouring Gail a cup. When Gail reached for the cup, her hands shook. She sloshed coffee onto the counter.

"Sorry, Marybeth."

Josephus also relates an infamous story about a kiss of betrayal by Joab: "When he reached Gabaon . . . he found Amasa there at the head of a large force, and Joab went to meet him with his sword girded on and wearing a breastplate. Then, as Amasa approached to greet him, he artfully contrived to have his sword fall, as if by itself, out of its sheath. And he picked it up from the ground, and with his other hand seized Amasa, who was now near him, by the beard as if to kiss him, and with an unforeseen thrust in the belly killed him. This impious and most unholy deed he committed against a brave youth, who was, moreover, his relative, and had done him no wrong, because he envied him his office of commander and his being honoured by the king with a rank equal to his own." (*Jewish Antiquities* 7.283-84 [first century C.E.]) (from LCL)

Marybeth pulled a towel out of her apron pocket and said as she wiped, "Hey, no problem. What's wrong?"

Gail asked, "Did you see the ambulance?"

"Yeah. Me and Pete were wondering what was going on."

Gail took a shaky sip of coffee and said, "An old man had a heart attack. I had just closed up the shop to take my break, like always. As I got to the corner, right by the courthouse, I saw an old man lying on the ground. He was jerking a little and his lips were all blue. Standing right by him was this young guy, late twenties, wearing a suit and clutching a briefcase."

Then Gail stirred some sugar into her usually black coffee. Marybeth, eyebrows raised, didn't say anything. She poured herself a cup of coffee and waited.

After another sip of the sweetened liquid, Gail continued. "I knelt down and loosened the old man's collar. I figured he was having a heart attack. I said to the young guy, 'You with him?' But the young guy didn't say anything. He was just frozen. He was holding on to that briefcase for dear life. So I started doing CPR. I yelled at the young guy, 'Go call 911.' But like I said, he didn't move."

Marybeth put her own cup down and said, "He didn't go call for help or nothing? He didn't even try to help?"

Gail said, "No. He was all white and trembling and he just stood there."

Marybeth said, "Well that's disgusting. I tell you, what is this world coming to? Some old man falls down on the street right in front of a young guy and he doesn't make a move to help."

Gail went on, "I looked over toward the hardware store and saw Billy by

160

the door. I yelled, 'Hey Billy! Call 911!' So he did, I guess. I kept doing CPR until the ambulance came."

"And what about the young guy?" Marybeth asked as she poured Gail another cup.

"That's just it," Gail said. "He never moved. He was terrified. He just stood there. I felt so sorry for him."

Marybeth said, "You felt sorry for him? Are you kidding? That jerk stands there while some old guy practically dies and you feel sorry for him?"

"Yeah. You didn't see his face. It was so white and still. Like he was in shock."

Marybeth said, "Well, I don't feel sorry for him. He should be ashamed of himself. Not helping."

Stirring another spoonful of sugar in her cup, Gail said, "You know, I remember reading somewhere that when people are scared they either kick into a 'fight' or 'flight' mode."

Marybeth scowled and said, "Well, that young coward sure didn't fight. You did, but he didn't. He must be the kind that runs from fear. The baby. You were afraid, too, Gail. But you didn't run."

Gail stared into her coffee cup. She stirred the long-dissolved sugar. "It was awful. That young man's face. You should have seen him. When they took the old man away I stood next to him. I could almost smell his fear. I looked into his eyes. It was terrifying."

Confused, Marybeth asked, "What was?"

Without looking up Gail said, "Don't you see? I've always thought that I might be someone who'd run away. You know, if a gang came after one of my friends or something. I was always afraid I wouldn't be brave enough to stand up for my friends and fight. But that young man on the street today, he won't ever wonder again. He's a runner. He knows. Now he'll always know. I can't think of anything scarier than that."   *(Pam McGrath)*

The Crucifixion

Jesus is crucified as an innocent martyr who, even in death, continues his redemptive work of forgiveness.

The Story

There were two others with him, criminals who were being led out to execution; and when they reached the place called The Skull, they crucified him there, and the criminals with him, one on his right and the other on his left. Jesus said, 'Father, forgive them; they do not know what they are doing.'

They shared out his clothes by casting lots. The people stood looking on, and their rulers jeered at him: 'He saved others: now let him save himself, if this is God's Messiah, his Chosen.' The soldiers joined in the mockery and came forward offering him sour wine. 'If you are the king of the Jews,' they said, 'save yourself.' There was an inscription above his head which ran: 'This is the king of the Jews.'

One of the criminals hanging there taunted him: 'Are not you the Messiah? Save yourself, and us.' But the other rebuked him: 'Have you no fear of God? You are under the same sentence as he is. In our case it is plain justice; we are paying the price for our misdeeds. But this man has done nothing wrong.' And he said, 'Jesus, remember me when you come to your throne.' Jesus answered, 'Truly I tell you: today you will be with me in Paradise.'

Comments on the Story

Luke 23:32-43 is the New Testament reading for the last Sunday of the liturgical year C of the Revised Common Lectionary. That day is designated "Christ the King" Sunday. Certainly this text is a fitting one for the church's celebration of Jesus' regal person and work.

Luke records that the inscription over Jesus' cross read: "This is the king of the Jews" (23:38). This truth about Jesus' royal identity is revealed also in the soldiers' mockery of Jesus: "If you are the king of the Jews, save yourself" (23:37). The audience cannot miss the irony of these characters uttering a truth that they themselves do not believe or understand (otherwise, they would know that the proof of Jesus' kingship is to be found in his saving others, not himself). Finally, the "good criminal" also recognizes the future reign of Jesus the

162

king in his petition, "Jesus, remember me when you come to your throne" (23:42). But there is much more to glean from this text in addition to its emphasis on the kingship of Jesus. The passage divides into two units. The first, 23:32-39, records the continued mocking of Jesus and contains parallels with Matthew 27:33-44 and Mark 15:22-32; the second unit (23:40-43) is about the so-called penitent thief and is uniquely Lukan.

By echoing various Old Testament passages, especially in the Psalms, the narrator highlights the rejection of Jesus in the first section. From the narrator's perspective:

> Luke 23:33 (Jesus crucified between two criminals) "fulfills" Isaiah 53:12 ("and [he] was reckoned among transgressors"; see also Luke 22:37);

> Luke 23:34*b* (casting lots for his garments) "fulfills" Psalm 22:18 ("They share out my clothes among them and cast lots for my garments");

> Luke 23:35 (religious leaders scorn Jesus) "fulfills" Psalm 22:7-8 ("All who see me jeer at me ..."; see also Wisdom 2:18); and

> Luke 23:36 (soldiers mock Jesus, offering him vinegar) "fulfills" Psalm 69:21 ("They put poison in my food and when I was thirsty they gave me vinegar to drink").

The narrator also presents the groups mocking Jesus in descending order of social status: first the religious leaders scoff at Jesus (23:35), next the soldiers mock him (v. 36), and finally, as the humiliation reaches its nadir, Jesus' fellow condemned man ridicules him (v. 39).

There are two points of relief in this otherwise stark story of ridicule and mockery, which Luke places in a setting identified simply as "The Skull" (23:33; see also Matt. 27:33; Mark 15:22, where the Aramaic name "Golgotha" is also provided). First, the people, in contrast to the religious authorities, are depicted as watching, but not participating in, these degrading events (23:35). This brief reference stands within a carefully developed portrayal of the role of the people in Jesus' death in Luke. At first they are implicated along with the chief priest and leaders in conspiring for Jesus' death (23:13), they join in the cries for the release of Barabbas (23:18), and finally, in response to Pilate's offer to release Jesus, shout "Crucify him, crucify him!" (23:21). But unlike the religious leaders, who maintain a consistent opposition to Jesus throughout the Lukan passion, the people show signs of a change of heart and mind. Even though they have clamored for his death, the narrator reports that "great numbers of people followed" (23:27) on the route to the place called "The Skull."

Whatever their reason for following along Jesus' path, the people, in contrast to their leaders, have placed themselves in a position to remain open to the plan of God. Our passage here, where the people watch rather than participate in the ridicule of Jesus, continues the contrast with the religious leaders. This "watching" turns into genuine spiritual sight at Jesus' death, the climactic scene for the characterization of the people in the Lukan passion: "The crowd who had assembled for the spectacle, when they saw what had happened, went home beating their breasts" (23:48). In Luke the gesture of beating the breasts is one of genuine repentance, as Luke 18:13 makes clear: "[The tax collector] beat upon his breast, saying, 'God, have mercy on me, sinner that I am.' " So here in 23:48 the crowd's transformation from co-conspirators to penitents is complete.

The second positive note in the midst of the portrayal of the extreme humiliation of Jesus (a humiliation that extends all the way back to the beginning of chapter 23) is found in Jesus' prayer for his persecutors in verse 34: "Father, forgive them; they do not know what they are doing." Not all martyrs were so forgiving of their enemies. The martyred sons in 2 Maccabees 7 heap a series of curses on their persecutors: "[F]or you [Antiochus IV] there will be no resurrection" (2 Macc. 7:14); "Wait, and you will see how [God's] mighty power will torment you and your descendants!" (2 Macc. 7:17); "[D]o not suppose you yourself will escape the consequences of trying to contend with God" (2 Macc. 7:19). Though many ancient manuscripts do not contain Luke 23:34 (leading some to conclude it has been added as a parallel to Stephen's prayer in Acts 7:60), the theme of forgiveness is consistent with comments by Jesus elsewhere in Luke. In his first public address at Nazareth, Jesus acknowledged in the words of Isaiah that he had been sent "to proclaim release [Greek *aphesis*, "forgiveness"] for prisoners" (4:18). He claimed that the Son of Man had authority to forgive sins on earth (5:23-24) and pronounced a sinful woman forgiven (7:47). He taught his disciples to pray not only for God's forgiveness but also to pledge "for we too forgive all who have done us wrong" (11:4; see also 17:3). So here at the cross Jesus now asks God to forgive his oppressors.

That the request for forgiveness should take the form of prayer is also consistent with Luke's portrayal of Jesus as one constantly seeking union with God through prayer. Jesus prays throughout his public ministry: at his baptism (3:21), in deserted places (5:16), on a mountain before choosing his disciples (6:12), by himself (9:18), with his disciples (11:1), and just before his arrest (22:41). Furthermore Jesus told parables to underscore the importance of prayer (Luke 18) and offered the following instructions to his disciples: "But to you who are listening I say: Love your enemies; do good to those who hate you; bless those who curse you; *pray for those who treat you spitefully*" (6:27-28, emphasis mine).

This theme of forgiveness is continued in the second unit, 23:40-43, which is unique to Luke's Gospel. Jesus assures the penitent criminal of a place with him in paradise (23:43). First, though, the penitent thief rebukes his fellow criminal for taunting Jesus: "'Have you no fear of God? You are under the same sentence as he is'" (23:40). By "reproving" the malefactor, the penitent thief fulfills the words of Jesus originally addressed to his disciples: "If your brother does wrong, reprove him" (17:3). The criminal then pronounces Jesus, in contrast to his fellow victims, innocent of all charges: "In our case [our condemnation] is plain justice; we are paying the price for our misdeeds. But this man has done nothing wrong" (23:41). This theme of Jesus' innocence is a major one in Luke's passion narrative. Three times Pilate pronounces the innocence of Jesus (23:4, 14, 22). In fact, the narrator makes it a point to note that the last attempt Pilate makes to release Jesus was the "third time" he had pronounced Jesus innocent of any wrongdoing (23:22a). Likewise Herod, to whom Pilate had sent Jesus (since as a Galilean Jesus was under Herod's jurisdiction), pronounced Jesus innocent and returned him to Pilate (23:15; see also vv. 6-12). Finally, the centurion in Luke, when he saw what had taken place, praised God and declared, "Beyond all doubt this man was innocent" (23:47; compare Matt. 27:54; Mark 15:39, where the centurion says, "This man must have been a son of God"). Luke emphasizes that the death of Jesus is the death of a martyr, the unjust murder of an innocent man by the religious and political establishment.

The penitent thief gets his name from his next utterance: "Jesus, remember me

> The ancient world was full of stories of exemplary "noble deaths" of heroes who freely accepted their deaths and never wavered from the cause that brought them to such a circumstance. One of the most famous of these stories was that of Socrates, who, like Jesus in Luke's story, is "innocent" of real crimes and is willing to face death rather than back down from his convictions. "You must know that the deity commands me this.... For I do nothing other than trying to persuade both young and old of you to care, first and above all, not for your bodies and your money, but for the perfection of your soul.... This being the case, O men of Athens, I would say ... whether you acquit me or not, I shall not act differently, not even if I were to die many times" (Plato, *Apology* 30a-b [late fifth to early fourth century B.C.E.]). (van Henten and Avemarie, 30)

when you come to your throne" (23:42). This is the only time any character calls Jesus by his first name only and creates a moment of intimacy between the two. The audience can only guess: did these two know each other prior to this unhappy day? But the narrator will not allow the hearer to linger long over that question as he presses forward the plea, "remember me." This request for remembrance echoes past petitions: Hannah (1 Sam. 1:11), Nehemiah (Neh. 5:19), Job (Job 14:13), the psalmist (25:7), and Jeremiah (Jer. 15:15) all cried out to God: "Remember me!" Some have viewed the plea of the thief as a request for a kind of "royal clemency," but Jesus in his response goes beyond that request for pardon: " 'Truly I tell you: today you will be with me in Paradise' " (23:43). As in some pagan (Plato, *Apology*, 39) and Jewish (*b. Avodah Zarah*, 18a) sources, Jesus' martyrdom produces a convert. Salvation here is depicted in terms of immediacy and solidarity. The use of the word "today" echoes especially the words spoken by Jesus to Zacchaeus: "Today salvation has come to this house—for this man too is a son of Abraham" (19:9; see also 2:11 and 4:21). Salvation is also expressed here as a kind of "with-ness," a solidarity with Jesus.

> When Jesus offers "paradise" to one of the criminals who died with him, he uses an unusual term, *paradeisos*, which the Greek language had borrowed from Persian. It originally referred to the royal garden of Persia, but came to be used for any magnificent garden. In the Greek translation of the Old Testament it refers to the garden of God in the creation story (Gen. 2:8-10, 16). It then came to be used for the promised bliss of the end time, which would be especially characterized by abundant and life-giving food and drink (the tree of life and water of life) and a bounteous banquet in the presence of God. (Jeremias, 765-67)

This powerful story has fittingly been called the gospel in miniature. It carries many of the themes so dear to Luke: the kingship of Jesus, his innocence, the importance of forgiveness, repentance, and prayer. Jesus does not seek this martyr's death (see 23:1-25), but when it comes neither does he refuse it (as noted by Justin, *Apology*, II.12). This text legitimates the mission of Jesus, the faithful and righteous martyr, whose life and death have saving efficacy.

Retelling the Story

> Jesus answered, "Truly I tell you: today you will be with me in Paradise." (Luke 23:43)

His mother had named him Moses after the greatest of the leaders of the ancient Israelites. Even as a youngster he was tall and strong for his age. His skin, as dark as onyx, revealed his Ethiopian heritage. He too had been sold into slavery in Egypt. He too had won his freedom from bondage, and he too had killed an Egyptian. When he had been driven away from his master's house, this young Moses began to plunder the Egyptians. He spent the years following his release stealing from his former captors and any other Egyptians who weren't watching their belongings carefully. He was so successful in his thievery that he surrounded himself with seventy-five other thieves, all of whom worked for him.

After a time Moses' success as a thief gained him a celebrity of sorts. His name was a household word, spoken with fear by the Egyptians and with admiration by slaves all across that land. He was filled with hubris (overweening pride) and arrogance because of his skill and reputation. Of course, he became well known to the authorities as well, and they searched tirelessly for Moses and his band of thieves. He had many close calls but was never captured.

Once when the authorities came searching for him he hid in a monastery. He decided that the safest place for him to hide was the chapel. Skulking in the shadows in a dark corner of the chapel he began to listen to the Gospel reading for that day. The phrase that caught his attention was "between two thieves." From that point on in the reading Moses listened intently. The reading told of someone named Jesus, who was being crucified by the Roman authorities. He was apparently some sort of troublemaker, someone they considered dangerous. Moses was someone the Egyptian authorities considered dangerous. Two thieves were being crucified with him, one on either side. Moses was a thief and deserved just such a punishment according to the laws of Egypt.

Then the reader launched into a conversation between one of the thieves and Jesus. The thief made a request. "Remember me when you come to your throne," the thief asked, as if this Jesus was some kind of royalty. Jesus' answer struck Moses like a blow to the stomach. "Today," he told the thief, "you will be with me in paradise." Paradise! A paradise where thieves were welcomed! Moses wanted to know more about this Jesus and his paradise. That day he left thievery behind and joined the monks in their study, prayer, and fasting.

As he studied the Gospels he discovered that Jesus must have known a lot about thieves. After all, he had compared himself to a thief who came in the night. Instead of taking the property of others, Jesus slipped into the world and stole lives for God, who was, after all, their rightful owner. Moses came to believe that, if Jesus could welcome a thief, then he could welcome anybody.

In time Moses became a celebrity again, but this time it was for his humility rather than his hubris. He lived among the monks at Scete in the Egyptian desert. Instead of seventy-five thieves, he now had seventy-five disciples following him. He tried to avoid the many visitors who came to see and listen to him. One day he heard that a group of pilgrims was coming to Scete. Very quickly he left but met them on his way out of the community. They stopped him and asked, "Where is the cell of Abba Moses? We have come to gain wisdom from him." He answered them in a booming voice, "Wisdom? From

Moses? Why, the man is a fool and a thief! Not only will he lead you astray, he is likely to take your purse while he is at it." Then he went on his way. When the pilgrims arrived at Scete and asked one of the monks about their recent encounter, the monk asked, "Was he a very dark-skinned man?" "Yes," they answered. "That was Abba Moses!" he told the bewildered pilgrims.

Once Abba Moses was called by the other abbas to sit with them and judge the case of a young member of the community who had broken certain of the rules. After refusing to respond to several ever more insistent invitations to appear, he finally gave in. He showed up at the hearing carrying a bucket that was riddled with holes and had sand pouring from the holes. He turned to the other abbas and said, "Here I stand with my sins pouring out behind me like sand, yet I presume to sit in judgment of another." Then he turned and left the room.

Moses continued to live at Scete until he was seventy-five years old. That year the barbarians overran the community and Moses was killed. Many of his sayings have been remembered. One that seems to speak of his continual amazement that he could ever be accepted into a community of God's people is this: "When you are continually aware of your own sins, it leaves you no time and energy to point out the sins of others."   *(Michael E. Williams)*

The Death on the Cross

As Jesus dies on the cross, he speaks his last words.

The Story

At midday a darkness fell over the whole land, which lasted till three in the afternoon; and at three Jesus cried aloud, 'Eloï, Eloï, lema sabachthani?' which means, 'My God, my God, why have you forsaken me?' Hearing this, some of the bystanders said, 'Listen! He is calling Elijah.' Someone ran and soaked a sponge in sour wine and held it to his lips on the end of a stick. 'Let us see,' he said, 'if Elijah will come to take him down.' Then Jesus gave a loud cry and died; and the curtain of the temple was torn in two from top to bottom. When the centurion who was standing opposite him saw how he died, he said, 'This man must have been a son of God.'

A number of women were also present, watching from a distance. Among them were Mary of Magdala, Mary the mother of James the younger and of Joses, and Salome, who had all followed him and looked after him when he was in Galilee, and there were many others who had come up to Jerusalem with him.

Comments on the Story

The so-called "seven last words of Jesus" have long played an important role in the church's understanding of Jesus' passion. And the seven last words have been the subject of countless sermon series and musical productions. The importance of "seven" last words has been recognized at least since Tatian's second-century *Diatessaron*, though the order of the sayings has varied. Tatian's order, reconstructed from the Arabic form of the *Diatessaron*, was:

1) "Truly I tell you: today you will be with me in Paradise" (Luke 23:43);
2) "Mother, there is your son ... There is your mother" (John 19:26-27);
3) "My God, my God, why have you forsaken me?" (Matt. 27:46; Mark 15:34);

169

4) "I am thirsty" (John 19:28);

5) "It is accomplished" (John 19:30);

6) "Father, forgive them; they do not know what they are doing" (Luke 23:34*a*);

7) "Father, into your hands I commit my spirit" (Luke 23:46).

It is interesting to note that of the seven traditional sayings, Matthew and Mark share one, Luke has three, and John has three. However helpful it is to the church's passion liturgy and theology to keep the seven words together as a unit, it is equally helpful for the storyteller/preacher to "recontextualize" these sayings in order to understand their literary and theological significance within their respective narrative contexts. We will attend here only to the one saying shared in common between Matthew and Mark, focusing most of our attention on its occurrence in Mark.

The last words spoken by Jesus in Matthew and Mark are "My God, my God, why have you forsaken me?" While these two Gospels share this one saying verbatim, the surrounding narrative context suggests that each narrator gives a distinct interpretation as to the meaning of the saying. We will first take up the Gospel of Mark.

The first point to note about Mark is that this verse is a quote from the opening line of Psalm 22. Many have argued that the opening verse invokes the entire message of the Psalm. Psalm 22 ends with the psalmist praising God's faithfulness:

> I shall declare your fame to my associates, praising you in the midst of the assembly.... For he has not scorned him who is downtrodden, nor shrunk in loathing from his plight, nor hidden his face from him, but he has listened to his cry for help.... my descendants will serve him. The coming generation will be told of the LORD; they will make known his righteous deeds, declaring to a people yet unborn: 'The LORD has acted.' (Psalm 22:22, 24, 30-31)

Thus, interpreters have insisted that by quoting Psalm 22, Jesus is demonstrating his belief in God's faithfulness, despite the current circumstances. This reading makes Matthew 27:46 and Mark 15:34 sound much like Jesus' words of assurance in Luke 23:46 ("Father, into your hands I commit my spirit"). Despite the attractiveness of this interpretation and its obvious solution to a very difficult logion, others have maintained that the saying truly is a "cry of dereliction" and indicates the darkest moment in the passion narrative, the moment when Jesus feels abandoned by God. This interpretation certainly fits the larger context of Mark's passion narrative. Jesus has been condemned by the political and religious authorities. He has been abandoned by the very crowds who ushered his entry into Jerusalem with the words "Blessed is he who comes in the name of the Lord." One disciple has betrayed him, another has denied him, and all of them have forsaken him (14:50). Unlike John's depiction of Jesus' death, where Mary and the Beloved Disciple stand at the foot of the cross, here in Mark Jesus dies in isolation. Only his fellow victims and his executioners are nearby; even the women who had followed him from Galilee to Jerusalem and will later return to the tomb on that first Easter morning watch his death, the narrator says, "from a distance" (15:40). Jesus dies what Harry Emerson Fosdick once called "the loneliest death in history." That he would feel abandoned even by God seems the most natural reading of Jesus' last words in Mark.

But two subsequent events demonstrate that, from Mark's perspective at least, Jesus was not abandoned. Immediately after his death, two things happen in Mark. First "the curtain of the temple was torn in two" (15:38a). That this was a divine act is indicated by the additional note that the curtain was torn "from top to bottom" (15:38b). Most interpreters agree that the authorial audience was to understand this curtain to refer to the one that separated the Holy of Holies from the rest of the temple.

For readers/listeners imbued with Jewish tradition, the storyteller's reference to darkness over the land raises the story of the death of Jesus to the level of an apocalyptic event by calling to mind such parallel texts as Amos 8:9-10: "On that day, says the Lord GOD, I shall make the sun go down at noon and darken the earth in broad daylight. I shall turn your pilgrimfeasts into mourning and all your songs into lamentation. I shall make you all put sackcloth round your waists and have everyone's head shaved. I shall make it like mourning for an only son and the end of it like a bitter day."

But what is the significance of this action in Mark? Throughout the Markan passion narrative, the point of conflict between Jesus and the religious authorities had to do with Jesus' relationship to and attitude toward the temple. Near the beginning of the passion narrative, Jesus entered the temple and drove out the moneychangers from the temple complex (Mark 11:15-19; see also Matt. 21:12-13; Luke 19:45-48). While many English translations and commentaries refer to this event as the "Cleansing of the Temple," implying that Jesus wished to cleanse and thus "reform" or "restore" the temple to its original purpose, the surrounding verses in Mark make it clear that for him the temple incident is better understood as a "cursing," not a cleansing. In Mark 11, the story of the temple (11:15-19) is bracketed by the story of Jesus' cursing of the fig tree (11:12-14, 20-25), which signifies that the cursing of the fig tree is meant to be a commentary on the story of the temple.

This focus on Jesus' relationship to the temple continues throughout the passion narrative. The section of Mark known as the "little apocalypse" begins with the disciples speaking admirably about the temple to Jesus: "Look, Teacher, what huge stones! What fine buildings!" (13:1). Jesus responds, "You see these great buildings? Not one stone will be left upon another; they will all be thrown down" (13:2).

Charges against Jesus regarding the temple also crop up in the passion narrative itself. During Jesus' trial, Mark reports: "Some stood up and gave false evidence against him to this effect: 'We heard him say, "I will pull down this temple, made with human hands, and in three days I will build another, not made with hands"'" (Mark 14:57-58). Later, during the crucifixion itself, the charge reemerges: "The passers-by wagged their heads and jeered at him: 'Bravo!' they cried, 'So you are the man who was to pull down the temple, and rebuild it in three days! Save yourself and come down from the cross'" (Mark 15:29-30). Jesus' judgment against the temple is dramatically vindicated with the tearing of the temple veil. Though the actual destruction of the temple will take place forty years later, its obsolescence as a means of access to God is already signaled with the death of Jesus.

Thus, despite Jesus' complete abandonment by all others and his despair at being forsaken by God at the end, Mark indicates by means of the confession of the centurion and the tearing of the temple veil that, in fact, God has *not* forsaken Jesus!

Matthew adds another layer of interpretive meaning to the death scene. Following Jesus' last words, which are the same as in Mark, Matthew records not two but four events, each of which is associated with the end times in Jewish thought: (1) the temple veil is torn in two (Matt. 27:51*a*; compare *Testament of the Twelve Patriarchs* 10); (2) there is an earthquake (Matt. 27:51*b*; compare *1 Enoch* 1:3-9); (3) the dead saints are raised (Matt. 27:52-53; compare Ezek. 37:12); and (4) the centurion confesses

> It was a common motif in stories about the deaths of heroic individuals to refer to omens and extraordinary events of various kinds, including signs in the heavens. According to Plutarch, the death of Julius Caesar was followed by a comet "which showed itself in great splendor for seven nights after Caesar's murder, and then disappeared." This was followed by "the obscuration of the sun's rays. For during all that year its orb rose pale and without radiance" (Plutarch, *Caesar*, 69.3-5 [late first–early second century C.E.]). Similarly, at the death of the philosopher Carneades "the moon is said to have been eclipsed, and one might well say that the brightest luminary in heaven next to the sun thereby gave token of her sympathy" (Diogenes Laertius, *Lives of Eminent Philosophers*, "Carneades" 4.64 [third century C.E.]). (Boring-Berger-Colpe, 160, nos. 212 & 213)

(Matt. 27:54; compare the end-time gathering of Gentiles at the mountain of God in Isa. 2:2-3).

The death of Jesus as apocalyptic event explains why in Matthew 10 Jesus gives his disciples strict instructions: "Do not take the road to gentile lands, and do not enter any Samaritan town; but go rather to the lost sheep of the house of Israel" (10:5-6). At the end of Matthew, though, Jesus gives explicit orders otherwise in the so-called Great Commission: "Go therefore to all nations [i.e., Gentiles] and make them my disciples" (28:19). What is different? From Matthew's perspective, it was not appropriate to reach out to the Gentiles during Jesus' lifetime because the disciples were still in the "old age/aeon." But with Jesus' death, a "new aeon," the messianic age, had begun and now it was not only appropriate but also imperative that the ingathering of the faithful Gentiles begin.

The last words of Jesus are significant. Taken together, the traditional seven last words have enriched the life and work of the church over the centuries. But there is merit also in taking them separately as well, seeking to understand their place in each of the stories that our respective storytellers of old have spun. And in the case of Mark and Matthew, the words of Jesus from the cross provide an invaluable window into the early Christian reflection on that most mysterious of moments—the death of Christ.

Retelling the Story

Jesus cried aloud, "Eloï, Eloï, lema sabachthani?" which means, "My God, my God, why have you forsaken me?" (Mark 15:34)

The charges against him had been untrue from the start. All he had tried to do was to organize farmers in the area so they could receive a fair price for their crops. These farmers were all descendants of slaves and did not want to return to that life again. They had seen their sisters and brothers who were tenants on nearby farms reduced to virtual slavery. In fact the advantage of the tenant system for the landowner was that both poor whites and poor blacks could be enslaved legally, with the blessing of the community and the silence of the church. Though these farmers, who had held on to their land, were powerless to help either the white or black tenant farmers, they did not wish wind in their shoes.

While he was not a farmer, he had grown up plowing and planting and harvesting on his father's farm. He served as pastor of a church that had many farmers among its members. He was different, however. His family had been free ever since they arrived on the shores of the New World. He had been educated at a college begun by the Methodists after the Civil War to educate ex-slaves and others of African descent. He could have gone to a city church to serve, but felt called to a country church. These folk were "like sheep without a shepherd" and had little to cling to except their religion. As an unmarried man he had few expenses and so had few needs. He moved from house to house, living for a month with one family and then a month with another. This arrangement actually helped him with his organizing efforts without arousing the suspicions of the white population.

That is, until night before last when he was awakened by shouts, pulled from the corn-shuck mattress on which he was sleeping, and dragged into the yard. There he had been struck with fists and sticks. Before his left eye had swollen shut he caught a glimpse of a figure standing in the shadows just outside the light of the torches his captors carried. In the half-light he could just make out the features of the neighbor from whose house he had just moved. Why would that neighbor do such a thing? He was a church member, someone the young preacher had been trying to help. Perhaps it was fear for his own family or some small reward that prompted the betrayal. It didn't really matter now. The deed was done.

This would not technically be considered a lynching. No, he had been dragged before a magistrate to be charged, then before a judge and jury for trial and sentencing. The entire process had taken less than twenty-four hours. Now "Old Sparky" was on its way to town. His home state was one of the last to have a portable electric chair. It would arrive before the sun set and would be placed in front of the courthouse on the town square. Men, women, and children would be allowed to gather around and watch as he was executed for something he had not done.

In some ways it seemed like years and in others it was just a few short seconds before the jailer called his name and said that everything was ready. He was marched between two deputies to the square and through the crowd that had gathered to watch his death. As he stood before the chair the jailer asked, "You have anything you want to say before your sentence is carried out?"

He looked around the crowd; his was the only dark-skinned face present. Then he looked at some of his accusers and said, "God have mercy on you. You have no idea what you are doing here."

With that he was strapped into the chair. Before the switch was thrown, those closest to him heard these words, "My God, my God, why have you forsaken me?" Then there was a buzzing sound. Fire flew from his fingers and bare toes. Smoke rose from the top of his head, and there was the awful smell of singed flesh.

As they walked away to their homes, where supper would be waiting, some in the crowd were heard to say, "Um, um, um, forsook by God. And him a preacher, too."   *(Michael E. Williams)*

174

The Empty Tomb

The women discover the empty tomb of Jesus and a divine messenger gives them the first Easter message.

The Story

When the sabbath was over, Mary of Magdala, Mary the mother of James, and Salome bought aromatic oils, intending to go and anoint him; and very early on the first day of the week, just after sunrise, they came to the tomb. They were wondering among themselves who would roll away the stone for them from the entrance to the tomb, when they looked up and saw that the stone, huge as it was, had been rolled back already. They went into the tomb, where they saw a young man sitting on the right-hand side, wearing a white robe; and they were dumbfounded. But he said to them, 'Do not be alarmed; you are looking for Jesus of Nazareth, who was crucified. He has been raised; he is not here. Look, there is the place where they laid him. But go and say to his disciples and to Peter: "He is going ahead of you into Galilee; there you will see him, as he told you."' Then they went out and ran away from the tomb, trembling with amazement. They said nothing to anyone, for they were afraid.

Comments on the Story

The women who were last at the cross in Mark's Gospel (15:40, 47) are first at the tomb on Sunday morning. One might have expected Jesus' disciples to give attention to the corpse; after all, John the Baptist's disciples attended to him after his martyrdom (Mark 6:29). But the disciples are long gone and only the women remain. Even they, from the narrator's perspective, come for the wrong reason—to anoint the body. The authorial audience knows that this act has already been accomplished when the nameless woman breaks the jar of alabaster over Jesus' head, and Jesus remarks to the dismay of the disgruntled disciples: "It is a fine thing she has done for me.... She has done what lay in her power; she has anointed my body in anticipation of my burial" (Mark 14:6, 8). What remains for these women—Mary Magdalene, Mary the mother of

175

A more extensive parallel story of the young man wearing the white robe was developed in the so-called *Secret Gospel of Mark*, which was another version of Mark that circulated in Alexandria in the time of Clement. A fragmentary text from this version of Mark is quoted in a recently discovered letter of Clement, which dates from ca. 150–215 C.E. The additional text, which Clement tells us was inserted between Mark 10:34 and 10:35, reads as follows: "And they come into Bethany, and this woman was there whose brother had died. She knelt down in front of Jesus and says to him, 'Son of David, have mercy on me.' But the disciples rebuked her. And Jesus got angry and went with her into the garden where the tomb was. Just then a loud voice was heard from inside the tomb. Then Jesus went up and rolled the stone away from the entrance to the tomb. He went right in where the young man was, stuck out his hand, grabbed him by the hand, and raised him up. The young man looked at Jesus, loved him, and began to beg him to be with him. Then they left the tomb and went into the young man's house. (Incidentally, he was rich.) Six days later Jesus gave him an order; and when evening had come, the young man went to him, dressed only in a linen cloth. He spent that night with him, because Jesus taught him the mystery of God's domain. From there [Jesus] got up and returned to the other side of the Jordan." The reference to dressing only in a linen cloth is thought to refer to the ritual of baptism, which, in the early years of Christianity, took place in the nude, after which one would often put on new white garments. As Mark's story continued, the same young man in the linen garment fled when Jesus was arrested, leaving his garment behind (Mark 14:51-52). His final appearance here at Jesus' tomb served to emphasize how the story of his resurrection at another tomb much like this one prefigured the story of Jesus' resurrection. (Miller, *Complete Gospels*, 402-5)

James, and Salome—is no less important. They are the ones who will discover that Jesus' tomb is empty.

They seem blissfully unaware of this mission, however, as they approach the tomb. The narrator reports: "They were wondering among themselves who would roll away the stone for them from the entrance to the tomb" (Mark 16:3). To their surprise, when they arrive they find the stone already rolled back and the tomb not altogether empty! As they enter the tomb, they see a young man dressed in a white robe sitting on the right side (on his identity see comments on "Jesus Taken Captive"). They become frightened, but the young man reassures them. He knows why they are there—they are looking for Jesus of Nazareth, who was crucified. But they are looking in the wrong place! "He has been raised; he is not here," he exclaims, and he offers proof: "Look, there is the place where they laid him" (16:6). He then gives them the message of that first Easter, a message that rings the old familiar bells of faith, love, and hope.

He first offers them a word of *faith*: "He has been raised." These words form the core of the Christian faith. And these women, so intent on anointing a dead body, are given the needed strength to renew their faith. No doubt their faith had been shaken. How deep their depression must have been as they watched Joseph place the body in a tomb cut out of rock. But now the messenger gives them new words of faith.

The message also contains a word of *love*: "Go and say to his disciples *and to Peter*." Jesus, who was forsaken by the disciples and denied by Peter, refused to forsake or deny them. Through the words of the young man, Jesus was offering reconciliation and forgiveness to those who least deserved it. Here was sacrificial love at its highest and most supreme state. Here was a word of love for the loveless and undeserving.

The message of Easter also contains a word of *hope*: "He is going ahead of you into Galilee." Just as Jesus led the way to Jerusalem (Mark 10:32), the place of suffering and death, so he also is leading the way back to Galilee, the place of power and new beginnings. It was in Galilee that Jesus performed great miracles and calmed the storms and was followed by great crowds. Even more, it was in Galilee that the disciples were appointed to preach and cast out demons. Galilee represents the hope of starting over, the hope of a second chance for the disciples. Galilee represents the hope that the power of the gospel will be restored. There is also hope in a promise fulfilled: "Just as he told you." Jesus promised the disciples that after he had risen he would go before them into Galilee (14:28). And now that promise is being fulfilled. The message of Easter, then, contains the great trilogy of Christian tradition—faith, love, and hope.

What remains to understand is the women's response to this message and how Mark ends his Gospel. The best manuscripts of the Gospel of Mark end at 16:8. Scholars generally agree that 16:9-20 is the creation of the early church to provide closure to the Gospel. Regardless of whether the Gospel actually ends at 16:8 or whether the last few verses were somehow lost, we have an unfinished story. We do not know from the Gospel of Mark whether the women ever delivered the message to the disciples. In fact, we are led to believe that perhaps they did not: "They said nothing to anyone, for they were afraid" (16:8). Of course, we know from the other Gospels and from the history of the church that the disciples did in fact get the message, but we cannot be certain from Mark's story. Mark's Gospel, then, is an unfinished story. But the gospel is *always* an unfinished story. After all, Mark only promised to give the "beginning of the gospel" (1:1). For Mark, only the audience, with their response to the text, could end this story. Either the audience remains silent and says nothing to anyone, as the women did, or they go and tell. The decision is as simple as that. Mark, like any good storyteller, knows that though the last line on the page has been read, this story is far from over!

Retelling the Story

> They went into the tomb, where they saw a young man sitting on the right-hand side, wearing a white robe; and they were dumbfounded. (Mark 16:5)

Angel Journal: Day 1

I have just completed my training for the Yahweh Express Messenger Service. They gave me my uniform, a white robe, and the special washing instructions for keeping it clean and bright. We learned many helpful things in our classes in addition to robe cleaning. How we were to greet people was a very important lesson, in order to get off on the right foot, you know. "Hail, O favored one" was my favorite one. But our instructors kept insisting that we should begin every encounter with a mortal by saying, "Don't be afraid." This seems a bit extreme to me, since I am young, slight of build and, all things considered, not a very imposing figure. That my presence would frighten even a small child is beyond my comprehension.

Angel Journal: Day 2

I received my first assignment today. At first, it didn't sound like the best one on the list. Still, what should I expect when I am just getting started? I am instructed to sit in a tomb waiting for a group of women to arrive. When I see these women, I am to tell them that the person they are looking for, a gentleman named Jesus, is no longer there but is risen. This confused me a bit at first. I assumed right off that their friend had risen from sleep, but what would he be doing sleeping in a tomb? I started to ask that question, but such inquiries are frowned upon when made by brand-new angels like myself. Then they told me this Jesus had been crucified, which cleared that up. Sort of. Crucifixion, what a nasty business; what sort of cruelty will these mortals think of next? I've never heard of anyone surviving a crucifixion before.

The rest of the message made more sense. The fellow they were looking for must be a rabbi since the women were to go tell all his disciples and a fellow named Peter what they saw. Or rather what they didn't see. Why this Peter fellow is singled out, I do not know. Perhaps he has a special place among the rabbi's disciples, or, on the other hand, may not be included among his disciples at all. Anyway, that is none of my business, as my instructor kept telling me in training when I would ask about the content of a message.

Then I was to tell the woman that, along with the disciples and Peter, they were to meet their rabbi in Galilee. Then I was to remind them that he had given them those instructions before.

178

The assignment seemed simple enough. I found the tomb without getting lost and took a seat inside, just to the right of the place that the rabbi must have been laid. I had allowed myself plenty of time, so I arrived early. I waited a long time, and while I waited, I started to think. How could a rabbi who had been crucified rise and walk all the way to Galilee? This was a mystery to me. I thought until my head began to hurt, but never made any sense out of it. I guess there are things that we angels are just not meant to understand.

Anyway, the women arrived and looked around outside the tomb for a while. I think they didn't expect it to still be open. I wasn't sure whether to speak to let them know that I was there, or if hearing a strange voice emerging from a tomb would alarm them. So I remained quiet until they looked inside. That was when all Sheol broke loose. They jumped back with such loud shrieks and howls of distress that it took a while for them to hear me saying, "Don't be afraid! Don't be afraid!" Now I think I understand what fearsome creatures we are to mortals. I will never question the wisdom of one of my instructors again. Believe me, though, those women frightened me as much or more than I frightened them.

When they had settled down enough and my heart had stopped racing, I delivered my message and retreated as soon as I could. My voice shook the entire time I spoke to them. I am not even sure that I told them everything I was supposed to tell them. I certainly hope I did. It doesn't

The young man in the white garment could also be interpreted to be an angel, since storytellers often referred to angels as appearing in the form of young men wearing splendid garments. One such example is found in 2 Maccabees (late second–early first century B.C.E.). When the king's chief minister, Heliodorus, was dispatched to plunder the treasures of the temple, "the Ruler of all spirits and of all power sent a mighty apparition," which included "two young men of surpassing strength and glorious beauty, magnificently attired," who flogged Heliodorus (3:24, 26). Similarly, when Josephus retold the story of the birth of Samson, he described the divine messenger who announced the birth as being "in the likeness of a comely and tall youth" (*Jewish Antiquities*, 5.277 [first century C.E.). The other canonical Gospels, Matthew, Luke, and John, all followed this reading and, each in his own way, interpreted the "young man" as an angelic messenger.

look good to get a bad report on your first assignment. The whole episode unnerved me so that I took to my bed for the rest of the afternoon. I'm already becoming anxious thinking of the sort of assignment I'll get tomorrow. In truth, I'm no longer sure that I am really cut out for this job.   *(Michael E. Williams)*

The Road to Emmaus

The resurrected Christ appears to two disciples on the road to Emmaus and reveals himself in the breaking of bread.

The Story

That same day two of them were on their way to a village called Emmaus, about seven miles from Jerusalem, talking together about all that had happened. As they talked and argued, Jesus himself came up and walked with them; but something prevented them from recognizing him. He asked them, 'What is it you are debating as you walk?' They stood still, their faces full of sadness, and one, called Cleopas, answered, 'Are you the only person staying in Jerusalem not to have heard the news of what has happened there in the last few days?' 'What news?' he said. 'About Jesus of Nazareth,' they replied, 'who, by deeds and words of power, proved himself a prophet in the sight of God and the whole people; and how our chief priests and rulers handed him over to be sentenced to death, and crucified him. But we had been hoping that he was to be the liberator of Israel. What is more, this is the third day since it happened, and now some women of our company have astounded us: they went early to the tomb, but failed to find his body, and returned with a story that they had seen a vision of angels who told them he was alive. Then some of our people went to the tomb and found things just as the women had said; but him they did not see.'

'How dull you are!' he answered. 'How slow to believe all that the prophets said! Was not the Messiah bound to suffer in this way before entering upon his glory?' Then, starting from Moses and all the prophets, he explained to them in the whole of scripture the things that referred to himself.

By this time they had reached the village to which they were going, and he made as if to continue his journey. But they pressed him: 'Stay with us, for evening approaches, and the day is almost over.' So he went in to stay with them. And when he had sat down with them at table, he took bread and said the blessing; he broke the bread, and offered it to them. Then their eyes were opened, and they recognized him; but he vanished from their sight. They said to one another, 'Were not our hearts on fire as he talked with us on the road and explained the scriptures to us?'

Without a moment's delay they set out and returned to Jerusalem. There they found that the eleven and the rest of the company had assembled, and were saying, 'It is true: the Lord has risen; he has appeared to Simon.' Then they described what had happened on their journey and told how he had made himself known to them in the breaking of the bread.

Comments on the Story

The story of the road to Emmaus is one of the most powerful stories in the Bible and certainly one of Luke's greatest achievements as a storyteller. The story divides into two parts, the walk to Emmaus (24:13-27) and the meal at Emmaus (24:28-35). The entire story is framed with a chiastic structure that initiates the movement of the story away from Jerusalem and brings it to a full stop with the Emmaus disciples' return to Jerusalem:

A Disciples going away from Jerusalem (13)
    B Disciples talk with each other (14)
        C Jesus comes near (15)
            D Disciples' eyes kept from recognizing Jesus (16)
            D' Disciples' eyes opened and they recognize Jesus (31*a*)
        C' Jesus vanishes (31*b*)
    B' Disciples talk with each other (32)
A' Disciples return to Jerusalem (33)

The scene begins with two travelers going to a village called Emmaus; that these two are followers of Jesus is suggested in the language "two of them," e.g., two of the followers of Jesus. Scholars have never been able to locate this village with any certainty, and in terms of the plot of the story, it is enough for the hearer to know that it is "about seven miles from Jerusalem." So the story begins with two as of yet unnamed followers of Jesus traveling to an obscure village outside Jerusalem "talking together about all that had happened" (24:14). As they are journeying, "Jesus himself came up and walked with them" (24:15). The travelers are unaware of this christophany since "something prevented them from recognizing him" (24:16). The theme of a deity appearing to unsuspecting mortals would have been well known to the ancient audience (see parallel stories). The text also implies that the disciples' blindness was the result of a divine act.

Jesus then inquires of them, "What is it you are debating as you walk?" (24:17). Before giving their response, the narrator builds the drama—"They stood still, their faces full of sadness"—and gives one of their names, Cleopas. The response is ironic, even comical: "Are you the only person staying in Jerusalem not to have heard the news of what has happened there in the last few days?" (24:18). Of course, the audience knows that, in fact, Jesus is the *only one* who *does* know the full details of what has transpired in Jerusalem over the past few days! Jesus seems to egg them on: "What news?" They take the bait and continue: "'About Jesus of Nazareth,' they replied, 'who, by deeds and words of power, proved himself a prophet in the sight of God and the whole people; and how our chief priests and rulers handed him over to be

181

sentenced to death, and crucified him'" (24:19-20). This summary of events would have been heard favorably by the authorial audience, who expected integrity between what a leader did ("mighty in deed") and what he said ("and word") before God and the people. The two explicitly claim that the responsibility for Jesus' death lay squarely with their chief priests and leaders rather than the "people" who witnessed Jesus' deeds and words (v. 20). The reference to Jesus being *handed over* to be sentenced to death" also effectively insinuates the role that the Romans played in conspiring for Jesus' death. The "objective" summary of events quickly gives way to their reaction to it: "we had been hoping that he was to be the liberator of Israel" (24:21a). Their despair is poignant, almost palpable. The hope they had once placed in Jesus for Israel's deliverance lay shattered by the events they had attempted to dispassionately describe. Like the child who, upon seeing colors refracted in broken glass on the pavement, remarked, "Look, mommy, there's a rainbow gone to smash," these disciples had seen their own messianic mosaic of hope gone to smash by the events of Good Friday.

This story follows the pattern of an ancient story motif about a divine messenger(s) coming to earth in disguise to test the hospitality of the mortals. The classic Jewish version is the story of Abraham entertaining the three divine guests at the oaks of Mamre. Because of his hospitality, he is rewarded with the promise of an heir. His neighbors at Sodom, meanwhile, because of their inhospitality, are severely punished (Gen. 18–19). The classic Greco-Roman version is the story of Baucis and Philemon. The two gods Zeus and Hermes, disguised as mortals, appear at the door of this aged couple one day, requesting hospitality. Though Baucis and Philemon are quite poor and have very little to offer, nevertheless they invite the strangers in and offer them what they have. For their hospitality, they are rewarded richly. Meanwhile, their neighbors in the village, who refuse to offer hospitality, are punished severely (Ovid, *Metamorphoses*, 8.618-724 [late first century B.C.E. to early first century C.E.]). Following this motif, Cleopas and his unnamed companion offer hospitality to an unknown stranger and are rewarded with a divine appearance and, subsequently, a promise.

The remainder of their speech, however, discloses to the audience that their temporary inability to see Jesus was more than physical. They glibly report, "What is more, this is the third day since it happened" (24:21), apparently unaware of the significance of the chronology, even though the audience could hardly miss the import of "the third day" (see references in Luke). Furthermore, they are "astounded" by but evidently unwilling to accept the testimony of "some women of our company" who reported that they could not find the body of Jesus and that "they had seen a vision of angels who told them he was alive" (24:22-23). Even though some of their other (presumably male) companions confirmed that the tomb was empty, the Emmaus disciples, lacking empirical evidence ("him they did not see"), simply cannot see the conclusion to which their story irresistibly draws the audience—Jesus has been raised from the dead, just as he promised, just as the angels had claimed, and just as the empty tomb indirectly attested. And, of course, they make this "non-confession" of faith to the very one whose presence in this story confirms his resurrection for the audience.

Jesus finally blurts out what the audience is feeling: "How dull you are!" (24:25). The resurrected Christ then proceeds to instruct the pilgrims in "all that the prophets said," specifically regarding the divine necessity: "Was not the Messiah bound to suffer in this way before entering upon his glory?" (24:26). Here is a clear example of early Christian messianic exegesis, delivered by the Messiah himself! "Then, starting from Moses and all the prophets, he explained to them in the whole of scripture the things that referred to himself" (24:27). This pattern of scripture exposition followed by a meal with the disciples is reversed in the scene that follows (24:36-49). Here Jesus eats a meal with the disciples, namely broiled fish (24:42-43; the Greek phrase *enopion auton* is best translated "ate *with* them" rather than "ate before their eyes"). He then explains to them "everything written about [him] in the law of Moses and in the prophets and psalms . . . [relating to] the sufferings of the Messiah and his rising from the dead on the third day" (24:44, 46).

The second section of our text, the meal at Emmaus, begins with another strange twist. As the travelers approach the village of their destination, Jesus "made as if to continue his journey" (24:28). Is he toying with them, trying to wrest a dinner invitation from them (which he does!)? Does the text echo the Old Testament scene where God disclosed his glory by passing by Moses (see

> The *Testament of Abraham*, which was contemporary with Luke (ca. 100 C.E.), was a retelling of the story of Abraham's hospitality. It is set in the lifetime of Isaac, when Abraham is visited once more at Mamre by a disguised divine visitor, this time the archangel Michael, and once more Abraham proves himself an exemplary host. At first Michael is unsure what to do, since "heavenly spirits are incorporeal, and they neither eat nor drink" (4:9), but God provides a way in which Michael can accept Abraham's hospitality (4:1-11). Here in Luke, Jesus at first reveals himself when he breaks bread. Later he will make a point of eating food to prove he is no apparition.

Exod. 33:18-23)? Whatever the motive, the travelers do urge Jesus strongly, saying, "Stay with us, for evening approaches, and the day is almost over" (24:29). He complies and joins them at table, but again an ironic situation quickly develops. The guest becomes the host! "And when he had sat down with them at table, he took bread and said the blessing; he broke the bread, and offered it to them" (24:30). These four gestures, taking, blessing, breaking, and giving the bread, recall earlier meal scenes: the feeding of the five thousand (Luke 9:16) and the Last Supper (22:19). The audience is not the only one to notice the similarities; the Emmaus disciples do as well.

No sooner have they recognized Jesus than he disappears from before their eyes. Immediately, they return to Jerusalem to tell the disciples what has happened. First, though, the disciples have news of their own: "It is true: the Lord has risen; he has appeared to Simon" (24:34). Cleopas and his companion then relate "what had happened on their journey and told how he had made himself known to them in the breaking of the bread" (24:35).

What is the meaning of this story, often referred to as the "beautiful story" in Luke's Gospel, for the authorial audience? Put simply, it is this. Luke's audience lived at a time when the apostles, the living links to Jesus, were dying or were already dead, and presumably none of them knew the earthly Jesus, including the author himself. They lived in a place far from Jerusalem. Yet the Emmaus story reminds them and us that one need not be an apostle to experience an epiphany of Christ. One could be so little known that one's name is forgotten. Indeed, leaving the one disciple unnamed is an invitation to the reader to participate in the story—to inscribe him or herself into the narrative. One need not sit at the feet of the earthly Jesus in order to know him. In fact, Christ continues to make himself known in the eucharist, in the "breaking of the bread" (on the use of this phrase as a shorthand for the Lord's Supper in the early church, see Acts 2:42, 46; 20:7, 11). One need not be in the religious center of Jerusalem (or anywhere else) for a religious revelation. Indeed, one might experience the presence of the resurrected Christ in one's own home.

So Luke encourages his audience, then and now, to take heart from the fact that the resurrected Lord revealed himself to little-known followers, in an obscure place, in a humble home, in a shared meal. So may our hearts also burn within us and may he, too, be made known to us in the breaking of the bread!

Retelling the Story

That same day two of them were on their way to a village called Emmaus, about seven miles from Jerusalem, talking together about all that had happened. (Luke 24:13)

I.

Our footsteps sounded like a death toll
As we walked the dusty road
From Jerusalem to Emmaus.
Both words and silences spoke for us
As our feet trudged toward home
In search of whatever comfort
A familiar place might offer.

Along that same road,
Our faces set for Emmaus,
We spoke of one dear to us
Who was no more. The journey home
Might help, but could not comfort,
Our broken hearts despite the offer
Of rest after grief's expensive toll.

While the place, Emmaus,
Still lay some distance from us
We met a stranger, going home
Like us. In need of comfort
Like us, perhaps. We hope the offer
Of company to reduce our toll
Of mourning along that sad road.

The stranger began to question us.
The words that accompanied us home
So far, held pain and sorrow, not comfort.
"Are you the only one that does not know? We'll offer
A story that will wring from your heart a toll,
A price, no tax collector along this road
Could match from here to Emmaus."

The rest of our long trek home
We told the stranger of Jesus, the comfort
Of God extended to the world, God's offer
Of grace to cancel the excruciating toll
Of death. But following Jesus' road
Had led us nowhere but back here to Emmaus.

II.

Arriving home
At dark in Emmaus
We offer
Small comfort,
Food to ease the toll
Of the long, bleak road.

III.

The bread is broken
Between familiar
Spike-torn palms.
Now we recognize the face,
The voice, the hands, the gait.
We start to speak.
Our voices reach toward
An emptiness across the table
Where our guest/our host had sat.
The question returns
To us and turns on us—
Are we the only ones who did not know?
Then we return
Along a moon-lit ribbon
Of road, saying,
"Were not our hearts on fire?
Were not our hearts ablaze?"

(Michael E. Williams)

Appearance to the Disciples and Ascension

Jesus appears to the eleven, commands them to wait in the city until they receive the Holy Spirit, and takes his final leave of them.

The Story

As they were talking about all this, there he was, standing among them. Startled and terrified, they thought they were seeing a ghost. But he said, 'Why are you so perturbed? Why do doubts arise in your minds? Look at my hands and feet. It is I myself. Touch me and see; no ghost has flesh and bones as you can see that I have.' They were still incredulous, still astounded, for it seemed too good to be true. So he asked them, 'Have you anything here to eat?' They offered him a piece of fish they had cooked, which he took and ate before their eyes.

And he said to them, 'This is what I meant by saying, while I was still with you, that everything written about me in the law of Moses and in the prophets and psalms was bound to be fulfilled.' Then he opened their minds to understand the scriptures. 'So you see,' he said, 'that scripture foretells the sufferings of the Messiah and his rising from the dead on the third day, and declares that in his name repentance bringing the forgiveness of sins is to be proclaimed to all nations beginning from Jerusalem. You are to be witnesses to it all. I am sending on you the gift promised by my Father; wait here in this city until you are armed with power from above.'

Then he led them out as far as Bethany, and blessed them with uplifted hands; and in the act of blessing he parted from them. And they returned to Jerusalem full of joy, and spent all their time in the temple praising God.

Comments on the Story

In the last major section of Luke's Gospel, Jesus makes his final appearance to the disciples. The scene begins where the Emmaus story left off. The disciples had been talking about the appearances of Jesus to Simon and to the Emmaus pilgrims. Suddenly, Jesus stood among them (24:36). Their response is typical of post-resurrection appearances (see Matt. 28:16-17): "Startled and terrified, they thought they were seeing a ghost" (24:37). Jesus responds with a gentle reproof and an invitation for them to touch him and see that he is no

187

apparition: "But he said, 'Why are you so perturbed? Why do doubts arise in your minds? Look at my hands and feet. It is I myself. Touch me and see; no ghost has flesh and bones as you can see that I have'" (24:38-39).

While they were still disbelieving for joy and wondering, Jesus asks a very strange question: "Have you anything here to eat?" Many commentators see in this question a continuation of the Lukan emphasis on the corporeality of the resurrection, previously seen in the invitation to the disciples to touch Jesus' body in order to disprove that he is only a phantom. In this view, Jesus offers to consume food before the disciples to demonstrate the bodily nature of his resurrection. Luke may be responding to some incipient Gnostic ideas that emphasized the spiritual nature of resurrection to the denigration of its corporeal aspects (see also the similar theme in John 20:24-29).

The Gospel storyteller's concerns, however, go well beyond establishing Jesus' bodily resurrection. After the disciples have responded to Jesus' request by giving him a piece of broiled fish (24:42), most translations read something like, "which he took and ate before their eyes" (*enopion auton*, 24:43; see also NRSV). Such a rendering suggests that only Jesus ate the fish, while the disciples were passive onlookers. The only other time this Greek construction is found in Luke's Gospel is at 13:26. There the phrase is translated, "We used to eat and drink with you [*enopion sou*]" and clearly refers to a shared meal. The same understanding should apply here as well, and the verse is better translated: "which he took and ate *with them*." So the image here is not simply of a resur-

> In other stories in the Jewish tradition about divine visitors who appear on earth, the point is regularly made that angels do not eat human food. In Tobit (third century B.C.E.), when the angel Raphael identifies himself, he offers as proof: "Take note that I ate no food; what you saw was an apparition" (12:19). In *Testament of Abraham* 4 (Recension A; ca. 100 C.E.), when the archangel Michael appears to Abraham in human form and is offered Abraham's hospitality at the dinner table, he has to exit secretly to inquire of God what to do next, since, he says, "all the heavenly spirits are incorporeal, and they neither eat nor drink." God tells him to return to Abraham's table and eat what is set before him, "For when you are seated with him," God says, "I shall send upon you an all-devouring spirit, and, from your hands and through your mouth, it will consume everything which is on the table" (4:9-10). Operating within this story world, Luke nevertheless makes the point that Jesus is different; he is not a mere apparition but, in fact, eats human food.

rected Lord raiding the refrigerator one last time before his final departure, nor even of Jesus seeking simply to demonstrate his "bodiliness" one more time. Rather, we find the resurrected Lord seizing one last opportunity to dine with his disciples.

This reading is consistent with the theme of food and meals that runs throughout Luke's Gospel. Only Luke reports that at Jesus' birth, he was placed in a manger, a feeding trough. The term "manger" occurs three times in Luke 2 (vv. 7, 12, 16) and provides a vivid image drawn from the very beginning of Jesus' earthly existence. For Luke, Jesus, born in a feeding trough, is food for the world!

To the ancients, the primary way in which one moved from the human realm to the divine realm was by ascending to the heavens. This motif was common in Jewish stories, as seen, for example, in the story of the ascension of Elijah in a whirlwind (2 Kgs. 2:11). In Tobit (ca. 100 C.E.), the angel Raphael first appeared in human form, then, after revealing his divine identity, announced that he was "about to ascend to him who sent me. . . . He then ascended and, when they rose to their feet, was no longer to be seen" (12:20-21).

Luke develops this theme in ways distinct from John. John favors the rhetorical device of "telling," that is, having his protagonist Jesus make explicit theological claims about being sustenance for the world: "I am the bread of life . . . I am the living bread that has come down from heaven; if anyone eats this bread, he will live for ever" (6:35, 51). Luke, on the other hand, employs the rhetorical device of "showing," that is, having Jesus engage in actions that demonstrate that he is sustenance for the world. This is not to say that John never employs the strategy of "showing" (see also the wedding feast at Cana, John 2:1-11, and the feeding of the five thousand, John 6) or that Luke never uses the technique of "telling" ("Blessed are you who now go hungry; you will be satisfied," Luke 6:21; "This is my body," Luke 22:19), but John clearly favors "telling" while Luke prefers "showing." Most of the showing in Luke occurs in the context of table fellowship. Jesus dines with Levi, a tax collector, and other sinners (Luke 5), and with Pharisees (Luke 7, 11, 14). He feeds the multitudes (Luke 9) and individuals (Luke 8:55). He eats with Mary and Martha (Luke 10) and presumably with Zacchaeus (Luke 19). He dines with disciples in Jerusalem (Luke 22) and Emmaus (Luke 24). The old adage is certainly true: in Luke, Jesus is either going to, coming from, or at a meal!

Such indiscriminate dining leads to sharp criticism of both Jesus and his disciples. The Pharisees complain to the disciples: "Why do you eat and drink with tax-collectors and sinners?" (5:30). Later they direct their objections at Jesus: "This fellow welcomes sinners and eats with them" (15:2). Jesus himself states the opposition viewpoint very clearly: "... you say, 'Look at him! A glutton and a drinker, a friend of tax-collectors and sinners!'" (7:34). To share a meal with someone, whether in antiquity or today, implies acceptance of that person. No doubt the significance of the table as an agent of social change is one of the key reasons that lunch counter sit-ins were among the first gestures of civil rights activists in this country in the 1960s. In Luke, the way Jesus eats—with sinners and tax collectors, with religious authorities and disciples—leads directly to his death. Such inclusivism was not to be tolerated.

Ascension stories were also told about heroes of the Greeks and Romans. For example, in stories about Romulus, the mythical founder of Rome, he was said to appear to humans by descending from heaven, then ascending back to heaven once more. "And Proculus, a man of eminence, took oath that he had seen Romulus ascending to heaven in full armor, and had heard his voice commanding that he be called Quirinus" (Plutarch, *Numa*, 11.3 [45–125 C.E.]). (Boring-Berger-Colpe, 164, no. 219)

Jesus does not want his disciples to forget how (or with whom) to eat. So in Luke, Jesus has two "Last Suppers"! At the first (Luke 22), Jesus, reclining at table, engages his disciples in a discussion reminiscent of a philosophical symposium (see, e.g., Plato's *Symposium*). The topic is true greatness. Jesus says, "Among the Gentiles, kings lord it over their subjects; and those in authority are given the title Benefactor. Not so with you: on the contrary, the greatest among you must bear himself like the youngest, the one who rules like one who serves" (22:25-26). The point is clear: "eating and drinking" at Jesus' messianic table in his kingdom (22:30) demands radical inclusion at the ordinary table, an inclusiveness that transcends racial, social, and gender barriers. And so the last "Last Supper" (Luke 24) where Jesus eats broiled fish with his disciples is a reminder not only of the corporeal nature of Jesus' own resurrected body, but, standing as it does in a sequence of suppers, it also serves to remind the disciples of the radical inclusivity of the "body," the church, which remains behind to continue the work of the resurrected Christ. And so he took fish and ate it with them!

Jesus then gives his disciples one final Bible lesson. "And he said to them, 'This is what I meant by saying, while I was still with you, that everything written about me in the law of Moses and in the prophets and psalms was bound to be fulfilled'" (24:44). He makes it clear that what the law, prophets, and psalms say about him deals specifically with his suffering: "Then he opened their minds to understand the scriptures. 'So you see,' he said, 'that scripture foretells the sufferings of the Messiah and his rising from the dead on the third day'" (24:45-46).

Commentators since Conzelmann have often overemphasized the lack of any notion of vicarious suffering in Luke. But here the suffering of the Messiah leads inevitably to "repentance bringing the forgiveness of sins," and this message must be "proclaimed to all nations beginning from Jerusalem" (24:47). Jesus' Bible study leads from exposition to application: "You [the disciples] are to be witnesses to it all" (24:48). And, unlike in Matthew, where the disciples are commissioned to "go and make disciples," in Luke, Jesus commands the disciples to "wait here in this city" (24:49). The delay, however, is only temporary. They are simply to wait until they are "armed with power from above" (24:49), a wait that ends with the events at Pentecost (Acts 2).

The last scene in Luke (24:50-53) brings closure to the story. Jesus leads the disciples to Bethany, where he completes his "exodus" (see also 9:30-31). He gives them one final blessing (doing what Zechariah was unable to do, Luke 1) and the disciples return to the temple in Jerusalem, where the story began (Luke 1:5ff). This literary circularity provides a sense of completion. "We return to the place where we began and know the place for the first time" (T. S. Eliot, *Four Quartets*).

Luke, however, cleverly employs another strategy to indicate that the story is now complete. He introduces some "space" between the audience and the scene. We are allowed close enough to see what Jesus is doing—lifting his hands, blessing the disciples—but not close enough to hear—there is no dialogue in this closing scene (contrast Matt. 28:16-20). The effect is to usher the audience out of the symbolic world of the narrative and back into the real world. The task of proclaiming "repentance bringing the forgiveness of sins ... to all nations," a theme reiterated in the book of Acts, remains for those of us who, having heard, now wish to be "servants of the gospel" (Luke 1:2).

Retelling the Story

"Wait here in this city until you are armed with power from above." (Luke 24:49*b*)

One of the most difficult tasks in life is waiting. I remember when I was a child waiting for my father to get home from work. Then there were those road trips and I would have to wait to arrive wherever we were going, all the time asking plaintively, "Are we there yet?" On holidays, when our relatives would come to visit I would stand by the window looking out. It seemed like they would never arrive. My mother would say things like, "A watched pot never boils." As I grew older her proverbial wisdom made less and less sense to me. Surely even a watched pot would boil eventually. Then as an adult I realized that she was wise in her own way. The more attention we pay to the process of waiting, the longer it *seems*.

The difficulty of waiting was underscored every evening as I waited for supper. I would ask, "When will supper be ready?" My mother would always reply, but never with a precise time. She would say, "Not long" or "In a little while." She knew from experience that I would continue to pester her unless she could distract me. So she would give me a job. These jobs might include setting the table, or mashing the potatoes, or cutting the round, cast iron pan of cornbread into pie-like slices.

What I didn't realize was that all the waiting I did as a child was training for discipleship. The last time Jesus appears to his disciples in Luke, he eats with them one more time. Two of the disciples have just returned from Emmaus with an incredible story. A stranger had accompanied them along their way home, then when he broke the bread at the evening meal they realized that the stranger was Jesus. Then he was gone. The two went back to tell their friends in Jerusalem.

Just as the two were telling their story, Jesus appeared again. Some of those standing there that day say they heard him greet them, "Shalom." He asked for something to eat, which assured them that he was not a ghost. Then he took some time to tell them about some of the stories they thought they already knew very well. But the way he talked about them helped the disciples begin to fathom how one who was executed like a criminal could still be the chosen one of God. The one who died like any common, run-of-the-mill sinner was really the Messiah who had come to offer forgiveness for the sins of others. The disciples would be the ones to retell his story and offer that forgiveness to people everywhere.

Then Jesus raised both hands in blessing. Do they see the open wounds on his wrists where the spikes were driven that pinned him to the cross? Luke does not say. All we know is that the spikes could not hold him, and the grave could not hold him, and the blessing he offers with open hands is a blessing of peace. The monarch butterfly that the world thought dead and pinned against a black velvet sky is alive.

Then Jesus tells his disciples what he wants them to do—wait. Stay in Jerusalem until they receive new clothes woven from the power of God's spirit. Then, once again, he is gone.

As they waited they did more than wait. They broke break together and knew Jesus once more in the breaking of the bread. They told the stories that later would be written down and given the names of four disciples. They made sure the widows and orphans among them were not neglected. And they walked throughout their lives in clothing woven from the very fabric of God's love.

Guess what. That's what Jesus' disciples have been doing ever since.

(Michael E. Williams)

Selected Bibliography

References in the text are cited by author.

Boring, M. Eugene. "The Gospel of Matthew," in *The New Interpreter's Bible*, vol 8. Ed. Leander Keck. Nashville: Abingdon, 1995.

————, Klaus Berger, and Carsten Colpe. *Hellenistic Commentary to the New Testament*. Nashville: Abingdon, 1995.

Brown, Raymond E. *The Birth of the Messiah*. New Updated Edition. New York: Doubleday, 1993.

————. *The Death of the Messiah*. 2 vols. New York: Doubleday, 1994.

Charlesworth, James H. *The Old Testament Pseudepigrapha*, vol. 1. New York: Doubleday, 1983.

Cicero. *De Oratore*. Books I-II. Trans. by E. W. Sutton. Loeb Classical Library. Cambridge, Mass.: Harvard University Press, 1988.

Crossan, John Dominic. *Who Killed Jesus? Exposing the Roots of Anti-Semitism in the Gospel Story of the Death of Jesus*. New York: HarperCollins, 1996.

Culpepper, Alan. "The Gospel of Luke," in *The New Interpreter's Bible*, vol 9. Ed. Leander Keck. Nashville: Abingdon, 1996.

Davies, W. D., and Dale C. Allison, Jr. *Matthew*. The International Critical Commentary. 3 vols. Edinburgh: T.&T. Clark, 1988, 1991, 1997.

Fitzmyer, Joseph A. *The Gospel According to Luke*. Anchor Bible. 2 vols. New York: Doubleday, 1982, 1985.

Garland, David E. *Reading Matthew: A Literary and Theological Commentary on the First Gospel*. New York: Crossroad, 1995.

Jeremias, Joachim. "*Paradeisos*," in *Theological Dictionary of the New Testament*. Ed. Gerhard Kittel. Grand Rapids: Eerdmans, 1967.

Josephus. *Against Apion*. Trans. by H. St. J. Thackeray. Loeb Classical Library. Cambridge, Mass.: Harvard University Press, 1997.

193

————. *Jewish Antiquities.* Books VII-VIII. Trans. by Ralph Marcus. Loeb Classical Library. Cambridge, Mass.: Harvard University Press, 1998.

————. *The Jewish War.* Books I-II. Trans. by H. St. J. Thackeray. Loeb Classical Library. Cambridge, Mass.: Harvard University Press, 1997.

Klassen, William. "The Sacred Kiss in the New Testament: An Example of Social Boundary Lines." *New Testament Studies* 39 (1993):122-35.

Lucian. *How to Write History.* Trans. by K. Kilburn. Loeb Classical Library. Cambridge, Mass.: Harvard University Press, 1999.

Miller, Robert J. *Born Divine: The Births of Jesus and Other Sons of God.* Santa Rosa, CA: Polebridge Press, 2003.

————, ed. *The Complete Gospels.* Sonoma, CA: Polebridge Press, 1992.

Newsom, Carol A., and Sharon H. Ringe, eds. *Women's Bible Commentary.* Expanded Edition. Louisville, KY: Westminster John Knox, 1998.

Plutarch. *Lives.* Book I. Trans. by Bernadotte Perrin. Loeb Classical Library. Cambridge, Mass.: Harvard University Press, 1998.

Quintilian. *Institutio Oratoria.* Books I-III. Trans. by H. E. Butler. Loeb Classical Library. Cambridge, Mass.: Harvard University Press, 1989.

Smith, Dennis E. *From Symposium to Eucharist: The Banquet in the Early Christian World.* Minneapolis: Fortress Press, 2003.

Talbert, Charles. *Reading Luke: A Literary and Theological Commentary on the Third Gospel.* New York: Crossroad, 1982.

Tannehill, Robert C. *Luke.* Abingdon New Testament Commentaries. Nashville: Abingdon, 1996.

Theissen, Gerd. *The Miracle Stories of the Early Christian Tradition.* Philadelphia: Fortress, 1983.

Tolbert, Mary Ann. *Sowing the Word: Mark's World in Literary-Historical Perspective.* Minneapolis: Fortress, 1989.

van Henten, Jan Willem, and Friedrich Avemarie. *Martyrdom and Noble Death.* New York: Routledge, 2002.

Vermes, Geza. *The Dead Sea Scrolls in English.* Fourth Edition. London: Penguin Books, 1995.

Index of Readings from
The Revised Common Lectionary

Matthew 1:18-25, Advent 4 (A)
Matthew 2:1-23, Epiphany (A, B, C)
Luke 1:26-55, Advent 4 (B, C)
Mark 1:1-8, Advent 2 (B)
Matthew 4:1-11, Lent 1 (A)
Luke 4:1-13, Lent 1 (C)
Luke 4:14-30, Epiphany 4 (C)
Mark 2:1-12, Epiphany 7 (B)
Mark 4:35–5:20, Proper 7 (B)
Mark 5:21-43, Proper 8 (B)
Mark 6:30-44, Proper 11 (B)
Matthew 14:22-33, Proper 14 (A)
Mark 7:24-30, Proper 18 (B)
Mark 8:27-38, Proper 19 (B)
Matthew 17:1-8, Epiphany Last (A)
Mark 9:2-8, Epiphany Last (B)
Luke 9:28-36, Epiphany Last (C)
Mark 10:46-52, Proper 25 (B)
Luke 19:1-10, Proper 26 (C)
Luke 19:28-40, Lent 6 Palms (C)
Mark 14:17-25, Lent 6 Passion (B)
Mark 14:43-52, Lent 6 Passion (B)
Luke 23:32-43, Lent 6 Passion (C)
Mark 15:33-41, Lent 6 Passion (B)
Mark 16:1-8, Easter Day (B)
Luke 24:13-35, Easter Evening (A, B, C)
Luke 24:36-53, Ascension Sunday (A, B, C)

Index of Parallel Stories

EARLY CHRISTIAN LITERATURE

GREEK AND ROMAN LITERATURE